KISSING ASPHALT

The Courageous True Story of One's Child's Unbreakable Spirit—From Kidnapping & Abuse to Self-Love

BY

DELICIA NIAMI

Trigger Warning: This book contains references to drug abuse, sexual abuse, rape, pedophilia, and suicide.

Published by ResilientAF Press
Distribution by Bublish
Printed in the United States of America

ISBN: 978-1-647047-60-3 (Paperback)
ISBN: 978-1-647047-71-9 (Hardcover)
ISBN: 978-1-647040-09-3 (eBook)

For my big brother, Nile. I'm not sure I could have survived the first six years without you.

And to The Go-Go's, thank you for making music that allowed me to "capture the light and keep it in my heart."

Trigger Warning:
This book contains references to drug abuse, sexual abuse, rape, pedophilia, and suicide.

SECTIONS

Author's Note i

She's Ugly 1

We're Going to Disneyland! 5

My Personal Archangel 25

Trustworthy Monster #1 51

I Should Be Angry, but I'm Not 73

The Night Stalker 123

Going To A Go-Go 127

Island Fever 151

Coming Out 157

Loneliness Averted 177

My First Drunken Blackout 219

AUTHOR'S NOTE

Several of my early readers wondered why I chose to tell my story in snapshots rather than in a linear fashion. The simple answer is because this is how I remember it. But life is never so simple. This is especially true when speaking about trauma.

Throughout my life, many people were astonished by my journey, often encouraging me to write my story. It took forty-eight years for me to be ready.

Once I felt ready, I pondered how I would fit all my memories and events of childhood into some sort of comprehensible order since memories do not come to me linearly but rather in bits and pieces that fit together like a jigsaw puzzle.

Suddenly, it occurred to me. The best way to compartmentalize my childhood was to write in snapshots. I envisioned writing chapters as nouns: important people, places, and things in my life.

It wasn't until I finished writing this book that I realized memories of trauma work differently.

There have been numerous books written about trauma, recall, and the fragmentation process. Intense traumatic memories can create mental fragments (or flashbulb memories) due to hormone overload in the hippocampus of your brain when serious or life-threatening trauma arises.

This is why so many people that have intense trauma can only remember snippets of what happened. During the writing process, I recalled memories that had been completely blocked out—until I began to write. A television in the background of a dark room flashed in my mind as I wrote. Then a large shadowy figure sitting in a chair. The flashes kept coming. Slowly, pieces started converging little by little.

Due to the nature of how my brain processes trauma, each chapter is a short story unto itself. This compilation of stories melds together to create the beginning of my journey to who I have become today.

It is important to note that this memoir is a snapshot of my life. Since my traumas and triumphs have spanned over many years I wanted to give my readers a full picture; In order to do that I had to write my story in three parts: Kissing Asphalt is the first. Followed by Not My Circus, which continues from the end of Kissing Asphalt through about age thirty-two where my world was changed and turned upside down due to yet another and the biggest trauma of my life. Not My Circus will be followed by The Queen of Silver Linings which will take you through my healing journey including more ups and downs but this will conclude with my triumph and finally victory, filled with self-love, self-worth and respect. Like a phoenix, I rise through the ashes!

SHE'S UGLY

Six a.m., February 9, 1971. My mother, eight months pregnant at the time, was jolted awake by one of Los Angeles's all-time biggest earthquakes. The epicenter of this quake was less than five miles from where she lived in Sylmar, California. Rolling out of her bed with the quake, she ran toward the nearest doorway. The tectonic plates collided and ground against each other, causing the earth to shake beneath her feet. Stretching out her arms with all her might, she braced her very pregnant body beneath the door, as if the doorframe alone would hold up the entire house if it were to come crashing down.

That was the earthquake protocol. Anyone living in California in the 1970s knew it quite well. If an earthquake hit, you ran for the nearest doorway.

My experience of this event was complete darkness. Sloshing around while amniotic fluid rushed over me like a tidal wave, crashing on a tiny fetus. Feeling the surge of adrenaline but knowing I was safe. It has been said that when you're in the womb, you feel no fear. Why should you? Isn't a mother's womb the safest place you'll ever be?

For then, it was. She was. Standing strong in the doorway, she rode out the waves of the quake, sheltering me from the violence of the outside world.

Twenty-six days later…

"Hazim, my water just broke!" she screamed as she waddled down the hallway. "WE HAVE TO GO TO THE HOSPITAL… *NOW*!"

My father rushed Nile, my three-year-old brother, out the door and into the car. The growing family flew up the 405 North to Devonshire Boulevard, exiting the freeway and traveling onward to Granada Hills Community Hospital.

I was ready to jump into this world headfirst. After several hours and a lot of stress on my little body, I finally popped my head out—the journey every human makes in our effort to squeeze out of that tiny pinhole from where the light beckons us. Shortly thereafter, out came my shoulders, torso, and legs, followed by my little feet. A spanking on my bare bottom was the first experience of my existence like most babies born in America. Not understanding what was happening or the emotions I was feeling, I cried. I was whooshed into my mother's arms. Ahh, finally, some comfort and a smell I recognized. I could relax.

As I settled into the warmth of my mother's supple skin, she stared into my eyes, uttering the first words I would ever hear—"She's ugly."

My father's immediate response was, "She looks like you, Laurie."

At this point, I imagine all I wanted to do was crawl back into the womb.

"She's ugly" was something I'd carry with me my entire life. In fact, I'd sometimes wonder whether those first words played a profound role in shaping my self-image. It's something I've internalized and a badge I've carried with me for as long as I can remember.

At the same time my mother pronounced, "She's ugly," my angels or some ethereal being whispered in my ear, "Find your joy." That is precisely what these books are about.

When I was a little girl, we would take trips with my mother during the summer. One year, when I was seven, we drove to New Mexico for our vacation. That summer, I experienced pink eye for the first time in my life.

When we were road-tripping, Mom didn't book motels ahead of time since we never knew how far we would get each day. This particular night, we couldn't find any place with a vacancy, so Mom found a local campground. We didn't have a tent, so we just slept in the old station wagon. Nile and Mom reclined in the front seats, and I made a small bed in the tiny back seat.

When I woke the next morning, I couldn't see anything. Panic set in, and immediate fear permeated my mind. I thought I had gone blind.

"Mom, help! I can't see anything!" I cried. "Am I blind? Mommy, help me!"

"What are you yelling about?" she asked, turning around to look at me. "Oh, wow!"

"What? What is it?" I knew my worst fears were about to be confirmed. I was blind. Somehow, the lack of concern in my mother's voice was not reassuring.

I guess because she spent a lot of time around kids as a teacher, my mother knew exactly what this was. "You have pink eye, honey," she said matter-of-factly.

"What's that, Mom? It's not pink. Everything is dark. I can't see anything."

"Just relax and let me go get a washcloth. Nile, keep an eye on your sister while I am gone."

"Okay," Nile replied as she left the car. The second she was gone, he teased, "Ewww, gross. What is on your eyes?"

"It's scary. Don't make fun of me."

"I'm sorry, but it looks gross."

My mother returned and got into the back seat. Grabbing my face, she gently wiped the boogers from my eyes. Slowly, I saw flashes of light. A trickle here and a trickle there. Small holes appeared where the light glistened. I realized I wasn't blind, and the panic in me settled. It took about forty-five minutes of wiping the gook from my eyes before I could see again.

This brief moment in time is the lens through which I view the world. Despite the challenges life continuously throws my way, I keep working my way through the muck of it all. Putting one foot in front of the other, I move forward. I do this knowing full well in my heart, spirit, and soul that when you come through the sludge that life dredges up, beauty and joy emerge... if you choose.

WE'RE GOING TO DISNEYLAND!

March 25,1975

It was a sunny day in Arleta, California. A layer of smog covered the sky, giving it the most illustrious orange hue. My brother and I were anxiously awaiting our five-day Easter vacation with our father. Our parents were going through a tumultuous divorce and had been separated for about a year at this point. I felt extremely sad because I never got to see my "dad." I thought it odd that he cut all ties with our family, especially his own children. At only four years of age, I couldn't understand the concept of a father wanting nothing to do with his kids. Imagine the excitement my brother, who was seven at the time, and I felt after almost a year of not seeing him. Now we were going to get to spend five whole days for Easter with our "dad."

Our mother was on a two-week ski vacation in Big Bear, a mountain resort town in Southern California. She planned a trip with her boyfriend knowing our father had plans to take my brother and me that week. Mom left us in the care of our aunt until our father, Hazim, arrived.

Nile and I were playing cops and robbers on our front lawn, and my brother pretended to shoot me. I fell in slow motion onto the lawn while wearing light blue polyester pants. Worried about a grass stain, I quickly jumped up as Nile noticed our father's car, a 1966 Oldsmobile, making a U-turn. We ran over to the car with glee. It felt like forever since we saw him last.

As we approached the car, our father smiled and shouted, "Hey, kids, let's go to Disneyland!"

"Yay!" we screamed.

"I'll go get our stuff," Nile said, turning toward the house. Our father stopped him.

"Don't worry, son. I already took care of everything. Let's go before the crowds hit."

At that time, entry to Disneyland was only six dollars, but you also had to buy ticket books to get on the rides.

Nile and I looked at each other, shouting, "Far out!"

We jumped into the car, excited to begin our journey to Disneyland. Being kids, I guess we didn't think much of telling our aunt that we were leaving. She was in the backyard at the time, and we figured she knew he was on his way.

When I was young, it always felt like it took forever to get to Disneyland. This time, the drive was much shorter. We parked in a large garage with what looked like thousands of cars. It didn't feel like Disneyland, but I didn't think much of it, nor of the planes flying above our heads. After exiting the car, our father unloaded luggage—presumably what he had packed for our trip.

Being three years older, Nile was more aware of what was going on than I was at age four. He asked, "What are we doing? This isn't Disneyland."

"Just wait, son," replied our father.

Standing in line while waiting to hand our luggage to the ladies behind the counter, Nile noticed something wasn't right. My head, on the other hand, was still full of hope and anticipation of our impending visit to "the Happiest Place on Earth."

Nile continued badgering our father. "Um, why are we at the airport if we are going to Disneyland?"

Hazim quickly replied as if it'd been rehearsed, "Well, son, I am surprising you and we are going to Disney World instead. We have to take a plane to get there."

Nile and I were thrilled and didn't question him any further as we got on the plane.

This was the longest plane ride of my life.

I kept falling asleep and waking up. Each time, it seemed like many hours later—and there was no Disney World on either side of the plane. I was tired, cranky, and just wanted to go see Mickey. Unbeknownst to me, I would not see Mickey for a very, very long time.

After falling into a deep sleep, I was awakened by my father shaking me. "Delicia, get up. Get up, Delicia. We are home." Beginning to slowly wake up, I saw my father's face about an inch in front of mine, coming in for a kiss on my cheek.

Hearing, "Time to get up—we have arrived," I eagerly darted up, looking out the window, naively hoping to see Disney World. All I saw were airplanes with funny writing on their tails, none that I recognized. They all looked unfamiliar and odd, unlike the plane we had boarded in California, which was American Airlines.

As we got off the plane and I looked up at Nile, a terrified look crossed his face. We were both exhausted and confused and didn't know what was happening. Everyone was speaking in a language neither of us knew. People dressed funny. All the women had clothes on their heads—you could only see their eyes. They looked like nuns.

Approaching the food court just beyond the corridor, everything was so different. Nile and I examined the menu but couldn't make out any of the characters.

"What would you like to eat, kids?" our father asked.

We shrugged our shoulders since we hadn't a clue what they were offering.

He scoffed. "I will order food."

Scanning the area, I checked out the signs. There was not a single one in a language I recognized.

Wandering through the halls of the airport, hand in hand with my brother, we knew we only had each other. We were all alone … together.

Knowing something was very wrong, we continued following our father for what felt like a mile-long walk. At the end of the journey, several strangers greeted us with happy smiles. Nile and I both wondered and speculated who they could be until finally it sunk in.

We weren't in Florida.

We were in Baghdad, Iraq.

The minute our father, Hazim, got us onto Iraqi soil, my mother lost all her parental rights. One moment, we were happy kids playing on the lawn of our San Fernando Valley home, and in the blink of an eye, we were ripped away and taken to a country we knew nothing about. Everything was new. New culture, new rules, new language—no mother, no mother, no mother!

I think my brother understood better than I did the consequences of being in Baghdad, but he was being strong for me. He had to protect his little four-year-old sister from knowing the reality of the situation. We had been kidnapped by our father and taken to another country far, far from home.

Meanwhile, our mother thought everything was fine. We were supposed to be enjoying our Easter break with our father. When we didn't return home, she became concerned. She quickly contacted her boyfriend, who was a police officer. He reassured her everything was probably fine.

Imagine my mother's astonishment when she received a letter in the mail, two days after returning from her ski trip to Big Bear. Postmarked from Los Angeles, written on Seven Seas Hyatt Hotel letterhead, it read:

> *Laurie:*
>
> *For twelve years I gave you everything I can.*
>
> *I took care of your brother and sisters for letting them live with us for many years.*
>
> *What you gave me for that?!?!*
>
> *You fucked me from the back. You cheated me. You betrayed me.*
>
> *You fucked another man behind my back.*
>
> *Now it's my turn to break even. To give you the biggest fuck you ever had in your life.*
>
> *By this time, I will be out of this country with my children who I love very much.*

If you will call the police or FBI, you will never see your children. If you do not than you can visit us sometime.

I will take care of them better than you. They will grow in a better society.

Hazim

For two months, my mother had no idea where we were, or if we were okay. During this time, my mother engaged the help of the police, the FBI, the CIA, local newspapers, and anyone she could find that might be able to help her find her children.

During our time in Baghdad, we lived with many of my father's family members: my grandmother, cousins, and some aunts and uncles. I don't remember much about them other than my grandmother loved to cook. She made the most incredible Arabic food! When I came home from school, I could smell our house from down the street. I'd run the rest of the way home while anticipating Grandmother's cooking. Once there, I'd toss my backpack to the floor as I hurried into the kitchen to see what she was making.

Tahdig (Hakaka) was my favorite. The essence of tahdig was rice cooked just to the point of being golden brown with a crispy crunch on the outside and a sticky chewiness on the inside. You could top it with almost anything you wanted. My favorite, fesenjan, was a pomegranate sauce that was cooked for hours along with freshly picked walnuts. The sauce simmered until it thickened and became a stew. Sometimes, kidney beans were poured on top of the tahdig. The flavor in combination with the texture of the rice made for a little bit of heaven on my tastebuds.

Grandmother also made a wide variety of amazing dolmas. In America, we mostly eat the dolmas that have rice and sometimes meat stuffed into a grape leaf, but in Iraq, they make them out of eggplant, squash, tomatoes, mushrooms... and they are fantastic.

My grandmother's cooking was really one of the only good things I can remember about my time in Baghdad.

We lived in a shoeless house. Everyone removed their shoes and left them in the front door foyer. Heaping piles of various shoes were assembled adjacent to the front door.

Every morning, in Iraq, I would begin my journey to school with my book bag in hand and a smile on my face. I'd move to the foyer to put my shoes on before heading out the door. Hunched over the small black leather bench that was adorned with gold buttons down its wooden legs, I'd frantically search for my shoes. It was the same story every day: no shoes.

I'd roam around the house calling out, "Has anybody seen my shoes?" in my best broken Arabic.

My cousins, aunts, and uncles would laugh and go about their business. Some days it would take me five minutes and others it would take what felt like hours to find my shoes, if I was lucky enough to find them at all.

My cousins always acted strange whenever I questioned them about my shoes. It wasn't until I'd endured weeks of finding them in various hiding places that I realized they were messing with me. In the beginning, my cousins would just do it as a joke. Everyone but me thought it was funny.

One night, one of my cousins figured out that my shoes fit her, and she wanted them. Frequently, after that night, she stole my shoes and wore them whenever she wanted. This was the only pair of shoes I owned, and my father wouldn't buy me another pair, no matter how much I begged. On numerous occasions, I trekked to school barefoot.

Walking barefoot was such a strange and sometimes nerve-racking experience. There were no sidewalks. Instead, the pathways were a mixture of mud, rock, and broken glass amongst other obstacles. Roaming along the streets while mud squished between my toes always disgusted me.

Having dealt with this for weeks on end, my only recourse was tattling to my brother.

Once I finally told him, he put a stop to this shoe thievery fairly quickly. The next morning, Nile intentionally got up early to hide in the hallway around the corner from where we kept all the shoes. He spied until he saw my cousin sneaking around the corner. She was about to grab my shoes when my brother jumped out of hiding and screamed in her face in Arabic, "What are you doing?"

She quickly turned around, snatched my shoes, and took off running, both shoes in hand. My brother chased her through the backyard, up and over a concrete wall into the neighbor's yard, finally catching her when the neighbor's pet turkeys cornered her.

Tackling her to the ground, he commandeered my shoes and screamed at her in Arabic, "Don't you ever touch my sister's shoes again!"

Nile carried my shoes to the front of the street and around to our house. When he came in, I was sobbing on the couch.

Putting his arm around me, he whispered, "Don't cry, sis. Here are your shoes. She won't ever take them again, and if she does, you tell me."

I felt so helpless. I was so little and hadn't ever been teased like that before. I was an outsider who didn't speak their language. I was just a little girl, and I didn't understand. What became clear to me from that moment onward was my brother was *the* person I could trust and count on most in the world.

Before we were ripped away from our mother, I attended Stancliff, a snooty private school in Pasadena, California. I started kindergarten the previous September of 1974, and I was the youngest person to have ever been accepted to kindergarten in that school. In April of 1975, I was required to attend kindergarten again—in Baghdad.

I went to a K–12 school where everyone was meshed together. I didn't speak the language at first and didn't have any friends. Many kids would make fun of me because I dressed, looked, acted, and spoke differently than they did.

Two girls who were much older than me were my only saving grace in that school. Every day, both of them would come and find me during lunch. They loved to speak English and wanted to practice with me. Whenever they visited me, they would buy me a Coke. I think this is where my affinity for Coca-Cola originated. That Coke was love to me at a time when I was shown no love on any other level, except by my brother and maybe when I ate my grandmother's cooking. These girls made me feel loveable when it felt like no one other than Nile cared about me.

Iraqi Independence Day, October 3, 1975

The family was celebrating in traditional style; food lavished the tables, and the youngsters were playing around the giant firepit in the backyard. As the night was coming to an end, the celebration began to wind down. Grandmother was telling the kids to "make it happen" in Arabic before going to bed. Encircling the large firepit, the children started blowing. At first, I was perplexed, but everyone looked like they were having so much fun, I wanted to join in.

Very eagerly pushing my way in between my cousin and my brother, I began to blow and laugh, having a good time for once. Suddenly, I felt heat on the right side of my face. I watched as my grandmother bolted up from her chair, screaming in Arabic and running straight for me. By this time, my brother and cousin had backed away. Feeling heat on my head, I hit my hair with my hand, which became hot. I cried as the high-pitched screeches got louder and louder until, after what felt like an eternity, my grandmother finally reached me.

She smacked my head with a towel as my cousins threw water on me, and the confusion in me grew. I still didn't completely realize that my hair was actually on fire! Grandmother immediately rushed me inside to see if I was burned. Miraculously, it only singed a good portion of my hair.

One of my aunts ran past us and into the kitchen, coming back within seconds with a pair of scissors. "Let me help."

She raised the shears to my head while the anguish and turmoil within me grew. There was so much chaos and commotion. I heard a strange sound next to my ear and looked as far to my right as possible, without turning my head, to see what the mystery sound was. The scissors coming right toward my head scared the living crap out of me.

I winced as my aunt held me down, lamenting in Arabic, "Sit still. We need to cut your hair."

Having never had a haircut before, it was a completely new concept for me. The shears continued coming straight toward my head as I was forcefully held down. Confused and scared, all I could do was cry. Suddenly, I heard the strangest sound next to my ear: *whoooshppp*. In shock, I watched my hair fall to the ground. I wailed as the adrenaline pumped through my veins.

I couldn't sleep that night because of the smell of burned hair. Every time I smell singed hair now, I flash back to my hair catching on fire in Baghdad.

I was often tasked with chores while living in Baghdad, even at four years old. One of my responsibilities was folding laundry. On a rainy night in November 1975, just past nine in the evening, I was watching TV and finishing schoolwork.

My father didn't like the fact that I was "wasting my time on television" and scolded, "Delicia, get up and stop watching TV. There is laundry that needs to be done."

Clutching my hand, he led me to the laundry room, where there were baskets and baskets of socks.

I looked up at him with sad eyes, asking, "Daddy, I'm so tired. Could I please do it tomorrow?"

"No!" screamed my father. "I need socks for tomorrow, so it needs to be done now."

At that time, I didn't have all my wits about me, or I would have folded one pair, handed it to him, and gone to sleep. Instead, my little four-year-old self stayed up in that laundry room past midnight folding socks. You can bet that when I was done, the only socks left were the stragglers. Seems I have always had the attitude that if you task me with something, it needs to be done right.

This was quite a traumatic event for me. It was in that moment the belief that nobody cared about me became deeply ingrained. My father cared more about his socks than me, his four-year-old daughter, getting sleep.

Christmas morning, 1975

By this time, Nile and I had been in Iraq for over nine months and were well immersed in the culture. We both were speaking, reading, and writing in Arabic. We were so eager for Christmas that year. The house was decorated, just like back home, with lights, a tree, and even some tinsel.

When Christmas morning came, Nile and I sprinted to the living room where our Christmas tree was. The house was empty, nobody to be found. We looked under the tree and saw many presents. None were for us. *Where was everybody? Why didn't we have any presents under the tree? Perhaps there was a bigger surprise in store. Maybe Mommy was coming for a visit. Or, better yet, maybe we were going home,* I wondered.

Anxiously awaiting the rest of our family under the eaves of our porch, I pondered these thoughts.

A few minutes later, a flashy new silver Mercedes came driving down the road. Seeing fancy cars in Iraq was an anomaly. The streets were full of beat-up cars, and few people were lucky enough to have a car at all. It came closer and closer, and then it pulled into our driveway. Our jaws dropped to the floor in shock. The entire family, including our father, gleefully exited the beautiful new car.

Our father proclaimed, "Look what I got myself for Christmas!"

Running over to the car, we checked it out in all its glory. A brand-new Mercedes ... WOW. I took a big whiff so I could smell the new leather interior of the car and ran my hand along the shiny paint job. I hadn't seen anything quite so pretty in a very long time. It reminded me of America. A wave of sadness washed over me. I missed home and my mom, and I'd hoped there was a bigger present in store for us. Everyone forged into the house with grocery bags in hand but no presents. Nile and I sat in bewilderment, wondering why there weren't any for us.

Following many hours of cooking, everyone gathered around the table to eat before opening presents. This was the longest my brother and I had ever waited to open gifts. Normally, we opened our stockings and presents as soon as Mommy and Daddy were awake. This year, Santa didn't even leave us a stocking. I thought I had been a good girl.

Our cousins, aunts, and uncles gathered around the tree, tearing into their gifts.

Nile and I waited until the very end. Looking at my father with tears welling up in my eyes, I asked, "Do we get anything for Christmas?"

"Oh yes, I almost forgot." Reaching into his jacket pocket, he removed two white envelopes, "Nile" handwritten on one of the envelopes, "Delicia" on the other. I eagerly opened my envelope, and I couldn't believe what was inside: one very crisp, green American dollar.

Thrilled to get a dollar, I hoped it meant we were going home.

I looked up at my father, and my eyes filled with tears. "Does this mean we are going home, Daddy?"

"Don't be ridiculous," my father snarked in Arabic. "It is for you to always remember where you came from, even though you have a new home now."

Speechless and heartbroken, I stomped away. I was incredibly angry, not only because we didn't get anything for Christmas, but also because what we did get was a reminder of the loss that made me extraordinarily sad on a daily basis.

However, I took an unpleasant situation and made it better. Although I didn't realize it at the time, that was the moment I created my first vision board. I put that dollar where I could see it every day—I taped it up and looked at it regularly, hoping someday we would be able to spend that dollar... in AMERICA!

One blustery January day, the doorbell rang. My cousin answered the door and returned with a strange look on his face. My father's expression turned terribly distraught as my cousin whispered in his ear. When my father approached the door, we were all curious about what was happening. My brother and I hid in the hallway. Peering around the corner, we saw our father standing in front of the door, which was opened only a crack. He was being very mysterious. We couldn't see who was on the other side of the door.

Somehow, my brother knew it was someone important. Perhaps someone who could help us get back to our mom?

Nile kept emphatically telling me in my ear, "Go ask him when we are going back to Mom. Go ask him when we are going to see Mom again. Go now... go now... go ask him NOW!"

Innocently, I ran over to ask our father.

"Daddy, when can we go back to Mo—" I felt a huge slap across my face and was yanked by my shirt collar into the kitchen and shushed.

My aunt bent over and whispered in Arabic into my ear, "You better keep your mouth shut and not say a word or you will be in big trouble."

I was crying inside, but the tears wouldn't surface.

After receiving Hazim's letter, our mother had more questions than answers. She ignored his threats and continued to work with the U.S. Embassy and FBI to track us until she was finally able to find the address: house #2630/3/3 Hay Al-Aqari Palestine Street, Baghdad, Iraq. This took some work, but my mother was relentless.

Once she was able to find out exactly where we were, she tried anything and everything to get us back, even threatening suicide. Hazim was adamant that he was keeping us in Baghdad and was in the process of getting us Iraqi citizenship. Researching for several months, she finally found an attorney in Baghdad who took mercy on her. Hence, the mystery man at the door.

Many of the attorneys she contacted wouldn't touch the case because our father had all rights in Iraq; the mother meant nothing. Luckily, this attorney was able to get Hazim to agree that he would send us back if our mother consented to his specific terms, which were as follows:

1. My mother must state that she gave him permission to take us to Baghdad for a year.
2. He owed zero court-ordered child support, both back support and moving forward.

3. My mother must state that Hazim owed her nothing (even though he left her with twenty thousand dollars in debt, which was a ton in 1975).
4. That she'd give up full custody and split custody with him equally.

The battle of our mother trying to get us back—letters between my mother and father, getting attorneys involved both in the USA and Baghdad, the FBI, CIA, police, and anybody else my mother could get to help her—commenced in April of 1975 and continued until our father finally agreed to send us back in March 1976, nearly a year later.

One night, shortly after the mystery man arrived at the door, Father gathered us both around the kitchen table to explain.

"Nile, Delicia, I want you both to know that I love you with all of my heart. My dream was that you would live here forever with me in Iraq and be part of my family. I even started getting you citizenship in your home country of Iraq."

"Our home country?" snarked Nile.

"Yes, this is your home country as much as America is."

"But we were born in America, so isn't *that* our home country?" Nile asked in a brusque tone.

"Sure, son, just listen." My father continued, "I love you more than anything, but your mother has been very insistent on getting you back."

Feeling happy flip-flops in my stomach, I tried hiding the burst of joy I felt because I knew that our father wouldn't like me being happy.

"Does that mean we get to go home?" The words shot out of my mouth before I could stop them.

"If your mother agrees to my terms, then yes, I will send you both back to America."

I felt a tight squeeze on my knee. My brother had reached his hand underneath the table and clutched my knee in excitement. Grabbing his hand, squeezing in solidarity, I gazed at my brother with a concealed smile.

"When?" Nile asked.

"I have to wait and see if she agrees to all of my terms."

Looking my father straight in the eye, Nile asserted, "I'm sorry, but I think I speak for both of us when I say we are going to be super happy to go home."

I agreed with a shit-eating grin like none had ever seen before.

"Well, sorry you kids were so unhappy here," our father snapped back. "I'll let you know if your mother agrees or not." Angrily, he left the table.

A few weeks later, we got word that our mother unreservedly agreed to everything my father had asked for. She would have done anything to get us back.

"YAY!" we screamed as we high-fived each other right in front of our father after he revealed the news that we would be going home. Home to America!

"When?" Nile asked anxiously.

"Well, we will have to figure that out. I don't think Delicia can fly alone, even with you, until she is five."

"Okay, can you book the flight for March sixth?" The words flew from my lips.

No unaccompanied minor could fly before the age of five, and my brother was only eight by that time; therefore, we had to wait to fly home. The date of our ticket home was March 6, 1976, my fifth birthday. We didn't want to wait a single day longer. I couldn't think of a better way to celebrate my birthday than boarding a flight and getting out of Iraq. It would be the greatest birthday ever, knowing my mommy would be waiting on the other end of the journey.

As we prepared for our flight, Nile and I were elated. We couldn't wait to go back to our real home, with our mother, in America. I was so happy I couldn't sleep the entire night before we left. We continuously told our father we were ready to go hours before we were slated to leave. It appeared to annoy and hurt him deeply.

When we arrived at Baghdad International Airport, we watched the planes flying overhead. But unlike the last time, we hoped we knew where we were going: home.

We processed our luggage at the ticket counter. At the security gates, we were met by two flight attendants who let us know they would be escorting us on the flight. Now was the time to say goodbye to our father. Giving him half-hearted hugs, we followed the flight attendants to the gate.

I couldn't fathom missing this man even though he was my father. Being kidnapped and mistreated for just short of a year by Hazim and the entire family had set me free from my desire to have "Dad" in my life, or so I'd thought. Much of my low self-esteem, insecurities, abandonment issues, and internal lack of self-worth stems from this time in my life.

That blissful day, I wore a pink jean jacket with a baby blue jumpsuit. Nile's hand clutched mine just underneath the cuff, holding my hand so tightly it seemed he was afraid someone might separate us. I felt anxious and nervous but also elated. My trust had been broken so many times, I wasn't sure what to believe, yet I was desperately clinging to hope.

As we boarded the plane, we were treated like royalty. Everyone acted like I was the most adorable thing ever, constantly bringing me food and ice cream. Finally, people saw my true cuteness! At that moment, I no longer felt invisible—a feeling I had grown unfortunately used to over the past year with my "family" in Iraq. The plane ride home felt like we were already in a different country.

When I stepped off the plane at Los Angeles International Airport, I could no longer speak a word of English, nor could I understand it. I was petrified I wouldn't be able to talk to my mom. I feared she would be disappointed that I wasn't able to understand or speak English.

My brother and I were escorted off the plane by a flight attendant before any other passengers. Nile and I walked hand in hand up the jetway toward the large open door that seemed like a possible safety portal for me. Upon entering, we saw a swarm of people crowding around, anxiously awaiting their loved ones from afar. None were more eager than my mother, whom I recognized immediately. She was wearing a baby-blue sweater with a pink collared shirt underneath and baby blue pants. Even though our day started thousands of miles apart, my mother and I were connected on such a deep level that the colors of our clothing matched that glorious day we were reunited.

Mom ran toward us with tears streaming down her face, grabbing and hugging us so hard I didn't think I would be able to breathe again. Everyone we knew from my mother's side of the family was there to greet us. That included both my mother's sisters as well as my uncle and his wife, whom we had only met on a handful of occasions.

That day, my fifth birthday, I was too tired from all the traveling to want to do anything but sleep. Mom brought us home, to our real home, in America. It's incredible how quickly your native language returns to you. Within a few hours, I was already speaking in broken sentences.

Christmas lights hung outside the eaves of our small home. I was in shock! I gazed over the entire house from top to bottom, and the colorful lights made me smile. Mom snuck a look at Nile and me so she could enjoy the excitement on our faces. Nile's mouth hung open while I couldn't stop glowing.

"Mommy, why Christmas?" I asked.

"Because I missed Christmas with you, and I never want to miss a Christmas with my babies ever again. So, we are going to have Christmas in March."

After removing our luggage from the car, we ran into the house. The biggest Christmas tree we'd ever seen stood before us, and we stared in awe. This tree was decorated to the nines; it had white lights, colored lights, glass ornaments, bulb ornaments, bubbling candles, popcorn strings, and tinsel. It was the craziest, most fun Christmas tree ever. Under the tree were what seemed like thousands of presents.

Dropping our luggage at the front door, Nile and I looked at each other with gigantic smiles, running to our presents—miraculously no longer tired from all the traveling.

"Can we open them?" Nile asked enthusiastically.

"How about we open one like on Christmas Eve and then in the morning you can open the rest and see if Santa left you stockings?"

My brother and I positioned ourselves in front of the tree, carefully choosing the one present to unwrap before bed. We both tore open our gifts while Mom joyfully snapped what felt like a million pictures.

Tucking us in that night, Mom read us each our own special bedtime story and gave us a thousand kisses, several for every day we were missing. It felt amazing to be at home with my mom, in my bed, in America. Still unsure if I was dreaming, I literally had to pinch myself.

The next morning, I lay in bed orienting myself. Skeptical of where I was, it took me a few minutes to realize this wasn't a dream. I was home. Grasping this, I quickly jumped out of bed and raced to the living room.

Running down the hallway, I saw the glow from the lights on the tree. I stared at the tree in all its glory, including the rows and rows of gifts, and was flabbergasted.

Looking up to our stockings to see if they were filled was my first clue that Santa came. Next, I began searching around the bottom of the tree because Santa always left presents wrapped in red tissue paper with our first initial in gold glitter. Sure enough, there they were—Santa came! I'd thought maybe our mom had some special phone number or something because Santa doesn't make trips in March. Our red tissue paper presents magically appeared while we were sleeping. Written atop in super fancy Santa handwriting were ornate, cursive *Ds* and *Ns*.

Unlike in Baghdad, where none of the presents were for us, *all* these presents were for us, every single one of them. My brother came running down the hallway as I shouted, "Nile, it's real, we're home, and all of these presents are for us!"

Kneeling next to me, wrapping his arms around me, he cried out, "We are home, Sis!"

Finishing up our Christmas in March, Mom went to the closet and took down more gifts. These were wrapped in birthday wrapping. Withdrawing presents, one after the other, she arranged them on the table.

Nile asked, "What's all this, Mom?"

"Well, I missed your birthdays, too, so today, we celebrate your birthdays *and* Christmas!"

"Far out!" I screeched, running toward the dining room table.

"Hold on a minute," said my mother while heading to the kitchen.

A few minutes later, she emerged from the kitchen carrying a large cake that looked like it had twenty candles on top, all aglow as she sang "Happy Birthday." The cake was split down the center, and each half was topped with

Nile's and my favorite things. At least, the last things my mother knew that we loved before being ripped away from her. Making a wish, we blew out the candles and opened our presents.

My brother opened his first since his birthday fell before mine. When it was my turn, Mom handed me my present with a giant smile. I was ecstatic and could tell she was looking forward to giving it to me.

"I made this for you while you were gone," she revealed with pride.

Ripping open the paper, I found a cardboard box underneath. Slowly opening the box with a bubbling spring of curiosity filling every crevice of my body, I could see white with tiny red plastic hearts.

"What is it?" I asked with fervor.

"Take it out. I hope you like it," she said.

Removing it from the box, I saw the most incredible dress I'd ever seen in my little five-year existence. Mom made it by hand—white chiffon with little rigid plastic 3D hearts that you could touch. A tiny heart glued onto my dress every inch or so.

I pled, "Can I wear it today?"

"Yes, of course. I would be proud to have you wear it today. I'm so glad you like it."

"Like it? I love it! Thank you, Mommy."

Putting that dress on made me feel like I was the prettiest girl in the world.

"Okay, kids, I have one more surprise," Mom said.

"Wow, Mom, you really outdid yourself," Nile said with a smile.

"Come on, let's go."

"Where are we going?"

"Just come on, let's go," she urged.

Jumping in the car, we took the 5 South. Mom did not say a word about where we were going, nor did we question her. It felt surreal to place that trust in someone again.

Getting off the freeway on Ball Road, as we veered right, I saw the Matterhorn in the distance.

"Are we going to Disneyland?" I asked enthusiastically.

"Yep, you got it, we are going to Disneyland!" my mom exclaimed.

"Yay, yay, yay, yay, yay!" my brother and I shouted in unison.

Upon entering the parking lot of Disneyland, I saw signs with Mickey, Goofy, Donald, and Pluto, and I knew we were actually at Disneyland this time. The excitement in me grew as I stepped out of the car. I was wearing the most delightful dress in the world and was finally going to Disneyland, feeling like an actual princess. We took a family photo next to the giant Mickey head that sits in front of the train station mere seconds before a moment I will never forget: the moment I knew I was finally safe. It was a feeling that had eluded me for nearly an entire year in Iraq.

Archways off both sides of the entryway with paths leading to the magical kingdom awaited us. We walked under the arch that read, "Here you leave today and enter the world of yesterday, tomorrow, and fantasy."

Upon entering, I knew this was it. I would never be ripped away from my mother, not ever again. It was as if walking through that small tunnel signified a magical passageway to my safety and well-being. At that moment, I knew I was finally home. For good.

Taking that dollar my father gave us for Christmas out of my tiny purse, I held it to the sky, proclaiming, "Mommy, I want some ice cream!"

"I'll get you some ice cream, my baby. Save your money."

"No, Mommy, please. I want to spend my money on ice cream. Here at Disneyland. At home in California."

The three of us continued down Main Street in search of some ice cream.

When I celebrate the day of my birth, I not only celebrate the miracle of being born, but I also celebrate that glorious day we stepped foot on American soil again, March 6, 1976.

MY PERSONAL ARCHANGEL

Much like the Archangel Michael, who is known for being the angel of protection, my brother Nile seemed obliged to be my guardian from an exceedingly early age. Even before we were taken to Iraq by our father, Nile was often put in a position where he was responsible for me.

Apparently, the Grim Reaper had it in for me in March of 1974, a year prior to being kidnapped. Thanks to Nile, my life was spared, not once but twice!

Our mom was a special education teacher at Woodrow Wilson High School in East Los Angeles, one of the toughest neighborhoods in all of LA. She struggled with two kids, a husband who was hardly ever around, and a full-time career. From the moment I was born, even though he was only three years older than me, Nile helped take care of me.

One particular night, Mom hollered at Nile from the bathroom, "Nile, I need to make dinner. Can you please come watch your sister so I can cook?"

"But, Mom," whined six-year-old Nile from the other room.

"Nile, please, I could really use your help. I'm making mac and cheese for you," she pleaded.

"Okay, okay," Nile finally caved.

"She is in the bath; all you have to do is watch her."

"Coming," he said.

"Delicia, Nile is going to watch you, so don't go anywhere."

"Yes, Mommy," I replied, distracted by the fun of my bubble bath.

I didn't notice Mom leave as I happily darted my yellow duckies in and out of the bubbles. Then suddenly, I lost the baby duck. Quickly sinking my body under the water open-eyed, I searched frantically. As I caught a glimpse of my duckie, my anxiety settled. Popping my head back up, I heard a *thunk* as I felt the bath spigot crack into my tiny skull. Immediate pain riddled my head as I passed out, sinking under the water.

Stepping into the bathroom, Nile saw me lying face down in the bathtub and swirls of blood forming around my body, the water slowly turning pink. He was sent straight into a state of panic.

"Mom, help!" he screamed.

Hearing terror in his voice, she rushed to the bathroom. My six-year-old brother had his arms around me, dragging me out of the tub. Mom helped him lay me on the cold tile floor. She put her ear to my mouth to assess if I was breathing.

"Delicia, Delicia!" she shouted in anguish while shaking my three-year-old body. "Nile, grab me a tissue!" she cried out.

When I finally came to, the first thing out of my mouth was, "Mommy, my head hurts."

Swooping my naked little body into her arms, hugging me as if there were no tomorrow, she screamed, "Let's go! Get dressed, Nile!"

"Where are we going?" Nile asked.

"The hospital. We have to make sure she is okay and doesn't have a concussion. And thank you," she paused to add. "You saved her life."

I was quite a curious child and often wandered the house and yard looking for random things I could play with. Money was scarce, so tea sets for my dolls were a luxury, and I was always scavenging the yard for arbitrary pieces of junk I could use for my tea parties. A piece of wood served as a plate, and an old tin can could be imagined as a fancy cup; oh, how my dolls and I would enjoy our time. The mud pies were always a big hit at my parties.

Later that year, in the summer of 1974 while scavenging in my backyard one sunny afternoon, I found a penny. Holding it to the sky, I watched it sparkle in all of its glory. It was shiny and new and quite intriguing. Curious about it in every way, I stuck it on my tongue. The taste was rather strange, but I kind of liked it.

Sticking the entire penny in my mouth, I sucked on it like it was candy until it went down my throat. Unable to breathe, I ran as fast as possible to find help.

Nile was in the kitchen and saw my little brown face turning blue. He began to scream. "Mom, help, Delicia is choking!" Bending me over his knee, he whacked my back as hard as he could.

Mom moseyed into the kitchen, asking nonchalantly, "What did you say?" Then, taking in the scene, she screeched, "What in the world are you doing?" And she snatched me away from his lap.

"Mom, she is choking!" he screamed, louder this time.

Finally recognizing my distress, Mom quickly bent me over her knee and pounded my back. The penny wouldn't dislodge. Turning me around and forcing my mouth open, she swept her finger into my throat as deep as possible.

Hysterical, she wailed, "I can't get it out! Call 9-1-1!"

Throwing me back over her knee, she hit me even harder. At last, that shiny new copper penny popped out of my mouth and rolled across the kitchen floor. My body collapsed on the floor, gasping for air and life.

"Slow down," Mom said. "You are going to hyperventilate. Take deep, slow breaths." Breathing deeply and slowly, she whispered, "Inhale and exhale."

Rolling onto my back and throwing my arms and legs out to the sides of me, I looked at my brother standing in the corner, terrified, and muttered, "Thank you." Looking at my mom, I moaned, "Mommy, thank you. I love you."

Nile was an entrepreneur by the age of six. The summer before our father tore us away from our mother was a particularly hot one in Southern California. We lived in the San Fernando Valley and, just to give you an idea of how hot summers in "The Valley" could be, you could *actually* fry an egg on the sidewalk.

Lemonade stands were a big deal when we were kids. On weekends, there would be a kid at every corner selling lemonade for five cents. One Saturday morning, we were out with our mom "garage sale-ing," as we normally did every weekend. This Saturday there were more homemade lemonade stands than usual. After scavenging through other people's trash for random things we could call our very own, we ventured home.

When we got home, I could see the wheels in Nile's head turning.

He dragged me aside, asking, "Did you see all those lemonade stands?"

"Uh-huh," I mumbled with a half-cocked head and one eyebrow raised. "Why?"

"We could do our own lemonade stand," Nile stated proudly.

"I'm *tree*," I said, incredulously, as I held up the three middle fingers on my hand.

"What good are you?" Nile replied, huffing off.

But once Nile put his mind to something, it was usually a done deal. Even at the immature age of six, he found a way to make it happen. Nile wasn't an ordinary kid. Always an out-of-the-box thinker, he didn't want a regular lemonade stand. In his six-year-old entrepreneurial mind, he knew he needed to set himself apart from every other kid on the block.

A few minutes later, Nile ran through the living room shouting, "Grape! Grape! I should do grape!"

As a structural engineer who worked on the famous Cinerama Dome in Hollywood, our father was rarely home. This Saturday, he happened to be around, watching a television rerun of *M*A*S*H*.

Nile marched up to him. "Dad, can you help me build a lemonade stand?"

"I have a lot of work to do, son. Ask your mother."

"She's not here," Nile argued.

"Then ask your sister," our father responded, anxious to get back to his show.

"She's '*tree*,'" he muttered, rolling his eyes and stomping away in a huff.

Breathing a big sigh of disappointment, yet determined to make it happen on his own, Nile wandered the neighborhood, searching for anything he could use to make a stand. Finding a large piece of paper he thought would make a perfect sign, Nile rushed home to finish the task, holding it up like a kite as he ran so it wouldn't get dirty. Running into the driveway, he noticed Mom's car.

I could hear him yell from the driveway, "Right on!"

Sprinting inside the house trailing a six-foot-long piece of butcher paper as if he had a giant white tail flowing behind him, he exclaimed breathlessly, "Mom, I'm making a grape drink stand! Wanna help?"

"What a great idea!" she said. "How did you think to do grape instead of lemonade?"

"Everyone does lemonade," Nile said dismissively. "I want to make more money, so I'm doing grape."

"Wow, I'm impressed! Let's get to work. What's that you got there?" Mom asked, spotting the paper.

"I found it down the street. I thought I could take a table and write a sign with 'Grape juice for sale, five cents.'" Nile waved his hand across the paper as he spoke, as if he could already see the words written on it.

Mom nodded in genuine admiration of her young son's ingenuity. "How about you write the sign, and I will find you a table?"

"Sounds good!" Nile replied with a big smile while reaching for a purple marker. "Thanks, Mom!" he shouted as she headed out the door.

I watched as he carefully wrote in large letters, "Grape Drink 5¢," big enough to fit the front of the table so people could read it clearly. When he ran out the front door, Nile saw Mom had already set up a little table and found a giant yellow umbrella. She plopped it onto the ground as she reached out to grab one side of Nile's sign.

"You have to tape it onto the side of the table, like this," she instructed.

Mom finished taping one side of the butcher paper to the table and handed Nile the tape. "Now you do the other side, and I will go make you some grape juice."

Nile carefully taped up the other side of the sign and positioned the umbrella so it shaded him from the hot sun. Running to the side of the house, he brought a folding chair back with him. Placing the chair under the sign, he stood, admiring his creation.

Mom came back, a pitcher of grape juice in hand, with some Dixie cups and a camera. She placed the pitcher on the table while I stood behind the fence, watching Nile construct his creation.

"Say cheese," Mom shouted proudly as he smiled for the camera.

That afternoon, I played on the front lawn, watching my brother sell many Dixie cups of grape juice to the neighborhood folk. Almost every car stopped to admire his adorable grape drink stand. Some even gave him a whole quarter. That weekend my brother made enough money to buy the RC car he really wanted at Toys"R"Us. This mindset was a small glimpse into the entrepreneurial success Nile would gain later in life.

When we first came back from Baghdad, we lived in a cute apartment in Burbank. A hallway led to a living room on the left that was open to the dining room. Around the corner from that was the kitchen. On the other side of the hallway was another corridor that connected to the bedrooms.

We didn't have central air back then, and the tiny air conditioner in the living room window basically kept your face cold if you were lucky enough to stand or sit in front of it. On scorching summer days, cruising to the store simply to enjoy the air conditioning was the thing to do. If we were lucky enough to have an extra fifteen cents, we would get an ice cream cone from Thrifty's.

Summer of 1977 was one of those unbearably hot times. At the time, I was six and Nile was nine. In an attempt to escape the heat, we trekked the eight blocks to the store. On our journey home, I was moseying about, not paying much attention to the ground in front of me, and I unexpectedly felt an immense sting in the bottom of my foot. I cried out in severe pain, my knees buckled beneath me, and I crumbled to the ground. I crossed one leg over the other in an attempt to look at my foot. In the center of my left flip-flop was a shard of translucent glass with about a half inch sticking out. Blood pooled between my foot and the flip-flop, forming a puddle on the sidewalk.

Nile was about twenty paces in front of me when I screamed, "Nile, help me!" with agony in my voice.

Hearing my anguish, he quickly darted back to me. "What happened?" he cried out in a bit of a panic.

"I don't know. I stepped on glass, and it went right through my flip-flop."

"Crap, let me think," he said, pacing back and forth on the hot sidewalk.

Cars went rushing by on the extremely busy street. We had cars on one side of us and a ten-foot concrete wall on the other. Once again, it was just the two of us relying on each other.

Kneeling down on the pavement next to me, Nile warned, "This is going to hurt, but we need to get the glass out."

"No, no, please, Nile," I begged. "Let's wait until we get home."

"How are you going to get home with that in your foot?"

"You can't pull it out. It will bleed like crazy. I learned that from *Code Red* on TV! And what if some gets stuck? Let's wait, please, and see if Mom is home."

Supporting me with his arm, he lifted me to a standing position. As I limped behind him, I held my foot up; it dripped blood every step I took, leaving a trail behind me. When my brother noticed how much I was bleeding, he panicked.

He knelt before me and said, "Get on."

"What?"

"I'm going to carry you home. We have to hurry. Jump on my back."

"Really? Are you sure you can carry me?" I asked.

"Just trust me and jump on my back," he responded.

I had a difficult time trying to hobble onto his back without touching my bloody foot to him. Bending down even lower, he shouted, "Get on!" He lifted me up while carefully placing my hurt foot around his waist.

He trudged as fast as he could the remaining six blocks home. When we arrived, Mom wasn't there. Figuring she was still working, we headed to the bathroom. Nile found a pair of tweezers and lifted my foot to his knee.

"This is going to hurt, so I will do it as quickly as possible," he warned.

There was about a half inch of the shard sticking out the foam bottom of the flip-flop. He found scissors and carefully cut right next to the glass, releasing the shoe from my foot. He now stared at a large fragment of glass inserted, who knew how deeply, into the bottom of my foot. Luckily, it was protruding and easy to grab.

"It's kind of numb now," I mumbled.

Carefully placing the tweezers on the end of the shard, Nile said, "I'm going to count to three. One, two—"

Immense pain ran through my body, and I let out a howl like a coyote caught in a trap on a summer's evening. In tears, I managed to muster up the energy to hit him on the arm, shouting, "You said you were going to count to three!"

Chuckling, he teased, "I'm sorry, I knew it would hurt."

He plucked out what was left of the shard, and blood gushed everywhere. He grabbed a towel and wrapped the bottom of my foot with it. "Put pressure on it," he instructed me. "I will go find a Band-Aid."

The white towel was slowly becoming pink. The blood wouldn't stop coming. He returned with an ACE bandage and wrapped it around the towel as tight as he could.

"Now, I have to call Mom."

I bellowed an appreciative "thank you" as he rushed out the door.

It wasn't long before Mom came home and swept me off the couch where I had been elevating my leg, per my brother's instructions. We rushed to the emergency room, where I got the first stitches I'd ever had in my life—eight, to be exact. The cut had been much worse than my brother or I thought.

"Where is the young man who saved her?" the doctor inquired. My brother beamed with pride and shyly raised his hand.

"Atta boy, way to take care of your sister," the doctor praised.

"Thanks, Doc," Nile replied with a smile.

A few months later, Nile and I were in our kitchen doing homework when Mom dashed in the door, shouting, "Let's go, kids!"

"Where are we going?"

"Never mind that. Let's go. Come on, quickly," she urged, ushering us out the door of our tiny apartment.

Nile, Mom, and I jumped in our green Opal GT—Mom and Nile in the front, me in the tiny back seat that made me feel as if I was living in a toy land every time we went anywhere. It was a bench that was, at most, two feet wide. To get in, I had to squeeze through the crack of the front seat leading to the back death trap, scrunch down in a squat position, and maneuver my body sideways. Once I finally managed to get in, I was able to sprawl my legs out and lie down. There, I'd stare at the ceiling, imagining a miniature world in our teeny car as we drove. In the summertime, my legs would stick to the seats, and I had to peel my skin from the dark green pleather to get out. The only view, other than the pinholes in the headliner, were the bottoms of the buildings through the infinitesimal triangular window in the back.

My mom drove for probably fifteen minutes or so, and I gazed either at the ceiling or through the window the entire time, not recognizing any of the tall buildings I saw. We passed what felt like blocks and blocks of hundred-foot-tall electrical poles. When the car slowed, then stopped, I popped my head up to see where we were.

Mom quickly turned around, pushing my head back down and hissing, "Not yet. One second." Then she handed me a handkerchief, demanding, "Put this on."

"Where?" I asked inquisitively.

"Over your eyes, silly," she mocked.

"Why?" I questioned with a bit of fear in my voice.

"Just trust me and put it on."

"Okay." Hesitantly, I tied the handkerchief over my eyes.

Then I heard Mom say, "Turn around."

"Me?" I asked. The confusion of the whole situation was disorienting.

"No, your brother."

Annoyed, he inquired, "What exactly are you doing?"

"Just turn around," she asserted, placing another blindfold on him. Curious why we were blindfolded in front of an electrical plant, we put our trust in our mother extremely reluctantly.

"Now, can either of you see?" she asked.

"No, what is going on, Mom?" Nile responded.

"Just a second." I felt her maneuver the car away from the curb, turn the corner, and drive a bit farther before stopping again.

"What is happening, Mom?" I probed once again.

"Just a minute," she insisted sternly, sounding like her patience was waning.

I heard the door open and shut and Nile utter, "Oh Jesus, what is happening?"

Shortly afterward, another door opened.

"Watch your step. Step up," Mom said to Nile as I waited helplessly in the back seat. "Okay, wait right there."

I had no idea what was going on at that moment, but oddly enough, I wasn't fearful. Somehow, I knew this was a good thing and I wasn't in danger. I could trust our mom implicitly, couldn't I?

The sound of the seat lever meant it was my turn. I am a bit claustrophobic, so being blindfolded certainly wasn't a picnic for me. I reached out for my mother as she took my hand.

"Come on, let's get you out of there," she said.

Mom placed me right next to my brother on the sidewalk. Feeling our arms touching, we stood in wonderment, anxiously waiting for the big reveal.

"Are you ready?" she asked with glee.

Impatiently, we cried out, "Yes, yes, please take these off!"

Mom gently removed our handkerchiefs simultaneously. Before us stood a pink house with white-framed windows and brick lining the lower portion of the house. It had a porch and a small front lawn with a "For Sale" sign, atop which perched a smaller "Sold" sign.

We stood in bewilderment.

Mom announced, "Come see your new home!"

My jaw practically fell to the ground. Nile and I looked at each other with astonishment. Laughing, we ran toward the house.

"Is this really ours?" I cried out with glee.

"Well, technically, it belongs to the bank right now, but someday it will be ours," Mom said as she inserted the shiny new key in the front door. We could hardly contain our excitement.

She slowly opened the door, and Nile and I stood in shock. We saw a dingy brown carpet that smelled like cat pee, paint that was peeling off the walls, and water stains along the stucco ceilings. My excitement dampened a bit—this place was a dump.

"How are we ever going to live here?" asked Nile.

"Oh, come on now, it will be fun! We can fix this place up ourselves, and it will be an amazing place to live. Look, come here: this will be your sister's room."

Behind the first door was a small room with a tiny, single-door closet. Gesturing for me to enter, Mom announced, "This is your room, Delicia."

Marveling at my very own room, I spun in circles with my arms open wide. I was amazed and grateful for the amount of space I had. No longer would I have to share a room with my brother.

"Come check out my room," Mom beckoned. We followed behind her to the end of the hallway. As we passed one door, she cried out, "Oh, and here is the bathroom!" and pointed it out as we passed it. "It even has a pink bathtub."

I peeked my head in and was surprised to see such a Pepto Bismol pink–colored tub. I was more eager than ever to indulge in a bath.

Nile and I began exploring when Mom gushed, "Let's go see the dining room and kitchen. There's even a small backyard and a garage."

I could see the place in a different light now; our new home was slowly revealing its potential. I was feeling the excitement once more. Nile, on the other hand, was pouting.

As we moved through the dining room and kitchen, I looked forward to the work we had ahead, even though the place was currently a disaster. I thought, *It can be cleaned, and it's bigger than any place we have ever lived before. But where is Nile's room?* Perhaps he was thinking that as well—hence the pouty face.

We walked out the back door and down the steps. Before us stood a separate garage to the right. The backyard was small, but it was bigger than any backyard I recall having. We'd been living in apartments since arriving back from Baghdad and were excited to have room to play.

Standing in the garage, Mom announced, "So, this is it. What do you think?"

Nile turned to her, tears in his eyes. "Where is my room?"

"Oh, silly me," Mom said, a mischievous grin spreading across her face. "I forgot to tell you—*this* is your room." She opened her arms wide, gesturing to the empty garage.

"What?" he exclaimed as his eyes sparkled like a kid in a candy store.

"Yep, I thought we could make this into your own little space. You will have to use the bathroom in the house, though. Decorate it however you like."

"Wow, far out! No way, Mom! For real?"

He was beside himself, a ten-year-old with his very own one-car garage for a room. The pouty frown had turned into the biggest smile I'd ever seen on him. I witnessed true joy in his eyes. He no longer had to share a room with his baby sister, and his room was completely separate from the house. Every kid's dream. By the look on Mom's face, I could tell how proud she was to be giving him such a gift.

The following day, Nile started on his room. The walls of the garage were wood slats, and the ground was concrete, so there was quite a bit of work to be done. He checked out construction books from the library daily and studied them. Over the course of the next few weeks, he made a list of what was needed to make his room super cool. On my mother's salary, we didn't have money to just go to the store and buy what he needed. He had to get creative with what he could find or what we already had.

A large piece of foam from a neighbor's trash can stuffed around the drafty opening of the garage prevented the frigid air from leaking in at night. A piece of packaging crate foam from a local business's trash provided soundproofing on the walls. My mother was able to get a couple of extra scraps of carpet from a friend of hers, and when puzzled together, they were just about the size of the floor. His walls displayed many of his favorite musical posters—mostly KISS. Nile even had his very own waterbed that we found at a garage sale and a fantastic stereo system. I was jealous, but he let me hang out in there sometimes. And when I was lucky, he shared his music with me. I looked up to my big brother and wanted the world for him, so it was easy to look past my jealousy.

However, after settling into our home in North Hollywood, it seemed my brother was done being my protector. Perhaps he had grown up too fast due to the obligation of looking out for me. The entire year in Baghdad, he felt responsible. Maybe he just wanted to be a kid again? Or maybe, because we had our mom back, he felt he could let go of that role. I wasn't sure. Either way, as I watched him make new friends, it felt like he was leaving me behind. Although it was a normal reaction for a kid his age, it was extremely difficult for me because I was used to having my big brother around.

Our father returned to the States only a few short months after Nile and I were reunited with our mother. Hazim was a nonexistent father who refused to pay child support and chose to completely abandon me.

Our father grew up in Baghdad, where daughters were not as important as sons; therefore, I meant nothing to him. It hurt me deeply believing in my heart that, simply because of my gender, he wanted nothing to do with me. Though I was desperately hopeful this wasn't true, his actions proved otherwise.

Not once did I receive a phone call, birthday card, or Christmas card. Nothing. There was zero communication with my so-called father. Nile, on the other hand, would get a phone call every blue moon asking if he wanted to play tennis or see a movie. Nile always politely declined the opportunity to even speak to him on the phone. Still, our father's feeble attempts at some sort of relationship with Nile was pure heartbreak for me.

Other than the occasional phone call to my brother, our father chose not to be part of our upbringing. Mom, wanting Nile to have a "father figure," signed him up for the Big Brother program, hoping to find someone to fill that role. After completing the required paperwork about my brother's background, what values were important for us, and a slew of other questions, she submitted the application to the Big Brothers Association of America. She hoped they would find a good match for my brother quickly.

Marvin came up as a fit for Nile. He was twenty-three and single and didn't have kids of his own.

They kicked off their relationship by having lunch once every couple of weeks. Shortly thereafter, they went to the movies, the park, and other seemingly fun things. Eventually, Marvin and Nile got together almost every weekend.

Marvin's BMW would pull into the driveway, and Nile would bounce out of the house as if he was going to play with the greatest friend ever. Gazing in awe, I wondered what fun things they would be doing. *What about me?* I ruminated. These were the days when Hazim abandoning me really hurt. I longed for someone to do father/daughter things with.

"Mom? Can I get a big brother too?" I asked.

"This organization is for young men who don't have their fathers, but you have a mother."

"But I don't have a father," I protested. I didn't understand what difference it made that I was a girl. Nile still had Mom, too.

"I know, sweetheart, but they don't have any place that can offer you an alternative father."

"I wish I could get a big brother," I said, pouting.

"I'll tell you what, how about we have a mommy and daughter day? We can get some ice cream and maybe watch a movie."

"Really, Mommy? That would be fun."

"Sure, let's do it!"

That appeased me until the next weekend when Marvin came for Nile again. Mom could only go on our special dates every so often, so when Nile and Marvin would venture out, I wandered the neighborhood in search of something fun to do. This got me into loads of trouble. I wanted a father figure, but there was no organization that had one available, so what was a girl to do?

Many of my musical influences came from Nile. One way we bonded as siblings was him introducing me to music he liked. When I was ten years old, Nile loved DEVO. Marvin was enthused to take Nile to a DEVO concert, but our mother wouldn't let him go unless Marvin took us together. At the time, Nile was thirteen, and the last person he wanted to tag along with him to a DEVO concert was his little ten-year-old sister. Reluctantly, he agreed, and Marvin purchased tickets for everyone.

The big day was December 10, 1981—our first concert ever. I could hardly sleep the night before, I was so excited. I knew I was going to be a third wheel, yet I was bound and determined to have fun. We gave our mom a quick kiss on the cheek while rushing out the door and hopped into Marvin's BMW.

My level of excitement made the cold shoulder from my brother sting even more. The ride was quiet from the back seat; I entertained myself while Marvin and Nile chatted the entire forty-minute journey. I knew we were close when we got off the 405 freeway and the off-ramp was packed with what looked like a thousand cars. Peering into the other vehicles, I saw people wearing funny orange traffic cones on their heads.

"Look, Nile, how funny!" I giggled, pointing to the hats.

Shrugging his shoulders, he said in a melancholic voice, "Yup, they're fans," then carried on his conversation with Marvin. The feeling of being unwanted washed over me. Ignoring it, I chuckled to myself and continued people watching. I recalled the DEVO album cover, which featured a bunch of guys wearing orange cones on their heads, and I realized all the people around us were going to the same place.

As we gave our tickets to the person wearing a uniform like I'd seen in the old movies—funny hat and all—I was in awe of how grand it was. He took our tickets, ripped them in half, and handed the other half back.

I was lured away by the merchandise booth, the crowds, glitz, and glamour. While checking out all the really cool posters and T-shirts, I heard my name being called in a panicked voice. Marvin thought he'd lost me. I could hear from a distance, "Delicia, Delicia, Delicia, where are you?"

I knew I'd better go find him quickly. I followed the voice through the crowds. "Delicia. Delicia. Delicia, where are you?"

The crowd thickened, and I felt lost in the sea of people. Fear arose within me. Luckily, Marvin kept yelling, "Delicia!"

Nile was yelling as well.

Finally, after what felt like hours to a ten-year-old girl in a sea of strangers, I was able to find them.

Marvin told me in a very stern voice, "It is super important that you stay right next to me. It is way too easy for you to get lost, and your mom put me in charge of you."

"Okay, Marvin, I'm sorry. I was just looking at the T-shirts."

"I know, but you can't do that without telling me, okay?"

"I'm sorry." The feeling of being a nuisance was amplified for me now that I had caused him strife.

As we approached our seats, the crowd came in from giant doors on every side of us. This place was huge! I felt like an ant in a colony of humans. There were so many seats and people. Seeing this many people in one place was something I'd never experienced. The closest I'd had come to it was at Disneyland, but they weren't all in one area like this. Realizing I was a ridiculously small fish in a giant pond, I wouldn't leave Marvin's side for the rest of the evening.

The stadium lights flashed, and an announcement was made overhead. People poured in through the doors, which closed behind them. The lights dimmed, and the crowd went wild, clapping, cheering, stomping their feet, and hitting the backs of the plastic chairs with their hands. It felt like an earthquake shaking the arena. The energy of tens of thousands of people cheering at the same time shot through my body like massive volts of electricity. DEVO emerged on stage, and I felt a surge of energy unlike any I'd ever felt before. Climbing up on my plastic seat, planting both feet on my chair bottom, I was able to catch a small glimpse. I maneuvered back and forth with the crowd, stealing a view under the armpit of the person in front of me as they raised their hands to the sky with delight.

DEVO played several songs I didn't recognize. Midway through the set, when they played the first beat of "Whip It," the crowd went nuts. Enjoying every minute, I danced like I had never danced before. A few times I nearly fell off my chair, and I hung on to Marvin's shoulder for balance. Since he was really tall—over six feet—Marvin was the perfect anchor in the large crowd. I was bopping around on that stadium seat like there were no tomorrows, cracking that whip and steppin' on the brakes. What an incredible experience it was, watching this band of men wearing cones on their heads while singing funky lyrics.

Regardless of how badly Nile treated me that night, I made it my personal destiny to have a good time. Which was precisely what I did, consciously choosing not to let anything or anyone ruin the first concert of my life.

From a very young age, I realized that no matter how badly something hurts your feelings, you still have the choice to ignore it, at least for that moment. Fun is something we don't get enough of in this lifetime, and most people take it for granted.

Nile and I didn't share the same friends or interests at this point in our lives. He was a teenager, and we were drifting apart. Nile listened to KISS, Madness, punk bands, and ska in his bedroom while I made mud pies and hung out in the backyard playing with my Holly Hobbie doll. The last thing my brother wanted to do was hang around with his kid sister. But for me, all I wanted to do was hang around with my cool older brother. I always thought he was so much more bitchin' than any of my friends in the neighborhood. I also often pondered the thought of having a dad. If that father figure had existed in my life, would I have longed so deeply for a friendship with my brother?

There were several occasions when Nile was forced to be with me. Our mom somehow managed to raise us single-handedly on a teacher's salary. She had to figure out a way to make ends meet. In order to achieve her goals and have additional income, my mother chose to purchase a bar.

She found a bar for sale in the local paper and was determined to give it a shot. The bar was in Burbank, within walking distance of our new home. She named it The Stein Club. Our mother was proud of owning her own bar. This purchase was a double-edged sword. No longer would we hurt for money. However, now she had to teach during the day and work at the bar in the evening. From that point forward, we were latchkey kids. We would be much better off financially, but she was rarely home, which made Nile my caretaker once again.

When I was lucky enough to have him around, he was quite the entertainer. His specialty was making crazy food, and I was his trusty taste tester. Spicy food was my arch nemesis, and he thought it was hilarious to promise me over and over that it wasn't spicy. Very aware that he was lying, he'd profess, "Just try it. I promise it's not spicy."

It was always spicy. So spicy I had to run to the fridge to wash my mouth out with milk. Nile just laughed.

On the plus side, he would make me delicious desserts like chocolate cake with Oreo cookies and gummy worms falling out the sides of it or pudding with Almond Roca on top. When my brother was watching me, I could always count on something entertaining or fun.

The Rocky Horror Picture Show was released in 1975, and midnight showings started in 1976. By 1978, the movie became a full-fledged cult classic, and Nile loved it. It was a musical parody of the classic horror film *Frankenstein* with a bit of a twist.

At the time, I didn't understand the film, but I loved the music as much as my brother did. Some of my favorite memories with Nile were chillin' in his garage for hours while he played me a variety of music and soundtracks, way beyond *Rocky Horror*.

Elementary school was an extremely difficult time in my life. Bullying was something that happened to me daily. Crying in my room after school because of this was the norm. One particular day was especially rough; feeling down and out, I didn't want to do much of anything. The harassment at school was overwhelming, and I broke. I was sulking on my bed when I heard Nile yelling my name from the backyard. Reluctantly, I got off my bed and went to see what all the fuss was about.

As I got to the backyard, my brother was still screaming my name. "Delicia!"

"What?!" I hollered back, irritated.

"Sit down!" he demanded with a mischievous look on his face.

"Why?" I protested, stomping my feet while I pouted. "I had a really bad day, and I just want to go lie down in my room."

"Sit down," he insisted.

"Okay," I relented, still annoyed and impatient as I obeyed, sitting on the concrete back step. "I'm sitting. Now what?"

"Just a minute," he barked in a stern voice. "Don't move. Stay there!"

"OKAY!" I shouted back.

Aggravated, I waited for whatever he had in store. I didn't want to be bothered with what he was planning and preferred to sulk in my room. I heard a beat of music come from Nile's garage room, and then he popped out of the door wearing a red silk nightgown he had grabbed from our mother's closet. His hair was spiked up high with grease, and he was wearing blue eyeshadow, bright red lipstick, and distinguishing pink blush. He looked like a drag queen straight out of a B-rated seventies film.

I burst into laughter the minute I saw him, my sullen, depressed attitude turning one hundred eighty degrees around.

"Stop! Be serious!" he pleaded with me through laughs of his own while trying to be profoundly serious at the same time. "I have to start over now. Wait... and don't laugh."

His outfit told me which song he would be singing—"Sweet Transvestite," the one about the main character in *Rocky Horror* creating a man for himself. We loved that song, but seeing my brother performing it in drag took it to a whole new level of enjoyment for me. I could hardly contain myself.

Jumping out again with a half-cocked smile, he sang, "How d'you do? I / See you've met my / Faithful handyman." He stopped himself. "Wait, I have to start over!"

The next time he popped out, it looked like he had taped his penis down and he didn't have one. *Wow,* I thought, *he went all out.* Seeing my brother with his penis disguised and wearing my mother's silk red nightie was something I never could have imagined.

I tried with all my might to get out the words: "Did you tape down your penis?" I was busting up so hard I couldn't get out half the sentence.

He continued to perform while trying to be serious, though he was still cracking up. "Yes, but just be serious!" he said. "Just watch."

Restarting the song, he came out once again. This time, I was finally able to watch the entire song. But we both knew there was no way I could do it without busting a gut. Of course, that was exactly what he wanted. These were the times Nile was the best big brother in the world, always making me smile, even on my worst days.

But then there were occasions where my brother did not make me smile.

The nine-hundred-square-foot "castle" my mom bought wasn't in the greatest of neighborhoods. Around the corner and down the alley from us lived a family with whom both my brother and I became quite close. Bud, the dad, stayed in a permanently parked RV, and three kids lived alone inside the house: Catherine, Jacob, and Jessica. Jacob was the same age as Nile, while Jessica and I were the same age.

Jacob was not the best influence on my brother. He was into drugs, stealing, and hangin' with the local gang bangers of the C14 street gang, one of Los Angeles's oldest and most dangerous Mexican street gangs.

One day, Nile and Jacob were hanging out in my brother's room. I was home alone. After Jacob and Nile realized this, being twelve and mischievous, they thought it would be funny to lock me in the room with Jacob and "see what would happen."

Jacob lured me into my room, and Nile closed the door behind us.

Jacob entrapped me with his body close to mine, cornering me with both arms against the wall. Panic set in.

"You look really pretty today. Looks like your boobies are starting to grow. Can I touch them?" he asked.

Feeling extremely uncomfortable, I retracted, shaking with fear. Jacob touched my shoulders, apparently thinking I was enjoying myself because my body froze. I couldn't breathe or move. Slowly running his fingers over the tops of my shoulders, he grazed my small, flat chest.

Knowing he was touching me in places where he shouldn't, I pleaded for him to stop. I felt helpless. I asked him several times to stop, but he wouldn't.

Jacob repeatedly stated, "There's nothing wrong with this. It's just exploring."

He ran his hand down my stomach and onto my thigh. Still frozen, I was sweating and trembling with fear as his hand crept in between my thighs and up toward my girl parts.

"Jacob, please, stop," I cried.

"*Please*, are you begging me for it?"

"No, *please* as in *please stop*," I asserted. "If you don't stop, I will scream." He didn't.

Reacting with more force, I urged, "I'm not kidding. I will scream if you don't stop."

When he touched the crotch of my pants, I forced his hand away, screaming as loudly as possible, "Nile, please help me!"

Nile opened the door immediately. But they both laughed.

I did not.

How could my brother, the person who protected me over and over in my lifetime, do that to me? Who could I trust if not my brother? Once again, my trust had been broken by the person closest to me. The back-and-forth of friendship and betrayal was something I sadly came to expect in life.

Our mom loved surprises. Holidays and birthdays were a big deal in our house. Nile's thirteenth birthday was Wednesday, February 25, 1981. He was planning a big party with his friends at Farrell's over the weekend and wanted to go to Sizzler the night of his actual birthday. Nile and I loved Sizzler—the steak and all-you-can-eat shrimp were the best, and so was the fluffy garlic bread, so soft and warm inside yet crispy with cheese on the outside, slightly toasted to perfection—yum!

"Hey, kids, go get dressed for dinner," Mom instructed, then added, "Put on some nice clothes, please."

"Mom, why are we getting dressed up? We are only going to Sizzler, right?" asked Nile.

"Just do what I tell you to and stop asking questions," Mom responded, always exasperated with our ceaseless inquiries.

Nile, Mom, and I dressed up to the nines that night. Being thrift store kids, it wasn't every day we dressed up. I picked out a blue-and-white satin dress Mom made for me earlier that year for a friend's birthday party, placing it to my chest while twirling in circles.

During our Sizzler celebration, Mom secretly told the staff it was Nile's birthday. We were finishing up our steak, breaded shrimp, potatoes, and yummy garlic bread when the staff came out from the back with a hot fudge sundae, candle burning on top. The leader of the group cupped his hand slightly over it, covering the glowing candle. They were singing as they approached us.

Nile leaned forward to blow out the candle, and Mom blurted out, "Don't forget to make a wish!"

Rolling his eyes, perhaps thinking this whole birthday wish thing was a sham, he blew the candle out.

After dinner we jumped in the Opal, thinking we were headed home. Mom drove over the railroad tracks on Chandler, turning right. When I quickly realized the direction of home was left, not right, I asked, "Mom, where are we going?"

She hushed me. "Shh, we will get there when we get there."

Nile wasn't saying much.

"But where are we going, Mom?" I implored.

"Just hold your horses, young lady!" Mom said.

We passed by the Hollywood Bowl, and I became even more curious. Upon arriving in Hollywood, we turned left. I watched the Sunset Boulevard sign as we turned. We drove several more blocks, then parked on a residential street. I was extremely confused but tired of asking what we were doing.

Nile finally spoke up. "What are we doing? Why are we here?"

"I have a surprise for your birthday," Mom replied, handing him a birthday card. "Go ahead, open it."

A group of young adults passed our car dressed like they were going to see a *Rocky Horror* show while he opened his card.

Nile noticed the crowd and got distracted, remarking with vigor, "Are we going to see *Rocky Horror*?"

"Open it!" Mom could hardly contain her excitement.

Three tickets fell on his lap. He picked them up, and his mouth dropped open.

"'Rocky Horror—*Live* ...'" he read. "What is that?"

"Come on, let's go, kids. I'm sure your sister wants to get out of that sardine can back there."

I was as happy about stretching my legs as I was about whatever we were doing.

Venturing up the street and turning the corner, we spotted a line of people waiting to get into a theater, many dressed as characters from the movie. Others were dressed up, fancy, like us.

"Are we going to see a midnight showing?" Nile asked.

"No, it's not a midnight show," Mom replied smugly.

"The movie?" he asked again.

"Nope." She was clearly enjoying the suspense.

"What the heck does 'live' mean?" Nile asked.

"You will see. Happy birthday, son."

This would be my first experience with musical theater outside of elementary school. I did not know as I walked through those grand doors of the Aquarius Theatre how inspirational and profound this experience would be for me. I felt small in that crowd of overzealous, devoted fans. The crowds, as interesting as they were, were not my favorite part of the evening; it was the grandness of everything else surrounding us. Giant chandeliers hung from the deep, crushed red velvet ceiling, and posters of various musicals were displayed on the walls. I imagined what it would be like to see the actors live on stage right in front of us. I could hardly wait. This may have been a birthday present for Nile, but it felt like a huge gift for me as well.

Nile saw the merchandise booth and pleaded, "Mom, let's go check it out!" He ran over to see all the cool stuff for sale.

Reaching out her hand for mine, Mom stated sternly, "Stay close to me. Don't go anywhere alone. I want you by my side the entire night, do you understand?"

"What if I have to go to the bathroom?" I whined.

"Then tell me and I will go with you. *Do not* do what your brother just did. It is far too easy to get lost in here."

"Okay, Mommy." I complied.

Hand in hand, we proceeded toward the merchandise booth. Nile was infatuated with a baseball-style T-shirt with a cartoon style picture of Frank-N-Furter, the main character in the film. The words "Rocky Horror" appeared above the picture.

"Mom, please, can I get it?" Nile begged.

"Sure, son. It's your birthday, and I budgeted money to get you something here, so, yes, let's get it."

Mom caught the attention of the young man wearing a black apron behind the counter.

"Excuse me, sir, it's my son's birthday, and he would like that one, please." She handed him the money, giving the shirt directly to my brother.

Holding it up in the air, Nile requested with a smile, "Can I wear it now, Mom?"

Sitting about twenty rows back, right in the center, we had fantastic seats—*if* you were taller than five feet, which I wasn't. Trying to figure out how I could peer in between people while closing one eye, I felt like a pirate looking for a buried treasure. The lights flashed and a bell chimed.

"Mom, what does that mean?" I asked excitedly.

"The show is going to start soon."

Once people settled into their seats, my view was much better. When the curtains rose and actors appeared on the stage, it was exhilarating. This was something I hadn't ever experienced in my life before. It was even grander than I had imagined it would be. The actors, the shimmering lights, the sets, the live orchestra, the audience being fully immersed—the entire experience was extraordinary. Never had I felt anything quite like it before in my life; it made me all aflutter inside.

The play had phenomenal music, all the songs my brother and I loved to sing together in his garage, live and larger than life. The orchestra vibrated under my feet. I was literally feeling it in my heart. Maybe someday I could be a live theater star. This had always been an unrevealed dream of mine, but unfortunately, if one cannot sing, one cannot be in musicals; it's kind of the nature of the game.

I remained mesmerized the entire first act. After using the restroom during intermission, we quickly made our way back to our seats as the curtains rose, and I watched, captivated once again. There was a square chamber filled three-quarters of the way with water, center stage. Rocky, the robot of a man that was created by Frank-N-Furter, and Janet, Brad's fiancée, materialized, singing. Janet wore white satin lingerie, and Rocky was in nothing but gold, shimmery boxer shorts.

"Touch-a, touch-a, touch-a, touch me..." they sang in unison as they climbed into a box filled with water. I was thinking to myself, *Oh, this is going to get good,* when I felt my mother's hand, before I could stop it, covering my eyes.

"Mom," I responded angrily as I grasped her wrist and tried moving it away.

Settling into my seat with my mother's hands wrapped tightly around my eyes, I realized there was certainly no way I was getting to see whatever was happening on stage, so I gave up.

From that night onward, my love for *Rocky Horror* and live theater flourished. I wanted to immerse myself in as many musicals and plays as possible. Coming away from *Rocky Horror,* I was secretly hopeful someday I could be bigger than anyone could ever imagine.

Although Nile and I were drifting apart, he continued playing the protector in my life. When I was in the sixth grade, Nile was in junior high school. Aware of the heavy burden I felt I put on the world, I tried to keep the heartbreak of being mercilessly teased on a daily basis to myself.

One day, while I was playing handball in front of my house, the girls who teased me incessantly at school suddenly appeared, riding their bikes. I'd never seen them near my house before, and fear set in. I ran toward the back of my driveway, hoping they didn't see me. Unfortunately, that wasn't the case.

I heard, "Hey, scummy," hollered from the street, and I hung my head and cried.

"What's the matter?" the shouting and mocking continued. "Why don't you come play with us, scumbag?"

Nile happened to be home hanging out in his garage. Curious what all the yelling was about, he came out. Seeing me in tears and concerned, he asked, "What's wrong?"

"Those girls who tease me all the time at school are here," I replied tearfully.

Fuming, he said, "What? Where?"

"Right in front of the house. Didn't you hear them calling me scummy?"

He ran down the driveway into the middle of the street, looking up and down, searching for them. I was watching him from beneath the eaves of our porch when he spotted them about a half block down.

He screamed, “Hey, leave my sister alone!”

They made a U-turn on their bikes. Nile stood in the middle of the street in his Dolphin shorts and IZOD T-shirt, skinny as a rail with bony knees.

Approaching him with a bullying tone, they shouted, “What are you going to do about it, skinny?”

Nile walked right up to the large girl’s bike, forcefully gripping her handlebars. She tried retracting her bike, but he was too strong.

He put his face about an inch from hers and hissed, “You better fucking leave my sister alone or I will kick your ass. If I ever hear her tell me that you so much as say hello to her again, I will come find you, and trust me, you will regret it.”

“Whatever,” she snarked as my brother released his death grip on her handlebars. That was the last time either of those girls ever said anything to me.

The distance between me and Nile grew the older he got, especially in his teenage years. Hanging out with Marvin introduced him to a whole new world, and his personality was very distinct from mine. We lost our common ground and liked doing very different things. It was heartbreaking for me, and it felt as if I was losing my brother. I was desperate to have a male figure in my life and was sad but figured I would try to find someone else to fill that role, somehow.

TRUSTWORTHY MONSTER #1

For as long as I can remember, school was an extremely difficult place for me, both academically as well as socially. Upon our return home from Baghdad, Mom re-enrolled me in Stancliff Elementary. The school decided it was best for me to enroll in kindergarten ... again.

Even though I had almost completed my entire year of kindergarten before being kidnapped and attended an additional year in Baghdad, they felt it best that I start over. Nonetheless, after a week or so, I was bumped up to first grade for being "far too advanced."

I attended Stancliff through almost the end of the second grade. This was the beginning of constant abuse throughout my school years, often enduring brutal teasing, not only from the students but from the teachers as well.

Since Stancliff was a private school, corporal punishment was something that was tolerated. One particular afternoon, I was approached by my teacher.

"Delicia, what is the answer to the question on the board?"

Straining to read the question, I quickly shrugged my shoulders and mumbled, "I don't know."

"You don't know?" she continued as she approached my tiny wooden chair/desk combo. "Why don't you know? Is it because you didn't do your homework or is it because you are stupid?" The kids in the class ridiculed, pointed fingers, and laughed.

Slouching down further in my chair from utter embarrassment, I couldn't speak. I was mortified.

"Get up! Get up right now and come here!" she shouted as she pointed to the small, dark blue plastic chair next to her desk.

I arose from my seat with trepidation and sauntered over slowly with my head hung low as all the kids in the class continued to laugh and make fun of me. Tears welled up in my eyes as I approached.

Reaching below her desk, the teacher pulled out a paper hat that looked like a homemade birthday cone. It had the giant word "DUNCE" glued on in cut-out black felt letters.

"Put this on and go stand in the corner," she instructed harshly.

"But Mrs.—"

"But nothing! I said put this on and go stand in the corner."

Reluctantly placing the dunce hat on my head, I walked slowly to the corner. There I stood with my face toward the wall. Sounds of laughter bellowed in my ears.

"Turn around, so everyone in the class can see you. I want everybody to know how stupid you look when you don't do your reading."

I was shocked and appalled at this behavior, but I was only six years old, so I obliged.

I stood in that corner wearing a dunce cap and facing all of the other kids in the class who continued to ridicule me while I hung my head in shame.

After the rest of the kids in the class were dismissed for recess, the teacher demanded that I approach her desk yet again. She grabbed a wooden ruler from the small oblong rectangular drawer and placed it on the top of the desk.

"Give me that hat," she demanded.

I quickly removed the paper hat and handed it back to her.

"Place your right hand flat on the desk."

"But I just stood in front of the entire class wearing that dunce cap. Isn't that enough punishment?" I inquired respectfully.

"I said put your hand flat on the desk," she demanded with a more rigorous tone, exuding her power.

I reluctantly laid my hand on the desk, knowing what was about to happen. Turning my head over my shoulder so I wasn't watching and squinting my eyes, I got ready for the pain.

TWHACK, THWACK, THWACK, THWACK, THWACK… five times that wooden ruler came flying down on my knuckles as hard as she could possibly hit me.

Quietly, I sulked back to my seat and held my hand that was throbbing in pain, trying to hold back my tears as the kids flowed back into the classroom from recess.

A few days later during recess, one of the largest girls in our school decided to pick a fight with me.

While I was minding my own business at lunch, she came up behind me and yanked my hair. This school, much like the school in Baghdad, was a K–12, and she was in the fifth grade and much older. I felt I had already endured enough and wanted to stand up for myself.

Raising my tiny body up from the table, I threw my legs over the bench and approached her from behind. Standing on my tippy toes, I tapped her shoulder. As she turned around, she hovered over me.

"What, you loser?" she said with a roar.

"Can you please stop picking on me and leave me alone?" I insisted.

Without speaking a word, she raised her hand to the sky and swung directly at my face, her open hand slapping it so hard, all I could do was put my hand to my warm cheek in shock.

While I stood still, feeling the burn, my temper fumed. Unable to control my reaction, I charged at her, ramming her directly in the stomach. She grabbed my hair and spun me around in circles.

Suddenly, I heard a loud crunching sound and felt an immense sting on the top of my head as my body flew backward onto the pavement. I reached my fingers up to where the pain was; I discovered a chunk of hair about an inch diameter had been completely ripped out of my head.

As she stood staring at me, a chunk of my hair in her hand, she laughed mercilessly. The school employee in charge of watching the playground finally put a stop to this and took us both to the office.

It wasn't long after this incident that my mother moved me from private to public school. Unfortunately, the teasing continued.

In the summer of 1978, we moved from Burbank to North Hollywood, the seventh move in my seven-year existence. Growing up, I often contemplated what it would have been like if my father was still in the picture. Would we have stayed in one place? I was desperately hopeful this would be the last of my childhood homes.

During this time in my life, my brother was, once again and very reluctantly, my caretaker. Mom was running the bar at night and teaching by day. In reality, Nile wasn't around much. He was more interested in hanging out with his friends than taking care of me. After all, he'd already had his fair share of being my "keeper."

Once we moved, I started at Oxnard Street School beginning in the third grade. Although I had been teased from the time I could remember, I always tried to start each day with a positive attitude: just because yesterday was bad didn't mean that today would be as well. One of my coping mechanisms as a child was believing that each day would be better than the last.

Arriving early was important so we could get the free breakfast in the cafeteria. The hash browns were my favorite. I was always so happy to get my hands on the greasy brown potatoes that filled those small pockets of wax paper. Breakfast in hand, I ate alone.

Two girls constantly badgered me on a daily basis. One was an exceptionally large girl who towered over everybody else in our third-grade class. I was petrified of her enormous size and football player stature. Her friend was blonde and skinny and was always there, right by her side. They made it a daily ritual to seek me out, often several times a day. I would be eating, minding my own business, and they would make extremely loud commentary on the outfit I was wearing that day.

"Look at her today. What a beautiful green polyester dress! Where did you get that from, the Salvation Army?" one would ask.

At the same time, the other would badger me, "Who does your hair? Your pet rats? It looks like they live in there."

Although I set out to have a good day, no matter how hard I tried to not let their words hurt, they always did.

Whenever we played dodgeball, I was the last one standing as teams were picked. Nobody ever wanted me on their team.

Often, I would try to get out of class activities on the playground by asking if I could play handball by myself.

There were a few kids who tried befriending me, but sadly, they would quickly opt not to be my friend once the two mean girls came by. Anyone and everyone who supported me became a victim of abuse.

The nasty girls would say things like, "Why would you want to hang out with her? She is so scummy," and, "Ewww, you like *her*?"

This happened daily. By the end of school, my cheerful outlook wasn't so positive, no matter how hard I tried. I never understood why they chose me to pick on. What was it about me that made me their target?

I recall conscientiously telling myself to let it go. They weren't worth it; it didn't matter what the mean girls thought. I knew I was a good person. I was only seven, yet somehow innately, I knew this was necessary.

We lived in our new home for a few weeks, and I was still optimistic for the possibility of having kids in our neighborhood that might like me. I had zero luck finding friends at school, so I decided to venture around the neighborhood one afternoon in search of new friends.

As I stood outside my house's front door and looked across the street, I saw a large concrete building. Beyond that was the Whitnall Highway Electrical Plant. Our new home was probably four hundred steps from it. When I say, "electrical plant," this was the mother of them. Giant metal towers stood what seemed five hundred feet high. Enormous arms with large conductors looked like massive metal robots. The towers were stacked six wide across the dedicated land, spanning at least two extraordinarily long city blocks. You could literally hear the electricity in the air, especially in the summer. We knew to stay as far away as we could, because we didn't want to get cancer from the towers. At seven, I was riddled with these thoughts.

Crossing the street catty-corner, I turned left down the alley where Jessica lived, a friend I would spend much time with but had yet to actually meet. The back sides of the houses were lined with gray brick walls, litter and garbage were strewn about, and weeds filled the cracks in the asphalt. The local gang, C14, tagged the concrete walls with graffiti.

I spotted a house that wasn't just a concrete block wall and approached. Detecting an open garage, I wandered past. There was a man painting a white board white. I thought that was odd. He was older than Mom, maybe in his late thirties or early forties. He had a short, well-kempt beard that was brown with some gray hair strewn throughout.

Sauntering past, I inquired, "Whatcha doing?"

I think he was taken aback. I was so little, wandering through that alleyway by myself, talking to a stranger.

Giving me a coy smile, he asked kiddingly, "Whatcha doing?"

That was the start of an almost wonderful friendship, such a juxtaposition.

I introduced myself. "I'm Delicia."

"Hi, I'm Isaac."

I stuck out my arm in a formal, more grown-up greeting. Having a paintbrush in one hand and a palette in the other, he put them down and politely shook my hand.

"Why are you painting a white board white?" I asked curiously.

"I'm painting this white board white so that I can paint another picture on top of it."

"Huh? That doesn't make any sense," I said, cocking my head sideways.

"Do you like art?" he asked. "Here, let me show you."

Artistic people really fascinated me, and from what I could see, he was an amazing artist. A painting of a woman riding a horse in a white flowing dress that was blowing in the wind hung on the wall. It looked so real, and I was intrigued. The details were incredible. Enamored with his talent, I really wanted to learn from him. I wanted to be an artist, too.

Getting to know each other over the next few weeks was fun for me. After school, I wandered down the alley on a regular basis to find Isaac. It was all very innocent... until it wasn't.

It only took a few weeks before I felt extremely comfortable around Isaac. Had I found someone who could be a father figure to me and teach me things that my mom couldn't?

I loved baseball and, specifically, the Dodgers. I longed to have my father in my life, if only just to play catch with me every now and then. Perhaps Isaac could fill that role? The thought was dreamy. After all, Isaac was already a dad to David, who lived across the country in Massachusetts at the time.

If I was hungry, Isaac would feed me. Sandwiches were our thing. Isaac invited me inside one day to eat my sandwich instead of hanging in the garage with him. Since I felt safe, I thought, *Sure, it is hot outside. We should eat inside,* I complied.

I noticed a very distinct musty odor upon entering. There were millions of books everywhere— piles and piles of books, stacked ten to twenty high. Dirty clothes were strewn throughout the house.

On the kitchen counter stood hundreds of vitamin bottles. They took up the entire counter, from one end to the other, five or six rows with ten to twelve bottles in each. The open cabinet right above the counter also overflowed with vitamins.

"What is all of this?"

"Vitamins," said Isaac. "They are good for you."

The combination of vitamins, musty old clothes, and old books was what I thought the aroma in Isaac's house consisted of.

Standing at the kitchen counter, Isaac mixed up something gross-looking to put on a sandwich.

"What's that?" My face contorted as though I had just sucked on a lemon.

"Wheat germ and honey," he replied. "It's delicious."

With my best seven-year-old "That looks disgusting" face, I blurted out, "Yuck! I will have ham and cheese, please."

Laughing, he made me a ham and cheese sandwich. We had a fun lunch before getting back to painting.

The next few times, we continued to eat lunch in the house, and I began feeling more comfortable as each day passed. I very much enjoyed his company, and I could tell how much he liked me as a person. I thought I'd found someone who actually wanted to hang out with me.

Being fatherless, I longed for someone who could fill Hazim's shoes. My mind was filled with the idea that maybe Isaac could be this person. He was an artist and a genius, and he could teach me things that I wouldn't and couldn't learn from my mother. We would talk about art, the world, karate, baseball, and other bitchin' stuff. Our conversations made me feel like my opinions mattered—something I hadn't encountered elsewhere.

One day when I went to visit Isaac, he was nowhere to be found. The garage was open, so I called out his name. No answer. Strolling up to the house, I knocked on the door, which caused the door to open. I heard a radio playing.

Shouting, I called, "Isaac?"

Again, no answer. Poking my head inside, I worried that something had happened to him.

"Isaac?" I called out a bit louder this time.

"I'm in the shower," he responded. "Come on in and I'll be right out."

Thinking nothing of it, I moved some clothes from a chair in the living room and waited.

He got out of the shower and went directly to his room. After what felt like twenty minutes or so, I called out again, "Isaac, are you coming?"

"I will be out in a second," he replied. "Actually, could you come here?"

I wandered down the hallway. "Where are you?" I asked.

"In my room."

"And where is that?"

"The door across from the kitchen in the hall next to the bathroom."

The door was cracked a little as I approached. Pushing it open a bit more, I saw Isaac lying down on his bed, covered with only half a sheet.

"Oh sorry," I shrieked, feeling as though I was somehow intruding and backing out the door.

"No, it's okay," he assured calmly. "Come back. I just want to talk to you."

Reluctantly, I went back into the room. Isaac stayed under the sheet, one leg protruding while the other remained covered. His legs were spread apart, and he was stroking himself ever so slowly underneath the sheet. Fondling his penis while squinting his eyes, he made an extremely pronounced *ouuuuhhh* sound while opening and closing his mouth.

I was stuck. My feet felt superglued to the floor. Isaac asking me to stay was perplexing. Out of respect, I felt I couldn't leave. Isaac had befriended me when I needed a friend.

I stood frozen at the foot of the bed watching him stroke his penis. Perhaps he thought I liked watching because I wasn't running away? He didn't realize that I *couldn't.*

He moved the sheet, his penis slowly protruding, and I stared paralyzed with confusion, wishing I had the strength to close my eyes. Fascinated by the excess skin, I gazed as he pulled the outer skin up and over the top. I'd never seen anything quite like it before. My brother didn't have that on his penis.

My curiosity grew, while simultaneously I knew whatever was happening was wrong, very wrong. It felt extremely dirty to me. Once I realized what was happening, a feeling of disgust washed through my body, a shiver only a molested child could imagine. I was repulsed. My stomach turned. I wanted to run away as fast as possible, but I was frozen, all the while feeling foul and nauseous. The first time I was molested, all it took was a look; he didn't even have to touch me, masturbating while he glared at me with lustful yearning.

Isaac's son, David, was living with his mother in Massachusetts during the first year Isaac and I were getting to know each other. Isaac wanted David to know he would have a friend about the same age to play with when he came to live in California. Because of this, I spoke with David on the phone several times before his big move to the West Coast. David and I were eager to meet in person. David, being an only child, was looking forward to having a friend in California, someone other than his dad. David was seven and although this wouldn't be the first time he had flown alone, it was the first time he was making the trip knowing that it would be permanent. I was hopeful the abuse would stop and Isaac, David, and I could have a "normal" relationship.

Once David came into the picture, Isaac rented an apartment in addition to keeping the place in the alleyway near my house. This way David could have his own room. Their new place was close enough I could walk there quite often.

However, my dreams of friendship and "normal" were soon shattered. David and I didn't have much time to become friends in person before Isaac was showing us what to do sexually and making us practice on each other. At that time, David was seven and I was eight. I blocked out a lot of that time in my life, but I do have a few vivid memories.

It was the summer of 1979. David and I were out all afternoon playing video games when we agreed to head back to David's apartment for a bite to eat. While David and I made sandwiches in the kitchen, Isaac was locked in his room.

He must have heard us because he popped out with a smile on his face.

"Hiya, kids, whatcha doing?" he said cheerily.

Isaac was wearing only a white T-shirt and his tighty-whities. His penis was erect underneath his underwear, so David and I became quite uncomfortable.

"Why are you dressed like that?" I sassed, attempting to mask my discomfort.

Isaac rolled his eyes and made a sucking sound with his teeth. "Relax, it's just hot outside and the air conditioning isn't working right."

We were trying to enjoy our lunch in the living room when Isaac materialized again, hair disheveled. He announced, "Delicia and David, today we are going to have a lesson in life."

"What are you babbling about?" I snapped.

"Come here, I want to show you."

Reluctantly, David and I followed half-naked Isaac into the kitchen. He placed a large hardbound book on the table. The cover had a naked man and woman, and when Isaac began to open the book, David and I looked at each other with trepidation and fear.

"Sit down and let me read you a story, kids. I want to tell you about the birds and the bees."

I huffed, "Um…my mom already had that talk with me, Isaac. I am good, thanks." I walked away quickly.

"Delicia, come here. I'm aware you already know, but I want David to know, and I want you to help me teach him."

I thought to myself, *Huh? What the heck is he talking about?*

I reluctantly returned to the kitchen where David was gawking at the scientific pictures of vaginas.

"Look, kids, here is where it begins. A man and a woman who love each other normally have sex because they want to make a baby. But sex is so much more than that. Sex can be pure pleasure, and that is what I want you to experience today."

Watching Isaac's penis becoming more erect with each page he turned, I felt extremely uncomfortable. What was I getting myself into? Once again, a fight-or-flight response came over me. I froze. Like a bird entrapped in its cage. If I tried to fly away, I was met by bars of shame, hatred, abhorrence, and terror.

I so desperately wanted someone to be a "father" for me and worried if I didn't comply Isaac would abandon me like Hazim had. Resuming the lesson, Isaac educated us on the parts of the human body, specifically the genitalia.

Once complete, he instructed, "Okay, kids, practice time."

Taken aback, David and I gazed at each other in terror.

"Come, come," Isaac said, gesturing to us to enter David's room. It was dark with one lonely window, no curtains. The window was high above the bunk bed and emitted only a sliver of light into the room. It reminded me of what jail cells looked like on TV.

Timidly, David and I sat on the bed.

Isaac called from outside the door, "How's it going in there?"

Neither David nor I responded. We didn't know what to say. Isaac, slowly opening the door, saw us sitting on the bed, shy and nervous.

Interjecting, he said, "Why aren't you doing anything? Here, let me show you. Delicia, you lay down on the bed. David, take off your pants."

David looked at him with concern. Isaac stared back with a "you better do it" look. Then David obeyed, standing in his Fruit of the Loom white underwear, cupping his hands over his private parts.

"Take off your underwear, David," Isaac said with a chuckle. "How can you do anything with your underwear on?"

Removing his underwear, David looked at me with empathy.

"Now, you get on top of her and put your penis into her pussy." Taking the book out again, he showed him where it was supposed to go. "I am going to be right outside the door. Get to it. Practice hour is almost up." He snickered.

David and I looked at each other awkwardly.

"I don't really want to do this, but I guess we should get it over with?" he proclaimed. I surrendered.

He got in the bed on top of me, just like Isaac showed us in the pictures. It felt uncomfortable. David tried putting his flaccid penis in me. Obviously, it didn't work.

From outside the door, Isaac hollered, "How's it going in there?"

Pretending so we wouldn't have to endure any more of this trauma, we shouted back, "Good, it's good." We were hopeful this would get him to leave us alone. We remained quiet until it felt safe to attempt to sneak away unnoticed. Isaac stood outside the door with an anxious look.

"How was it?" he asked excitedly.

We intentionally passed him without uttering a sound, trying to forget what just happened, and wandered around the neighborhood in search of more video games.

In many ways, Isaac was that "dad" I was missing. Knowing I loved baseball, Isaac suggested that David and I sign up for the local Little League. I was nine by now and had known Isaac for over two years. Mom inquired several times who he was but never pushed it. Figuring now would be a wonderful time, I introduced Isaac and my mother so we could discuss joining Little League. Observing my excitement and passion, Mom swiftly signed the forms before leaving for the bar.

I hadn't been this enthusiastic about anything since I could remember. Some of my happiest childhood times were surrounded with baseball and the Dodgers. The league had never had a girl player before, and they weren't quite sure what to do with me. Coaches constantly encouraged me to transfer to softball since "softball was for girls." I refused.

Isaac was there before, during, and after every game. Win or lose, when the game was complete, we ran to find Isaac. Nachos, hot dogs, Snickers, and sodas were waiting for us following every game.

One special game uplifted my spirit and self-esteem unlike anything had thus far in my lifetime. It was the spring of 1982, only a few years after David and I joined Little League.

We weren't on the same team that year. I was on the KC Royals, and David got picked to be on the Dodgers. I was jealous. In the San Fernando Valley, every kid wanted to be on the Dodgers.

The Royals made it to the playoffs that year, and I was elated. At this point, becoming the first woman baseball player was a dream of mine. This was, of course, my backup plan since it wasn't a real possibility. I'd dreamed of becoming a judge from the time I was five and knew I had to become an attorney first. That was always my "what I want to be when I grow up" answer.

I was older and bigger than most of the boys on the team. I could hit harder, and I was, frankly, just a better player. Even as a girl.

The final game of the playoffs, the Royals and Tigers were tied. Bottom of the ninth inning, two outs, the winning run-on base, and yours truly was up to bat. Trying not to buckle under the pressure, I stepped up to the plate. Giving the pitcher my best stink eye and trying to intimidate him, I gave the bat a few good, hard swings. Winding up, the pitcher threw the ball, and it swooshed past me, straight down the middle. Flabbergasted, I gathered my wits about me.

"Here batter batter, here batter batter, here batter batter, swing," the other team bantered in the background, trying to mess with my concentration.

Full count, this was it, the final chance, make it or break it, do or die. Taking a deep breath, the pitcher wound up and chucked the ball in my direction. The ball came closer, and I swung and closed my eyes, hopeful I would hear the incredible sound of tin hitting the ball. Feeling the vibration on my arms and the sting in my hands, I heard a loud pinging noise. I quickly opened my eyes and watched the ball soar up and over the back fence of the field. I stood at the plate, staring in awe, relishing my moment of glory. The crowd jumped to their feet, cheering and clapping. I heard Isaac screaming in the background, "GO, DELICIA, GO! ALL THE WAY HOME!"

Running the bases as fast as I could, I watched the center fielder run toward the back gate while the other two outfielders collapsed to the ground in dismay.

As I stepped on home plate, I was beaming with pride, something I had only felt a handful of times in my life thus far.

The entire team, including the coach, leapt from the dugout and ran toward me. The coach lifted me up, spinning me around and hugging me. The team was cheering, lifting me in the air while they carried me halfway to first base.

It's too bad my mother wasn't able to witness these moments of glory I had—it was always Isaac. He was a staple, always cheering me on in whatever endeavor I tried.

Isaac's best friend was Bill. Bill was married to a nice lady named Ethel. They lived in a converted Victorian house in East Los Angeles. Compared to the world in which I lived, Bill and Ethel appeared extremely wealthy. The gargantuan Victorian was split into a triplex, but as a kid, I thought they owned the whole house. It even had a swimming pool.

With David and I being "thrift store kids," we would get free lunches from North Hollywood Park in the summertime. Sometimes, if we had an extra fifty cents, we would buy entry into the pool that was part of the park. David and I loved to swim. Once I was old enough, I volunteered as a junior lifeguard at the public swimming pool in the park so I could swim for free. North Hollywood Park was a very public and popular place. Therefore, having a semiprivate pool was like a dream. Spending days in the summertime swimming in Bill and Ethel's pool were some of the best memories David and I shared that summer. While Isaac visited with his compadre, David and I would splash and play in the pool for hours.

Late summer 1981, I was ten. David, Isaac, and I were invited to go swimming at Bill and Ethel's place, so of course we were overjoyed. Ethel was on a business trip, and Isaac and Bill prepared dinner while David and I swam in the pool.

Hours in the hot sun made David tired. Wanting to rest before getting ready to eat, he went to lie down on the couch in the living room. In the same room, Bill had a recliner chair positioned directly in front of an old television set. The TV was the kind where you had to physically get up and turn the dial to change the channel.

Noticing David was sleeping on the sofa, Isaac realized I was swimming alone and headed out to get me. "Delicia, do you want to get out and dry off before dinner?" he asked.

"Sure, I will be right in."

I dried off and entered the apartment. By this time, Isaac was resting in the bedroom.

"Hey, get dressed and we will eat in just a bit," he shouted.

"Okay, will do," I said as I looked around, trying to find my clothes.

Bill called out from the living room, "Are you looking for these?" He held my things in his hand.

I ran over and attempted to grab them.

"Just a second," he said with a depraved look. "Can I have a hug?"

Bill was a tall man; he stood over six feet. He had a scruffy salt-and-pepper beard. He was much older; to me he looked like he was in his sixties.

"Sure." Thinking nothing of it, I gave him a hug.

"You look mighty cute in that suit," he said with a chuckle, then followed with, "Hey, I'm a poet and don't know it."

"Thank you," I responded, trying to be polite.

"Here are your clothes," he said, holding them above his head.

Jumping up, I attempted to grab my clothes. He jerked me close to him, hugged me again, and picked me up and put me on his lap.

He whispered in my ear, "I see your little titties are starting to grow. They are pretty."

I didn't know what to say; there wasn't much I could say. David was sleeping on the couch right next to us, and I was a guest in this man's house. Completely tongue-tied and mortified, I had no words, or they just wouldn't or couldn't come out. I wasn't sure which.

He asked, "Can I touch them?"

Time froze, I froze, everything around me froze. I went into a black vortex that I created for myself to help me escape these moments of sheer terror.

Something moved in my peripheral vision. David, awakening from a dream state, saw what was happening. He was only nine, and I imagine he was uncomfortable and unsure what to do. Isaac wouldn't help since he was as much a degenerate when it came to little girls as Bill.

The molestation continued while I sat staring at the television, numb. He fondled my private parts while I remained frozen in time, holding my breath, until he was finished.

The kitchen timer went off, and I quickly used that as an excuse to get off his lap.

"Dinnertime," I said, acting as if nothing had happened.

Dinner was quite an uncomfortable experience for me, although I acted as though I wasn't bothered and all was "normal." I was extremely relieved when it was time to leave.

Bill started to give me a hug goodbye, and I rushed past without making eye contact, hoping I would never have to see this man again in my life.

Isaac, David, and I never spoke of that night. It was as if it had never happened.

Isaac's molestation progressed over time, but that was the last time Isaac "shared" me with his friends, at least that I can remember.

One of the most frightening nights of my life was a night when I was suddenly awakened by loud screaming and banging on the wall. Shooting up in my bed, I stared at the ceiling for a few minutes, trying to figure out what exactly it could be. I was bewildered. The noises were loud and scary. Hearing my mother screaming had me perplexed because it didn't sound like she was in danger. I couldn't figure it out.

Collecting my wits about me, I somehow gained the courage to get up and investigate. Being in Little League and not having a father to protect us, I slept with my bat close to my bed.

Bat in hand, I cautiously proceeded down the hallway. Nile was sleeping in the garage outside and too far to help. The sounds were coming from my mother's room. Sneaking down the hall, I approached slowly. The closer I got, the louder the sound became. As I drew nearer, I heard more than just my mother screaming. Something else was making odd sounds. More confused and scared than before, I forged onward so I could make sure my mother was okay.

It felt like an eternity before reaching her room. The lights were off, except for a small sailboat lamp, which stood on her night table. The light glimmered, and I saw the silhouettes of two people. They were huffing, puffing, and panting, making sounds like dogs. Getting closer, I saw my mother's legs sticking straight up in the air spread out like an acrobat. The light flickered faintly on the other person's butt doing push-ups.

I looked closer, wanting to know that my mother was okay. The person on top of her noticed me, and the fear in me grew. Acknowledging I was there, he looked at me intently, straight in the eyes, continuing to do whatever he was doing. A feeling of filth washed over my body, and I froze.

I had the same reaction as the first time Isaac molested me. I was petrified in the hallway, trying not to breathe. The man on top of my mother stared right at me, allowing a good look at his face.

I quietly hurried back to my room, put my head underneath the covers, and cried.

The person looking back at me while I watched him have sex with my mother, was Isaac.

Seeing my mom and my molester having sex engulfed me like scorching hot embers from inescapable flames. I was scared, grossed out, confused, but most of all hurt. It felt like a betrayal.

I'd introduced my mother to Isaac only a few months prior to this incident, and my mother was unaware of the molestation I'd endured with Isaac. Out of shame, I never shared this with her.

Mom was completely oblivious that the man she was having sex with that night had, earlier in the day, inappropriately touched her nine-year-old daughter.

It took me a few days to muster up the courage to ask Isaac if that was him. When I finally had enough bravery to broach the subject with him, timidly, I probed, "Isaac, I have a question to ask you."

"You can ask me anything, sweetheart," he replied.

"Um, the other night, um, in my house... I saw you having sex with my mother, and I know it was you because you looked right at me."

His face turned beet red; he was mortified. I wasn't sure if he was embarrassed that I'd witnessed this abhorrent act or just that he'd had us both on the same day.

"Well, you caught me," he said with a chuckle, trying to brush it off as nothing.

"Excuse me?" I asked as my eyes bulged out like a pug in heat.

"I'm sorry, sweetheart. We were just having fun."

"Well, I don't want you to do that with my mother, ever!"

"If it is that important to you, I promise you it won't happen again. I'm so sorry that I hurt your feelings. Come give me a hug," he said as his arms opened wide.

There was an anticipation in his eyes that I would run straight to him... and I did.

Wrong as it was, I had an extremely trusting relationship with Isaac. It felt like I had found someone who actually liked me for who I was. He didn't think I was a stupid kid; he thought I was smart, pretty, and creative, but most of all, he thought I mattered! At least, that's how it felt at the time.

Isaac was the closest thing to a father that I would ever have. He was my go-to guy. If I needed a ride, I would call Isaac. If I wanted to do something, I would call Isaac. He was always there for me.

I can still hear his voice in my head teasing me about times I would call him at three a.m. from Hollywood when I was a teenager: "Isaac... come get me."

There were two sides of Isaac, and I think I separated them in my mind so that I wouldn't lose this "father" I had finally found. One side of Isaac, the father figure, was one of the nicest people I'd ever met in my life. Others would constantly take advantage of him because they thought he was a pushover. I have many memories I could share, but the most important is the juxtaposition of my feelings for this man and the fact that I loved him on such a deep level but was also petrified about when the next "session" might be.

Eventually, Isaac graduated to fondling my girl parts on several occasions, as well as my flat seven, eight, nine, ten, eleven, and not-so-flat twelve-year-old chest.

When we lived in Sun Valley, I loved to roller-skate. Our house was too far for me to walk and visit Isaac and David, so I spent most of my time at the roller rink, which was only a couple of miles away.

I'd go skating every weekend, and I could even rex. This is almost like dancing on roller skates, crossing one leg over the other as you propel yourself forward—or backward.

I was also in a breaking crew at the roller rink. Between skating, the lights dimmed, and our crew would break-dance on the roller rink floor. I wore hot pink from head to toe: hot pink sweats, a sweatshirt, and hot pink All-Star Converse, of course. Being the popper of the group, I would lock and pop, moving my arms either with a wavelike motion throughout my body or locking each joint so it looked robotic. I could break-dance as well, spinning on my head, and the worm was my specialty.

Between break dancing, I would skate with my friends. Sometimes David would come as well. If we weren't on the floor skating, we were getting pizza, ice cream, or munchies from the snack shack.

When they dimmed the lights, that meant slow couple's skate. Skating alone to a couple's song didn't sound fun to me. I wasn't coupled up with anyone, nor was I interested in that.

One night, during a couple's skate, I decided to take a break. I rounded a corner, approaching the steps, hopping up one step and then the next. On the second step, the stopper of my roller skate snagged a small piece of tape that had come undone.

Before I knew it, I was flying, landing face first on the floor in front of me. I don't remember much, except that it hurt. I was confused and writhing in pain; it was unlike anything I'd ever felt in my entire twelve-year existence. The manager ran over to me.

"Are you okay? What happened?"

"It hurts," I moaned as I wriggled on the floor.

"Let me call your mom. What's the number?"

I rattled off the number. He held a cordless phone in his hands, trying to reach her.

"There's no answer. What should I do?"

"Call Isaac," I replied.

After giving him the number, I heard Isaac answer. The call ended rapidly, and the next thing I knew, the manager of the roller rink was contacting 9-1-1.

I thrashed about while confusion was compounded with excruciating pain.

"Did I break my arm?" I moaned.

The ambulance showed up, and finally the EMT stood by my side, holding my left hand.

"You dislocated your elbow. Normally I can pop it back in place, but this one is really bad. We are going to have to take you to the hospital."

As they were putting me on the stretcher, Isaac came running into the roller rink. He immediately saw the EMTs and came over to see what was happening.

"That's my daughter. Is she okay?"

Even in my agony, those words resonated within my soul. Isaac had never referred to me as his "daughter" before this moment in time.

"Yes, sir, she dislocated her elbow. We are going to have to take her to the hospital. Would you like to ride along?"

"Absolutely," Isaac replied.

Following the gurney out of the roller rink and into the back of the ambulance, Isaac sat with me, holding my hand.

The EMTs must have given me some good pain medication because Isaac told me I was cursing like a sailor the entire ride to the hospital.

"I never heard words like that come out of your mouth before. To be honest, I was a little shocked. I didn't even know you knew some of those words."

Isaac stayed with me until my mother showed up hours later.

When I was twelve, I'd finally had enough. Mom had given me permission to spend the weekend with Isaac and David. While sleeping at Isaac's, I woke up feeling a heaviness on top of me and Isaac trying to position his penis to penetrate me. This was something that I had never let transpire in the past and wasn't about to let happen. Isaac was a triple black belt in karate, but the rage of awakening to this man trying to insert his penis into me was a force to be reckoned with. I kicked him so hard in his stomach he flew about three feet backward, knocking his back on the bedroom wall. Quickly standing up, I puffed my body up like a giant. Coming within a quarter of an inch in front of his face, I screamed as loud as my voice would go, "AND DON'T YOU EVER TOUCH ME AGAIN, MOTHER FUCKER."

Marching about four miles home, I pondered the years of our relationship and how I allowed it to get to this point. Several months passed by before I spoke to Isaac again. Throughout the years, he would still "come get me" whenever I called him.

This man, on every level, was more a father to me than my own father. Did that negate the fact that he molested me for many years? Besides my brother, Isaac was the only other man I had been able to truly count on in my life up to this point. Unfortunately, he was also the one who molested me the most and for the longest. Don't get me wrong, there were others, as you will see, but Isaac was not just my molester; he was my "dad," the "dad" I never had in Hazim.

To this day, I still remember the stench in his house. Over the years of abuse with Isaac, I came to realize the smell was not just musty clothes and vitamins but also the aroma of sex. This combination of smells haunts me. Smelling it in closets or places that don't get a lot of airflow makes me nauseous, and every time, I have to run away.

It wasn't until I wrote this chapter and re-read it numerous times that it hit me: Isaac was never the man that I made him out to be, nor was I the daughter in his eyes that I had hoped to be. After reviewing this chapter over and over, I finally realized that all I was to Isaac was his victim. I was his toy. This realization has been, by far, the most hurtful, gut-wrenching awakening of my writing process.

These events were so painful for me that the only way my psyche as a child was able to deal with this immense trauma was by putting Isaac on a pedestal. I had to convince myself that he was the greatest companion and safety net that I had during those crucial years in my life. However, now I recognize the truth—as agonizing as that may be.

I SHOULD BE ANGRY, BUT I'M NOT

I've seen pictures that tell a story of my mother's life as a little girl; what wonderful memories they paint. The stories she told would reveal a very different version.

My mom moved thirteen times before landing at the family's quiet little duplex in North Hollywood, CA. The living situation was barely passable. Piles of dirty clothes were scattered about with cockroaches everywhere. My grandmother, Betty, worked three jobs to make ends meet; therefore, the kids had no adult supervision. Various men were in and out of the home in between my grandmother's husbands. None of these men had any interest in her children.

As a single mother in the 1940s and '50s, Betty's life was challenging. Her lifestyle choices led to my mother being the caretaker for her younger brothers and sisters.

Betty was married several times. Bradley was the longest lasting of the chosen gentlemen, allegedly the father of both my aunt and uncle, siblings number two and three respectively. According to my mother, Bradley was an abusive man, both physically and emotionally.

Growing up, I heard stories of Bradley's abuse. The one my mother told me most often was about when she tried smoking for the first time. She was twelve. Since Bradley smoked, she thought it would be easy to steal a cigarette, "just to try it," so she devised her plan.

Laurie knew if she waited until the sun was setting in the smoggy Southern California sky, Bradley would doze off in his crushed-velvet, puke-green recliner, as he always did around this time of day. He slept with his soft pack of cigarettes just beside him on the folding metal TV tray. Next to the cigarettes lay a glass of whiskey, and reading glasses rested atop the *TV Guide*.

Innocently doing her homework, she anxiously waited for him to doze off.

Hearing snoring noises, Laurie peered around the corner and realized he'd finally fallen asleep. She knew this was her window of opportunity. She thought, *Now is the perfect time.*

She snuck into the living room, squishing her toes through the weaves on the brown shag carpet. Meandering past the back of his chair, she pretended she was heading to the bathroom.

ZZZZZZFLMPZZZZZFLMP, was all she heard.

Stealthily, Laurie knelt next to the wall and reached her hand out as far as possible, trying with all her might to reach the soft pack of cigarettes near the corner of the TV tray without waking him up. One was sticking out of the pack ever so slightly. She reached for the very end of that cigarette, taking it out of the cellophane wrapper, making a slight crinkle noise along the way. Immediately, she retracted her hand in fear that Bradley would awaken. She eyed them again and noticed that when she had yanked her hand back, one had popped out even more than the other she'd tried to grab. Certain she could get this one, she stretched her hand out as far as possible and snatched it, then snuck away quietly.

Realizing she needed something to light it with, Laurie sought out the giant box of matches her mother kept in the kitchen drawer. These were the matches you could strike anywhere, so she took a few and headed to the backyard.

Crouching down behind the giant metal dumpster just behind their house in the alleyway, Laurie put the cigarette to her lips. *It has a funny smell,* she thought. She took it out of her mouth and ran it under her nose, sniffing while she moved it back and forth, smelling every part of it. Putting it back into her mouth, she lit the match and held it while she inhaled. She'd seen Bradley do this on a regular basis, so she knew exactly what to do.

She inhaled the smoke from the cigarette, immediately coughing uncontrollably. Having suffered from severe asthma from the time she was small, Laurie became suddenly concerned—she didn't have her inhaler on her.

She ran back to the house, hacking her lungs out in the process. Laurie was desperate to reach her inhaler without being seen. She coughed her way through the house until Bradley was awakened by the noise.

"What's wrong with you, girl?" he hollered.

Coughing, Laurie couldn't answer. Finally, she reached her inhaler and took a puff. She let out a huge sigh of relief—she could breathe again.

Bradley was up and on his way to her room to see what the dickens was going on.

Looming in the doorway, he called out a bit louder this time, "What the hell is wrong with you, girl?"

"I was having an asthma attack. I just needed my inhaler."

Laurie brushed past him as he halfway blocked the door. He detected the smell of smoke. Quickly following behind her, Bradley glanced at his cigarettes and noticed something wasn't quite right. He immediately approached Laurie in the kitchen. "Laurie, have you been smoking?"

"No, why would I smoke? Yuck," she emphasized.

Bradley knelt, and with his face right next to hers, he hissed the words, "Breathe on me."

Laurie let out the tiniest breath she could in hopes that he wouldn't smell the cigarettes. Marching back to his metal TV tray, he shook his case, and what was left in the pack fell onto the tray. Watching with growing regret, Laurie wished she never had this plan and prayed he wouldn't notice. Growling, Bradley turned to her.

"There were nine cigarettes left in this package, and there are only eight now. Where is the other one?" he demanded.

Crouching lower and lower into her chair, she shrugged her shoulders and mumbled under her breath, "I don't know."

Knowing she was in trouble whenever Bradley had that crazed look in his eyes, she cowered, fearing the strike of his hand. Par for the course, my grandmother was working and therefore unable to protect my mother.

Bradley barked to Laurie, "So you want to smoke? Here, come with me. We are going to smoke."

"What?!" Laurie questioned with trepidation. "No, I don't want to smoke, but thank you."

"I said, let's go smoke."

"No, thank you," she declared.

Puffing up his chest and raising his voice several octaves, he screamed into her face, "It's *not* a choice. Come here!"

Reluctantly, Laurie followed Bradley outside. Bradley lit a cigarette and handed it to her.

He shouted in her face once more, "Inhale the damn thing! Don't waste it!"

Taking another puff, she couldn't control the hacking. Several minutes passed, and her cough finally eased.

Between her coughing spurts, she muttered, "Are you going to have one as well?"

Bradley looked at her, an eyebrow raised, and said, "Nope, they are all for you."

When she finished her first cigarette, Bradley removed another one out of the pack and handed it to Laurie.

"No, thank you," she replied with a sweet tone in her voice, attempting to lighten the mood.

"Take it," he fumed.

She snatched it from his hand, regretting ever thinking about smoking. She continued to hack while smoking the second cigarette. As soon as she could put out that cigarette, Bradley had another in hand ready for her.

"No," she screamed, "I don't want it!"

"You don't have a choice," Bradley roared. "Either you smoke it, or I will rip every hair out of your head."

"No," my mother protested, trying to escape the abusive situation. She quickly turned to run inside the house. This made Bradley's anger bubble up inside of him. He yanked her by the ponytail, forcing her head backward.

Having Laurie in a vulnerable position, he screamed in her face, "You do what I tell you to do when I am in charge of you! I said smoke and you are going to smoke. In fact, you are going to smoke all the cigarettes in this pack. You are going to smoke until you are green in the face and throw up, so you never want another cigarette again. Here," he said as he handed her another cigarette.

Laurie smoked until she couldn't take it anymore and threw up for the next several hours. My mother despised cigarettes after this.

It's interesting how parallel this story is to the time I smoked my first cigarette. My mother's reaction was almost identical, if not exact.

By spring of 1979, Nile wasn't around much, and it was a rare occasion I would see my mother before bedtime.

Having lived in North Hollywood for over a year now, I finally had an opportunity to make some friends in the neighborhood. Jessica, my best friend at the time, lived just a hop, skip, and a jump away. She was my age and lived with her older sister, Catherine, and their brother, Jacob. Their dad, Bud, lived in the RV parked out front.

The pungent aroma of marijuana filled the air whenever you came within a hundred feet of that RV. At first, I didn't recognize the smell, but it wasn't long before I knew exactly what it was. Bud not only smoked weed but he dealt it as well.

When Jessica and I first hung out, we weren't interested in smoking marijuana. I didn't even know it existed. There were no D.A.R.E. classes back then. Parents had to teach kids about drugs, and the only thing my mother taught me was that smoking cigarettes was bad.

Shortly after my eighth birthday, I wandered over to Jessica's house after school to play. We were bored and rummaging around her house when Jessica reached into a drawer and found a soft, cellophane-wrapped pack of cigarettes—Camels, I think. The pack was open, and a couple were falling out the top.

Jessica looked at me and her eyes grew larger. "Should we?" she asked.

My heart was palpitating rapidly, and my brain felt like a thousand bees were swarming around the neurons. I understood this was wrong and I shouldn't smoke. Having zero desire, I was shocked at the words that flew from my lips: "Sure, why not?" I regretted it before completing my sentence. *Why did I say that? Oh boy, what have I gotten myself into?*

Handing me a cigarette, she took another for herself. Retrieving a book of matches that had come from Circus Circus Liquors, we went searching for a place where we could sneak a smoke.

The alleyways in North Hollywood offered seemingly endless options. One block over were more residential areas with a lot of carports. Finding a spot with an abandoned car, we crouched down in front of the bumper. We knelt on the concrete parking stopper while using the front bumper of the car to prop us up. We placed the cigarettes in our mouths, and Jessica struck the match. My heart felt like it wanted to pop out of my chest. I knew how much my mother loathed smoking, and the guilt was eating away at me. My heart was beating harder and harder with each passing second. My hands were sweating as she lit hers, then she lit mine. Sucking in, I immediately hacked.

"That tastes like shit!" I declared. "Why do people smoke?"

Jessica seemed to be enjoying her smoke as she exhaled. She looked like an old-time movie star. I could picture her in a gown with a fancy plastic cigarette holder on the end. She was having so much fun, I tried another hit.

Again, I coughed my lungs out, and it tasted disgusting to me.

"I don't like it," I declared, happily putting the cigarette out on the concrete.

"Really? I love it," she boasted. She took another long hit and exhaled slowly.

A strange battle inside of me transpired. I wanted to like it so Jessica would feel we had something else in common and want to hang out with me more, but in reality, I hated everything about smoking.

Eventually, I said awkwardly, "I should go home."

"Oh poop," she sighed and snuffed out her cigarette. "Okay, let's go."

As I strolled the half block or so home, I noticed my mother's car in the driveway. *Why is Mom home?* I pondered. Thrilled that I'd get to see my mom before going to sleep, I ran to the house, completely forgetting I'd just taken a few puffs off a cigarette.

Excited, I ran directly to her and gave her a huge hug. Sniffing me during our embrace, she immediately took a step back, accusing, "You smell like smoke."

I shrugged my shoulders and threw up my hands, murmuring, "I don't know why."

"Breathe on me," she stated sternly.

"No." I stood my ground, looking her dead in the eye.

"BREATHE ON ME!" she bellowed. Hearing the rage in her voice, I felt my body recoil, letting out the tiniest breath.

"NO, I SAID *BREATHE* ON ME!" she roared.

Moving farther back, I blew out another tiny breath. She moved her face closer to mine, and with fury in her eyes, she declared, "You've been smoking."

"No, Mom, you don't understand."

"What don't I understand? You have been smoking."

"But Mom, it wasn't like that," I protested.

"What was it like, then? Tell me?" Her voice raised several octaves.

"Jessica was smoking, and I was next to her," I pleaded.

"Don't lie to me. I smell it on your breath."

"I tried a hit, and I hated it."

"You were smoking, just like I said!" She was furious.

"But Mom—"

"But Mom, nothing! Do you know what Bradley did to me when he caught me smoking?" she asked.

"Yes, Mom, you have told me this story a thousand times."

"Well, I'm going to tell it to you again. He made me smoke an entire pack of cigarettes until I was green in the face and threw up."

"But Mom, I didn't even—"

"I DON'T CARE!" she shrieked, but it wasn't loud. One of those screams where you don't even have to raise your voice—scarier than yelling, a whisper scream.

Somehow between teaching and the bar, my mother found time to rehearse a routine she was planning to perform at the high school talent show. Helping her with this over the past several months had been a complete joy. Quality time with my mother was something I longed for. Assisting in the choreography for a roller-skating routine to "Disco Duck"—a fun disco song sung in the voice of Donald Duck—was fulfilling that longing. She prepared for months, practicing on roller skates. I was looking forward to watching her.

While smoking that ill-fated cigarette, I had completely forgotten what day it was.

"I am so disappointed in you. I can't believe you would do something like that. This on my big night," she lamented.

My heart dropped and sweat dripped from my forehead. I knew what was coming, and I didn't want to hear it.

My mother came closer to my face, expressing her utter disappointment. "Your punishment will be that you don't get to come to the talent show and watch me perform."

I felt as if a bowling ball was thrown straight into my stomach. My eyes welled up with tears.

I begged, "Please, Mom, you don't understand. I didn't even—"

"THAT IS FINAL," she asserted.

Running to my room, I slammed the door, threw myself on the bed, and sobbed, crying into my pillow for what felt like hours.

When I emerged from my room in an attempt to beg her again, my mother was gone.

When my mother was seventeen, she dated a Middle Eastern man. This boyfriend arranged a double date with a friend of his, Hazim. According to my father, this was an intentional pass-off. The man she was dating was leaving the country and wanted to introduce Hazim to her so he could "take care of her."

Hazim and Mom hit it off immediately. It was only a few short months before my mother moved out of her house into an apartment with Hazim. Finally, she had a chance to escape her dysfunctional family and focus on herself, building a life of her own. Although she loved Hazim, this was a relationship of convenience. He was her getaway plan.

When my mother was only eighteen, my grandmother died of a brain aneurysm at the young age of thirty-nine. Once that happened, the children were split up and put into the foster care system. My mother made sure all three of her siblings knew they were welcome in her home. Every holiday would be spent with her siblings. In between foster homes, my mother's brother and sisters would often stay with her while waiting for their next placement. The only reason my mother was able to offer them a roof over their heads was thanks to Hazim, who supported her.

My mother married my father when she was eighteen, the same year my grandmother passed away.

My parents waited four years before having my brother, Nile. A few years after my brother was born, Mom was ready to try for a girl. She read everything she could get her hands on and prepared accordingly before trying to get pregnant.

In the 1960s, a doctor named Landrum Shettles researched sperm and its influence on the sex of a developing fetus. He proposed that each sperm had key differences based on the sex chromosome they carried. Shettles suggested ideal times to have intercourse, preferential sexual positions, and specific pH of bodily fluids to determine which sperm reached the egg first; even the food you ate could be a precursor to figuring out the sex of a baby. Mom was convinced that if she followed this method to a T, she would be blessed with a little girl.

Diligently, she took notes and made charts and maps. She would take her temperature throughout the day and mark down everything she ate as well as when she urinated. Meticulously, she followed Dr. Shettles's advice, plotting and planning until the exact moment. When it happened, she did the deed, demanded my father leave the room, and stood on her head naked for fifteen-plus minutes, just like the book said.

Mom was elated when she found out it worked. On March 6, 1971, she had herself a newborn baby girl.

Having both her children kidnapped and taken to another country made Mom realize how special our time together was. After we returned home from Baghdad, Mom did everything she could to make our lives amazing. Holidays were the most magical times. Christmas was always great, but Mom made every holiday extremely special. Trying to make up for the year we'd lost while we were in Baghdad, she gave us everything any child could imagine wanting—in my eyes, anyway.

On Easter she would create the most outrageous egg hunts. When we were little, we colored eggs, and my mother would hide them. Once we got a bit older, Easter became truly amazing. My mother would stay up all night painstakingly creating coupons by hand (or by computer once that was an option).

She would stuff plastic eggs with these coupons—or money—and hide them all around the yard before we woke.

The coupons were ingenious. They were for things like, "Good for one batch of Mom's homemade brownies," "Good for one trip to the movies with Mom," "Good for your favorite homecooked meal." If you found the big grand gold egg, you got a whopping five-dollar bill. That was the one Nile was happiest to find.

Special treats from Mom and quality time with her were the best presents I could ever wish for. We had to find clues and solve several riddles before finding our Easter baskets, wherever they were hiding.

My mother's favorite holiday was Saint Patrick's Day. She was extremely Irish and proud of it, as am I. Saint Patrick's Day was always a grand celebration. She'd get gussied up to the nines, and she had a famous plastic green hat she always wore. She wore it every Saint Patrick's Day to the bar or out to celebrate. When she acquired a new button or pin wherever she went, she placed it on her hat and proudly displayed it on her head at each bar or party she attended. I still have her green plastic hat, which has about thirty Saint Patrick's Day buttons that have Irish sayings such as "If you aren't Irish, fake it," "Touch my blarney stone," and various other funny aphorisms.

Wearing green on Saint Patrick's Day was super important to our mother. If we weren't wearing green, she would pinch us and make a huge deal.

"It's Saint Patrick's Day. Go put on something green," she would demand.

There was no year in which my mom wouldn't celebrate Saint Patrick's Day.

Halloween has always been my favorite holiday. While living in Burbank when I was seven, my family wanted to have a haunted house instead of passing out candy that year.

We prepared for weeks on end, plotting the story line, peeling grapes to use as eyeballs, cooking spaghetti for brains, and setting up the long table with the fancy table cover and cutting the holes.

Then the big night finally arrived.

Having worked so hard to prepare everything, we carefully laid out all the ingredients.

Upon entering, visitors were greeted by a table with a black plastic bag that had holes cut out of it. The room was dark, so you couldn't see. One by one, kids would slip their tiny hands through the holes in the table, feeling the brains (spaghetti) and the eyeballs (peeled grapes) in the cold metal mixing bowls.

While neighborhood kids entered, Mom told a tale, in a spooky voice, of a child who died in that very house back in 1924.

"Food was scarce, and nothing would be wasted. Each part of this little child was to be eaten. Dinner is served!" my mother screeched in her best witchy voice.

Being the main guide, I was responsible for getting kids into the house from the street. Convincing many of the kids it wasn't too scary, I was able to lure them in. I led them through the house, step-by-step, flashlight in hand. This was the only way to a possible escape. Throughout the tour, I often turned to the group, having only my face illuminated with the flashlight, telling the next frightening part of the story. We had a small coat closet next to our back door, which was the end of the haunted house. Our aunt was in the closet with chains. As kids would run out the door screaming, she would rattle the chains and scream like a scary monster. This was one of my favorite family memories and one of the best Halloweens ever.

To say holidays were special to me is an understatement. Within my mostly dark and overwhelming world, holidays were the bright lights that kept my spirits lifted throughout my childhood. At those times, our home was aglow with light and love. Family actually *felt* like family. Mom would have time off work, cook meals for us, play games with us, and spend quality time with me. As magical as these times were for me, I believe they were just as spectacular for my mom. Yet, in the back of my mind, I still longed for my father, never understanding how he could completely abandon me.

Summer vacations were always family time for us. Every summer, Mom would take time off from the bar and school so we could go on a road trip. Whether we went to San Francisco or Tijuana, Mom would always plan our trip to include stops at "tourist traps" along the way. She couldn't pass up a chance to see the Mystery Spot in Santa Cruz, where we watched balls roll uphill, or to stop at a tepee on Route 66. We were always looking for the next outrageous and most ridiculous thing.

Two summers after returning home from Baghdad, we took a road trip to New Mexico. I was six at the time, and we saw some amazing things along the way. Beginning at Universal Studios, we travelled onward to Sea World, Arizona, and then New Mexico for our final and grand destination, Carlsbad Caverns.

When we crossed into New Mexico, our first stop was a roadside taco stand. We have tacos in California, but I'd never seen a taco quite like this before. They were called Indian fry bread tacos, and they originated with the Native Americans. Handmade bread was deep fried and then stuffed with all the fillings of a taco, like seasoned meat, cheese, sour cream, lettuce, and tomato. The bread was crispy on the outside and chewy on the inside.

"Mom, this is awesome. What is it?"

"Do you like it?" she asked.

"Like it? It is the greatest thing I have ever tasted in my life!" I declared emphatically, savoring each bite.

"Well, then, it was worth the side trip."

"Side trip?" I asked.

"Yep, people say these are the best Indian fry bread tacos in all of New Mexico."

"They are delicious." Smiling, I took as big a bite as my mouth could hold.

The following day, we ventured out to an abandoned desert. Mom borrowed an old 1966 dark brown station wagon from a friend for our long summer trip; that way I didn't have to cram into the back seat of our other tiny car for hours on end. Veering onto a wide-open dirt road, Mom suddenly yanked the steering wheel as far right as she could. As we spun in a half circle, she pulled the steering wheel to the left, making the car spin in the opposite direction. Nile and I couldn't stop giggling. It felt like we were on an amusement park ride, the adrenaline making us laugh so hard I almost peed my pants. While spinning in circles, I didn't realize that the back door was ajar. As we turned sharply to the left, then quickly to the right, the door flung open, and I went flying. The world spun in wild bursts of color as I went tumbling over rocks and hard earth.

By the time I got up, it felt like my mother was about half a mile down the road. I felt pain in every limb as I slowly rose to my feet, only to see a billow of dust with a faint car in the distance.

I rubbed my eyes, attempting to discern if anything was beyond the dust. I feared having been left alone in that vast desert of nothingness. Feeling like a forsaken tumbleweed, I stood waving my arms, making myself as big as possible, attempting to get my mother's attention.

How could she not notice that I fell out of the car? I was little, but I wasn't that little. How could my mom forget me? How could they miss that I was no longer in the back seat? A million questions ran through my head.

It felt like a thousand years before the car turned around. My body was scraped up. I had bruises on my hands and scratches on my arms and legs, but mostly my heart was broken. It felt like my mother had forgotten me.

Abandonment is a recurring theme in my life. At times, feeling like everyone, including my own mother, could forget me was unbearable. As I watched that car return from a distance, something in me knew that I would overcome and that the choice was mine to be happy regardless of how many times I was left forgotten in the dust.

Often, if I was feeling particularly down or lonely, or just needing some "Mommy" time, instead of going home, I would head to the bar. At eight years old, I wasn't actually supposed to be in a bar, but since my mom owned the place, she made an exception. Sometimes, I even worked there—helping with the dishes, putting out the peanuts (I learned that people put them out because the salt makes you thirsty), cleaning the pool tables, and whatever else I could do just to be around my mother.

Often, having been mercilessly teased at school, I would head to the bar feeling extremely down and depressed. Mom could always tell when I was having a distressing day. Feeling included was a core need for me, and my mother was well aware of this. Since I spent much of my childhood feeling excluded, it really meant a lot to me when people would embrace my presence.

Having spent so many days there, I naturally became curious why people enjoyed alcohol. I often begged my mother to let me try it, but she never let me—until one day. I was in the fourth grade, and I'd had a particularly rough day at school. The girls who picked on me and gave me grief regularly were really on a roll that day. I endured teasing from the start of breakfast until the school day finished.

Walking to the bar that day, I felt sullen and cried most of the way. Upon my arrival, my mother could tell something was going on. Embarrassed about being picked on, I never really mentioned it to her. I knew she could get enraged easily, and I feared that, had I mentioned anything, it wouldn't be long before the principal would hear from her, and somehow, I knew this would only make things worse.

"Hi, Mom," I greeted her wearily, heading straight for my usual barstool, backpack in hand. Taking out my homework, I hung my head over my book in an attempt to hide my current mood.

Noticing something was off, she inquired, "What's wrong?"

"Nothing," I lied.

Stepping away, she quickly returned with a can of 7Up.

"Here, honey," she offered. "Have a 7Up. It will make you feel better."

"Thanks, Mom," I responded with a long, slow drawl.

I took a sip, then I glanced up at her, then back at the drink.

"This isn't 7Up..." I stated with a questioning look under an angled brow.

"Well, it is actually 7Up," she said matter-of-factly. "But it's mixed with a little beer. It's called a shandy, honey."

Wow, I thought, *this is good!* And I took another big sip.

"Don't drink it too fast," she warned.

I'm not really sure how much beer was in that shandy, but it did make me forget about those mean girls at school for a while. This was my first lesson that drinking could make your problems go away, at least temporarily.

I became a real pool shark since Mom owned The Stein Club. What else was a kid to do at a bar other than play billiards or darts? Pool quickly became my thing. I had my own custom-made pool cue, two pieces that screwed together. It was personalized with my initials carved in the natural, clear-coated wood. My cue had its very own hard plastic case so I could carry it with me. A closet at the back of the bar was where I kept this prized possession.

It wasn't long before the regulars knew me by name, but everyone called me Kiddo. Whenever I came into the bar, all the guys would shout, "Hey, it's Kiddo!"

Raising their glasses in the air, they celebrated just having me there. That made me feel wanted and loved. The bonus was I got to spend time with my mom.

One of my favorites, Jim, would often be there when I showed up.

Jim would greet me with, "Hey, Kiddo, there you are. Let's play some pool."

Jim taught me tips and tricks and would let me beat him so I could get a taste of success—a fantastic feeling and one that I rarely felt. Eventually, I was good—so good that I would bet the old guys that I could beat them at pool. They would just laugh and accept the challenge. On most occasions, I would win. I'm not completely sure if they just let me win because I was little, but in my mind, I beat them. I ached for love and praise in my life, and that feeling of accomplishment and pride was something I would cling to long after each game ended.

In the fourth grade, I really wanted to be part of drama and chorus clubs. The holiday play was coming up. Raring to go the day our teacher handed out the songs, I eagerly scanned the list.

There were about ten songs to choose from. After school, I ran to the bar, extremely excited, and found Mom working behind the bar.

Taking a seat on one of the stools, I said excitedly, "Hi, Mamma."

"Hi, baby, how was your day?"

"Mom, I am so stoked about the holiday play," I told her eagerly. I slid the paper onto the bar. "Look at these songs. Do you think I would be able to sing one?"

"Of course, let me see," she said, snatching the paper out of my hand and scanning the songs.

Sam, one of the regulars, sat a few barstools down from us, sipping from a large stein filled with a very dark and frothy beer and munching on peanuts. He stared at the football game that was playing on the TV, trying not to eavesdrop on our conversation.

Reading the songs to herself, she suddenly proclaimed, "Oh wow, they want someone to sing 'Silent Night' in German."

Quickly, Sam turned to us and volunteered, "I can help her with that!"

Mom and I looked at each other inquisitively, simultaneously asking, "How?"

"*Ich kanne Deutsch sprache,*" he revealed.

"Now that's cool," Mom replied. "Do you think you could teach her?"

"Of course," Sam responded with a wave of his hand.

Looking at my mom with a huge grin, I confirmed, "I know I can't sing that great, but if I can sing in *German,* I don't think anyone else will be able to do that!"

Sam and I got to work.

In celebration, Mom placed a can down in front of me.

"Here, dear, have some 7Up," she said, winking very intentionally.

Knowing it wasn't just 7Up in that soda can, I felt happy. We all raised our glasses and cheered to me, hopeful I would land this song in the holiday play. I drank my shandy while Sam taught me the words to "Silent Night" in German:

"*Stille Nacht, heilige Nacht / Alles schläft; einsam wacht...*"

Getting the part, I sang my little off-key heart out in German. I felt extraordinarily proud of myself; it didn't matter how off-key I sang.

I was learning from quite an early age to drink when I felt bad, when I felt good, when I wanted to celebrate, and when I wanted to wallow in my sorrow. Drinking during the day was fine, as was drinking at night. I can recall when drinking and driving was legal in some states and my aunt would drive around with a tumbler full of vodka with me in the front seat. Drinking had always been just "something you do" in our family.

Every summer, my family would go to Camp Fox, a Christian camp, run by the Glendale YMCA. Since it's located just off Catalina Island, we could only arrive via ferry. I was just a toddler when we began attending Camp Fox. As I grew older, my brother and I went together until Nile got "too old."

The first year I attended alone, I was eight. My brother wanted to hang out with his friends instead of coming with me. Though I was terrified to go by myself, I knew the time had come to put on my big girl boots and go at it alone. I wasn't sure if there would be anyone I knew that year or not, since many of the kids we knew were getting too old for camp. Luckily, there were some familiar faces when I got on the bus headed for the ferry.

At camp, everyone had to do their part; daily chores were expected. That year, I volunteered in the kitchen. On the fourth morning of camp, my turn for chores arrived. I rose with the sun, ready for kitchen duty. I felt in my bones this was going to be a totally awesome day.

The smell of fresh-cooked oats lured me inside. *How exciting, it is oatmeal day,* I thought. Before letting my mouth water too much, I checked the menu posted on the corkboard just outside the cafeteria. I loved oatmeal. Especially at camp. On oatmeal day, campers were greeted by all the fixings they could imagine. I was always a simple girl—a heaping spoonful of butter along with just the right amount of brown sugar and maple syrup was all I needed. The saltiness of the butter brought out the flavors of the maple syrup, brown sugar, and oats. It all blended so remarkably in my mouth.

Doing the dishes was my job when I had to work kitchen duty. Today was special—the manager was going to let me serve the oatmeal to other campers. When campers wanted oatmeal, we had to bring the bowl to the chef, who would scoop it into the bowl, and then we would deliver it to their table. Essentially, this was my first waitress job.

One of my friends from my cabin, Annie, ordered oatmeal, and I was eager to bring it to her. At the back of the kitchen, the chef scooped the steeping hot oatmeal into the bowl. Making sure my hands were securely wrapped around the bottom of the bowl, I strode out to my friend. Flinging open the door with my foot, I stepped into the dining hall, being incredibly careful because the oatmeal was extremely hot.

Since it was beginning to burn my hands, I put a bit of pep in my step so I could put down the scalding bowl. A piece of carpet stuck up in a spot on the floor. Not paying attention, I continued walking rapidly. It caught the tip of my shoe, and I went flying headfirst, hands stretched out in front of me, my face planting on the ground. The piping hot oatmeal flew out of my hands and crashed to the floor. The bowl shattered; oatmeal sprayed everywhere. I lay there for a few seconds, but I soon felt a burning sensation and realized oatmeal was scorching the side of my wrist.

Someone handed me a towel soaked in icy water. I held that on my burn for hours. Some of the staff took me to the nurse while others cleaned up my mess. The oatmeal was hot enough that it would leave a scar on my wrist for life. Somehow, the worst part about that morning for me was that I never did get my oatmeal.

Other than this unfortunate incident, camp was great that year. Mom sent her famous brownies, we sang unforgettable camp songs, I made tons of new friends, our cabin came up with the most awesome skit, and that burn got me out of any more chores for the rest of my stay.

Whenever we started our journey home, I always felt a bit sad, as Camp Fox was the one place I felt consistently welcomed, loved, and—more importantly—liked by others. Those special weeks of the summer I spent at camp were and have always been some of the calmest and best times of my life, no drama or trauma—unless you count the oatmeal burn, which, all things considered, isn't the worst thing to leave a permanent scar on my body or my life.

To prepare for the ferry trip, I'd take my ginger capsules a few days before we left. Mom would make these herself, taking dried ginger powder and funneling it into capsules. Somehow, long before there was internet, she'd found out that ginger helped with sea sickness. Ginger really did make boat rides bearable for me.

Back at the dock in San Pedro, we were ushered into a big yellow bus back to Glendale. This was the last little bit of time we had to spend with the other campers before reuniting with our parents. It was always an eventful bus ride back.

As usual, that year I was sad to leave my friends but overjoyed to see my mother and very much looking forward to sleeping in my bed again. Being gone for two weeks felt like an eternity to an eight-year-old girl.

Mom was waving enthusiastically with a big smile on her face as the bus entered the Glendale YMCA parking lot. My brother was there as well, also waving vigorously. He kind of even looked happy to see me. As I moved with the crowd, it took forever to get off that bus. I finally reached the stairs and practically skipped off the bus. Running directly to my mom, I gave her the biggest hug.

I squeezed my brother, and he actually embraced me back, which was not the norm. Nile had a devious look on his face.

I wondered what was going on all the way home; I could tell they were jittery about something but couldn't put my finger on it.

"So, how was it?" Mom asked.

"Fantastic! Oh, except for this." I showed her my bandage.

"How did that happen?"

"It was stupid. I was serving oatmeal and I tripped."

"We will have a look at it when we get home," she said.

Upon arrival, everything looked the same. I got out of the car while clutching my duffel bag. Nile took my sleeping bag, and Mom and Nile trailed behind me, giggling. A mischievous look crossed their faces. My bedroom door was closed. I turned to look at them when Mom pointed a camera at me and snapped a quick photo.

"What are you doing?" I queried.

"Go on, open your door," Mom requested.

Curious and confused, I slowly opened my bedroom door. Peeking my head in the doorway, all I saw was pink. I closed the door, my head cocked to the side like a confused cocker spaniel. With a furrowed brow, I questioned, "Mom, what is going on?"

"Just go. Open the door." She beamed.

Thinking to myself, *When I left my room was a boring white,* I opened the door again, and all I could do was stare. What I saw left me breathless. I looked quickly at Mom as she snapped a photo of my exuberant face.

While I was at camp, my mother and brother had completely revamped my room. A fresh, light-pink coat of paint covered the walls. The old dingy carpet was gone, revealing a beautiful hardwood floor underneath. A small pink-and-white braided rug rested at the foot of my bed. The bed itself had grown from a tiny twin to a full-sized canopy bed. The frame of the bed was steel and painted white. The bedposts were fancy, with elaborate brass pieces on all four corners. I always wanted a pink-and-white checkerboard canopy, and I couldn't believe I was staring right at it, on my bed, in my room. I even had matching checkerboard curtains. My boring old dressers had been replaced with pink-and-white ones. I loved it. My dream room. *What did I do to deserve this?* I pondered.

Tears began welling up in my eyes as I hugged my mom and brother so hard, I think I squeezed the breath right out of them.

"Oh, thank you! Thank you! Thank you!" I shouted as I twirled around my new room in circles.

Throwing my body on my bed, I rolled around and around until I was on my back looking at the underside of my beautiful pink canopy.

This was one of the most joyous days of my life. It was amazing what a little makeover could do. Times like these made life worth living and instilled in me that the little things in life are truly what matter. I don't take anything for granted and have a huge appreciation for things people do for me.

When you go through everything I had been through by the young age of eight—constantly teased and tormented by other children, kidnapped and ultimately abandoned by my biological father, sexually molested by individuals I trusted—you grow to appreciate the little things in life more than you might otherwise.

It makes the trivial things that people do for you seem huge. Finding out my mom and brother spent two weeks of their time and hard-earned money on this surprise really meant the world to me.

By now, I think you get the picture how terrible our neighborhood was when we moved to our "amazing pink castle house." The kids that we hung out with weren't the greatest. There wasn't much to do, and we always had to be inventive when it came to keeping ourselves entertained.

Two houses down from ours, there was a house for sale. It was unoccupied for many months, and the kids in the neighborhood were curious about the place. One day, a couple kids were bragging to the rest of us how they had broken into the house a few days prior. Because they were able to do it, the rest of us, naturally, wanted to do it too. We were determined to break into that house.

Among all of us—about ten in total—Jacob had the worst reputation of the bunch, and he was the one we chose to break in. We knew if anyone would be able to get into the house, it would be him. Waiting outside, we watched as Jacob snuck over a fence and through the backyard, glancing over our shoulders anxiously to see if anyone was coming. Holding our breath, we waited to see if Jacob would be able to get in. Suddenly, the front door opened, and Jacob was standing there with a big smile on his face.

Making a play on the famous words, he mimicked Bob Barker on *The Price is Right*: "Come on in."

Hoping no one would see us, we rushed inside. The house was empty; it had beautiful hardwood floors, and a fireplace in the living room.

"Hey!" Jacob shouted. "Let's play truth or dare."

Looking at each other, we agreed that sounded like fun. We sat on the floor next to the fireplace, and the game began.

Angie started, "Jess, truth or dare?"

Jessica chose truth, and Angie asked, "Is it true you kissed a boy last weekend?"

"No," Jessica answered, giggling. "I've never kissed a boy."

Embarrassed, she laughed harder, her face flushed because her brother was in the room. Next, Jessica asked, "Okay, Nile, truth or dare?"

"Dare," he answered.

"I dare you to go pee in the bathroom and not flush the toilet."

"That's stupid," my brother said, rolling his eyes. "No problem."

The game went on for thirty minutes or so until it became a bit risqué.

Jacob and Jessica's older sister, Catherine, had had an accident when she was three years old. Their father, Bud, and Catherine were playing hide and seek. Counting to ten, Bud looked everywhere but couldn't find her. When he finally found her, she was inside of a closet and had managed to wrap a trash bag around herself and wasn't breathing. It had been three to seven minutes, and he wasn't sure how long she had been unconscious. Quickly, he performed CPR and was able to get her breathing again. Catherine was never the same. The lack of oxygen caused major brain damage, and she was mentally challenged from that moment onward. Although I didn't know this at the time, everyone just thought she was born that way.

Catherine was playing with us when Jacob's friend asked Catherine, "Truth or dare?"

"Dare," she answered.

"I dare you to take off your shirt."

Catherine thought that was funny, so she complied. The next turn was hers.

"Truth or dare, Jacob?" she asked her brother.

"Truth."

"Is it true that you broke into this house?" she asked, clearly cracking herself up and thinking that was a very funny question.

"Duh, obviously it's true. We are here, aren't we?"

"Okay, my turn." Jacob turned to us and whispered, "Watch this. She will do anything I say. Truth or dare, Catherine?" he asked his sister.

"Dare," she answered with a giggle.

"I dare you to take off your pants."

"*What?*" she asked.

"I dare you to take off your pants," Jacob affirmed.

"Okay," she said and dropped her pants to the ground.

I was feeling extremely uncomfortable and could tell I was not the only one. I looked at Jessica, Yoli, and Angie, hoping they would understand what I was asking without words. They looked back at me with the same gaze. What could we do? We carried on with the game since our big brothers were having fun. Still, it felt wrong. We thought it odd that Jacob would ask his sister to take her pants off in the middle of a room filled with people.

The game continued, and within the next fifteen minutes, Catherine was naked in the middle of the living room. Not knowing what to say or do, Yoli, Angie, Jessica, and I sat stunned and feeling terrible for Catherine. We felt helpless since our older siblings were the ones in charge.

Someone must have seen us break into the house because at that moment two police cars appeared, blocking the driveway. Jacob had a record as a juvenile. He was the first to detect them and darted out the back door and over the fence so he wouldn't get caught. Scared shitless, we didn't have much of an option. Catherine was naked, and we didn't know what we were going to say to the police.

"Put your clothes on," we whispered to Catherine as we handed her the pile of clothing. The police pounded on the door while Catherine got dressed in a frenzy.

Extraordinarily frightened, Nile opened the door. The police saw Catherine half naked in the middle of the room.

"What's going on here?" one of the officers asked angrily.

"We were playing truth or dare," my brother answered.

"Why is she half naked?" the officer snipped.

"Because she was dared," my brother replied honestly.

The officer told Catherine to get dressed while they jotted down everybody's information—names, birthdays, parents' names, addresses, and phone numbers, as well as filing a police report for breaking and entering.

Knowing she would be livid, we were scared yet hopeful the police officer would not contact our mother. With bated breath, we meandered the quarter block home.

When Mom came home early that day, we knew we were in trouble. Flying in the door in a complete fit of rage, she left no opportunity for explanations.

Fuming, she screamed, "Who the fuck do you think you are? What kind of children did I raise? I'm mortified by your behavior. I have been thinking about your punishment all day, and you're both grounded for three weeks. No friends, no phone, no anything! You will go to school, do your homework, eat breakfast, lunch, and dinner, and go to bed, and that's it. In addition to that, I am going to give you both a good whipping."

Mother made my brother and me lay on her lap, butts up in the air, while she spanked us, one after the other, bare bottomed, repeatedly, hitting us so hard that her rings cut into her own fingers, making her bleed.

Nile and I stood together in solidarity after being beaten within an inch of our lives. Our mother approached, shoving her hands in our faces and screaming, "Look what you did to me! Look what you did. You made me bleed!"

My brother and I had no words. Retreating to my room, I cried myself to sleep.

Coming home from school to an empty house wasn't unusual growing up. One day, after completing my homework, I was watching *The Facts of Life* on TV when the telephone rang. Getting up off the couch to answer the phone, I didn't think much of it.

"Hello?" I casually spoke into the phone.

"Hi, is your mom home?" a woman's voice asked on the other end of the line.

"No. Can I ask who is calling?"

"This is a friend of hers, Mary. I haven't been able to reach her today. Do you know when she might be home?"

"I'm pretty sure she is at her bar, The Stein Club, working. She should be home later."

"Oh, okay, thank you. Can you please let her know Mary called?"

"Sure, will do. Bye." Getting back to my show was the only thing on my mind at that moment.

After homework and some TV, I tucked myself in bed around nine when, shortly thereafter, I was awakened by a loud, mysterious sound outside my bedroom window. Never sure if Nile was home or not, I assumed he was sleeping in the garage. Cautiously, I went to investigate when I saw a large body, dressed in black, lying on our front porch. The body was positioned sideways with the face toward the street so I couldn't see who it was. Frightened, I ran out back to Nile's garage. I pounded on his door, scared and screaming.

"Nile, Nile, get up, please. Nile, get up, there's somebody on the front porch." I was terrified.

Barely awake when he opened the door, he questioned in a groggy voice, "What are you babbling about?"

"I heard a *thunk*, and there's someone on the front porch."

"*What*?!" he screeched as we ran back to the house to see who it was.

Nile opened the door in trepidation. He moved toward the body and poked it with his finger—it didn't move. He poked at it again, still nothing. Rolling the body over, I saw long brown hair that looked like our mother's.

Nile cautiously rolled the body from her side onto her back, and that was when I saw that it was indeed our mother. A frothy foam oozed from her mouth, and her skin was cold, clammy, and pale. Her hand clung tight to a note. Picking the note up, Nile read it silently.

Without speaking, he threw the note down in anger. Then he rushed into the kitchen, picked up the phone, and dialed frantically.

From the porch, I heard my brother say, "Auntie, my mom committed suicide."

"What?" I screamed, sobbing while holding my mother's lifeless body in my arms.

Sirens wailed down the street as I watched the ambulance lights approach from the distance. I was praying like never before, hoping and wishing with all my might that our mom wouldn't die.

The ambulance arrived, and the EMTs went straight to work. Watching in agony, I saw the crumpled-up note on the ground. I picked up the note and read it.

I can't take it anymore. I have tried and I don't want to live any longer. I'm sorry, kids, I love you very much. Mom.

The EMTs rushed my mother onto the gurney and into the ambulance that took her away. Sobbing in the street, I felt my heart literally ache. What had just happened? Was our mother dead?

It felt like hours passed before our aunt showed up, although it was probably only twenty minutes in real time. Speeding to the hospital, nobody uttered a word, but we all felt the chill in the air.

About three hours had passed by the time the doctor finally came out. Taking my aunt aside, he whispered something. We watched her facial expression in torment, knowing her face would tell us if our mother was alive or dead. Believing her expression was relief, we hoped it meant our mother was still alive.

We held our breath as she approached.

"She is okay," our aunt said at last.

Letting out a huge sigh of relief, we exclaimed, "Thank God."

"But it's not going to be easy. Your mother tried to kill herself. We really need to be there for her right now."

The aftermath of this was reeling for me. I didn't understand how my mother could have wanted to die on the trail of getting us back. We had only been home for three years. *Are we that much of a burden? Is it our fault? Does she not love us?* So many unanswered questions ran through my mind. This was not something I ever had an opportunity to speak with my mother about because it wasn't something she ever wanted to discuss.

Having found her on the porch with a note in her hand and foam coming out of her mouth was one of the scariest moments of my life. It wouldn't be until later in her life that we discovered her depression was caused by a hormone imbalance.

A few months after her suicide attempt, I was, once again, home alone. I did my chores and homework, then went to the kitchen to make myself Hot Pockets and Top Ramen. Finding a note on the countertop, I wondered what it was. It looked spotted with paint.

Coming in for a closer look, I noticed it wasn't paint—it was blood.

Written in my mother's cursive handwriting: *I was in an accident, went to the hospital.*

Panicking and having no idea where my brother was, I felt terror set in. I called my aunt, hopeful she knew more than I did.

When she answered, I heard dread in her voice. "H-heello?"

"Auntie?"

"Yes... Delicia, your mother has been in an accident. I just got off the phone with the hospital."

"I know. She left a bloody note here on the kitchen counter."

"Don't worry," she said. "She is okay."

A sigh of relief surged through my body.

"She was on the 101 when she crashed her bike."

"Oh my gosh."

"Yeah, luckily, she wasn't hurt too badly, even though she rolled across all of the lanes. She said when she stood up, all of the cars were lined up, the drivers just staring at her."

"Oh geez, but is she okay? What hospital is she at?"

"Kaiser."

"Do you have the number?" I asked. When she gave it to me, I hung up and called the hospital immediately.

"Mom, are you okay?" I asked once I got her on the line.

She laughed. "Yeah, I'm fine. I was wearing all my gear, luckily, everything except gloves. My hands are pretty roughed up, though. I rolled across all lanes of the freeway."

"Yeah, Auntie told me. That is so scary!"

My mother's hands were scarred from that day forward, and I was reminded every time I ever wanted to get on a motorcycle, moped—anything with two wheels, except a good old-fashioned bicycle—the answer was always a hard no.

My mom met two of her three husbands at her bar, The Stein Club: Ron, her third and final husband, and Joshua. Once she met Joshua, we moved to Sun Valley, and they were married in the backyard. It was clear to my brother and me that she married Joshua because he had money. Joshua was average height, even a bit shorter than my mother. He had dark hair that was always slicked back, and a receding hairline accentuated the extreme V on top of his head. He wore cheap suits and frilly shirts, usually light blue or pink.

Joshua owned and operated a pirated video game company. He was installing a new video machine at the bar when they met. He would write the code to create copycat games exactly like *Pac-Man, Galaga, Defender,* and all the most popular games.

Essentially, he was stealing proprietary information and using it for financial gain. During that time, I had no idea what Joshua actually did; I just knew that I had unlimited life-sized video games that I could play free anytime at Joshua's work. Indeed, it was a little slice of heaven for me.

By this time, Mom had switched schools and was working as a resource specialist at Madison Junior High School, where I also attended school. My thirteenth birthday was around the corner, and I convinced her to let me have a pool party at our house. As in grade school, I wasn't popular, but I was determined to be cool, for once. I was thinking about the ways I could draw kids to my pool party when a light bulb went off in my head: Joshua!

At dinner, Mom talked about her day and some of the challenges at The Stein Club and school. Joshua ate in silence, and Nile, well, he reluctantly sat ignoring us. This was the perfect time to bring up my brilliant plan.

"Um, Joshua?" I began timidly. "Um, do you think, um, for my party that maybe I could borrow a video game?"

"Sure," he answered with glee.

The next day, Joshua brought home a full-sized *Defender* machine. I was thrilled.

"I thought you could hook it up and practice before your party."

"Wow, thank you!" I exclaimed.

Opening the door of his van, he rolled the giant game in on the dolly, placing it in the hallway just next to the entryway. Watching him kneel over and plug it in, I was beside myself. I couldn't believe it, my very own video game in my living room. What a dream!

Hearing the beep while watching the lights on the game flash, I knew this party was going to be the best one ever. He had an odd-looking short and fat key that opened the main door of the video game. He inserted the key and turned it; the door opened. The insides of the video game fascinated me. Peering inside, I saw red, green, blue, yellow, and black wires going everywhere. Joshua was eager to show me how it worked.

Pointing his finger to the slot inside, he said, "This is where the coins go down. They hit this little wire right here, and that's how you get a credit."

Being a video game junkie, I spent the majority of my free time either at the liquor store playing *Asteroids,* at the local burger shop for *Donkey Kong,* or at the store next door to In-N-Out. That was where I hung out the most, because they had *Pac-Man* and my personal favorite, *Galaga.* I spent all my allowance on video games, so much so that I was recruited to be on a show called *What Ever Happened to Childhood* on PBS. *Defender* was an okay video game, but I knew people loved it and it would be a big draw.

"Boy, Joshua, that is so bitchin'. Thank you," I said sincerely.

"Check it out," he announced as he pushed the little lever down repeatedly. "You get as many free credits as you want."

Twirling around the living room, I jumped for joy, shouting, "This birthday is going to be the greatest!"

I went straight to my room, grabbing paper, colored pens, and other art paraphernalia to make the invitations. Drawing a picture of the video game and adding the date and time, I wrote: *Come to Delicia's 13th birthday... FREE full-sized video games, pizza, swimming, and more.*

Boy oh boy, was I stoked. Mom made copies of the invitation, and I passed them out. Word spread like wildfire that there would be an arcade-style video game at my house. Suddenly, everyone was interested in me. Funny how one video game could change my world. The kids came to my party that year, and I made a few friendship breakthroughs. The memories would last me a lifetime.

Joshua, on the other hand, didn't last long. Within six months of living in that house, my mom married and divorced Joshua, leaving behind no trace of him or the video games.

Junior high school was an interesting time for me. I was at an entirely different school in a new neighborhood, so it was a fresh start. I no longer had to deal with the bitter and bullying girls teasing me on a daily basis since I attended school outside of that district now. It was a fantastic opportunity to make new friends, people who didn't know me as "the scummy kid."

I never considered myself book smart. I wasn't interested in learning about history or science, but I loved math. Electives were the best classes but had never been an option in elementary school. Woodworking and electronics were two of my all-time favorites.

In the eighth grade, our final project in electronics was to make a lamp. We were allowed to use anything we wanted, so long as we came up with a good plan. Mountain Dew was my favorite soda when I was a teen. I decided to make a lamp out of a Mountain Dew can. Studying books, learning how the wires worked, and determining exactly how I would put this together, I came up with a plan. After a few weeks of research, I approached the teacher with my idea.

"A lamp made from a soda can, huh? Sure, I don't see why not."

Looking at my drawing that showed where to put the wires, the conduit that held the wires together, and other specific details, he made sure everything looked right and approved my project.

Working on that lamp for weeks, I painstakingly cut holes in the aluminum, careful not to make them too large. Several Mountain Dew cans later, I finally got it right. This trial and error was fine by me—the more cans I used, the more I drank.

Threading wires through the metal bulb holder, I made sure everything was tightened. When I grasped the plug, my hopes were high. Praying it would work, I slowly plugged the cord into the socket. Squinting my eyes just enough to still see, I turned the knob on the lamp with a mountain of hope in my heart. Excited, I opened both eyes, but nothing happened. I jiggled the bulb a little, yet still nothing. Back to square one. This happened two or three times until I finally plugged in my lamp and saw that shimmer of light I had worked so hard for. I was elated. I created light! Well, with a little help from my teacher, Edison, and electricity, that is.

Fast-forward a few months...

Minding my own business, I was watching *Happy Days* in the living room when I heard yelling coming from the kitchen. This was a daily occurrence in my house, so I didn't think much of it.

"How dare you try and keep me from going out tonight? What right do you have? I am sixteen now. You can't tell me what I can or can't do!" I heard my brother shouting from the kitchen.

"You better lower your voice, boy. You don't have the right to talk to your mother like that."

The fighting got louder, and I could tell this was escalating to a point of no return.

I was frustrated and tired of the nonstop fighting. I got off the couch in a huff, annoyed I wasn't able to sit and watch my show in peace. The screaming had reached an extremely voluble and harsh level.

"You better get your finger out of my face!" I heard my mom shout in a fit of rage.

Marching into the kitchen, I demanded, "What is going on in here?"

Looking at me with fury in her eyes, my mother shot back, "This doesn't concern you. Go back and watch your show."

Sheepishly, I slunk back to the living room. I knew I'd better stay out of their way.

At that moment, Nile turned to my mother and screamed in her face, "You are such a bitch! I HATE YOU!"

"You hate me? You HATE *me*? How dare you, you ungrateful bastard! If you hate me so much, why don't you hit me?" Mom shouted, pushing her face closer to his.

Nile took a step back, brusquely turning toward her, and planted a slap across her face so hard I heard it from the living room. Worried, I ran back to the kitchen. I swore I witnessed actual steam rising from my mom's nostrils while her eyes became violent red.

She screamed at the top of her lungs. "How dare you hit your mother?"

Comprehending the madness growing in her, Nile ran away, fast. Mom chased him at full speed. Nile turned left, directly into my room. *What the… Why did he go into my room?* I ran down the hallway to make sure everything was okay and watched my mother tackle Nile, beating him with her fists over and over and over again, hitting him anywhere and everywhere she could as he wriggled and writhed underneath her in a fetal position, trying to avoid her wrath.

As our mother released her rage on my brother, I stood at my door screaming. "Please stop, stop it, you guys."

My gaze focused on the lamp that I so painstakingly made in electronics class sitting just above my bed on the wooden headboard.

"Please, Mom, stop! You are going to break the lamp I made."

She took another swing at my brother's face and hit my lamp, and it went crashing onto the floor. It's amazing how time slows down when something of importance is about to be destroyed. Watching my lamp fall in slow motion from the top of my bed, I dove headfirst with both arms out, hoping and praying I would catch it. I heard the crash of my lamp as I landed face-first on the hardwood floor.

Just as the bulb shattered into hundreds of pieces, so did my heart. My lamp was broken, the internal wires hanging out of the can.

"STOP IT! GET OUT OF MY ROOM!" I screamed at the top of my lungs.

My shouting finally got through to them. Mom dragged herself off my brother. Nile ran out of the room, down the hall, and out the front door, while my mother retreated to her room.

Tears welled up in my eyes as I slowly picked up the pieces of my shattered lamp. My pride and joy, strewn about in a mess of broken glass, a smashed Mountain Dew can, and a heap of loose wires. Fixing it was not an option. I threw myself on my bed and cried. Nobody cared about me, my things, or the things I did in life. This was just another nail in my proverbial self-esteem coffin.

Perhaps the real tragedy of this event was that my main concern was the lamp rather than my brother. Violence in my house was such a regular occurrence that I overlooked my mother beating the living shit out of my brother right in front of me.

One friend I could always count on in junior high was Alon, my best friend and secret (or maybe not-so-secret) crush. Alon's family owned a restaurant in Sun Valley, Lady Munchies. The restaurant was closer to our new house than the bar. Alon and I took the bus home and walked to Lady Munchies on almost a daily basis.

In the middle of an outdoor strip mall, right next to Mervyn's, stood a small restaurant with heavenly smells gliding past my nose. The sweet aroma of chicken adobo filled the air. We normally missed the lunch and dinner rush, so there weren't many customers while we were there.

When I walked to Lady Munchies with Alon the first day, I had no idea what an impact it would have on my life. Upon arrival, Alon introduced me to his family.

"This is my sister, Jocelyne; my brother, Jay; my father, Papa; and my other sister, Sally."

"Where is your mom?" I asked.

"Oh, she passed away," Jay quickly answered.

Saddened for Alon and his entire family, I didn't know what to say.

From that moment onward, my connection with Alon became even more profound. Although we had not lost our parents in the same way, we were both one parent short.

It didn't take long for Alon's papa and I to start bonding. From my first visit, he began teaching me specific words or phrases in Tagalog.

"*Kamusta ka?*" Papa asked, while staring at me as if he wanted an answer. I looked at Alon, shrugging my shoulders.

Giggling, Alon replied, "He is asking how you are doing."

"Oh, good," I responded, smiling at Papa.

Leaning forward with a hearty chuckle, Papa raised one eyebrow and declared, "*Mabuti.*"

I looked at him inquisitively, slanted my head to the side, and asked, "Your booty?"

Busting up, Papa jiggled in his seat, he was laughing so hard. Alon was chuckling as well. Sally, Jocelyne, and Jay came out from the kitchen.

"What's so funny?" Jocelyne asked.

Hardly able to contain his laughter, Papa answered between breaths, "Mabuti."

Laughter turned into hilarity.

"Oh, Dad." Sally smirked, retreating to the kitchen.

What was so hilarious about Alon's dad's booty? Confusion set in.

Grabbing my hands and coming close to my face, grinning from ear to ear, Papa said, "*Mabuti* is 'I good' in English."

Finally getting it, I was busting a gut now, along with the rest of the family.

Papa was inspiring and had such a great sense of humor and attitude about life. Although he had lost his wife, he continued to find so much joy.

While playing Go Fish with Papa and Alon, I took a gander at the Lady Munchies menu. I searched for something that would tantalize my taste buds, but there was nothing on the menu I recognized—chicken adobo, lumpia, bulalo…

Probing, I asked, "Alon, what is this stuff?"

"Are you hungry?" he asked, chuckling.

"A little, but I really just want to try it. Maybe I could try the lumpia?"

This was the only thing I somewhat recognized; it sounded like an egg roll and was cheap—one dollar for two of them.

"Hold on," Alon declared, sauntering into the kitchen. When he returned to the table, he said, "My sister is going to make you something."

"She doesn't have to do that, really. I can order from the menu. My mom gave me money so I can get something." I was pleading with desperation while trying to feel grown-up and hoping they believed I had money to spare.

"Don't even think about it, this is my family, and you are not paying," he said with finality as he picked up his cards to finish the round of Go Fish.

It felt like hours passed. Mouthwatering aromas wafted from the kitchen, totally awesome smells I hadn't ever experienced before. Emerging from the kitchen, Sally brought a folding tray, the kind they had in hotel rooms for luggage. Jocelyne and Jay following behind, several plates in hand. Setting everything on the tray, they pushed a few more tables together. One by one, dishes of amazing food kept coming, what looked like chicken in stew, noodles, rice, another square patty of something accompanied by various sauces.

"Oh boy!" Papa exclaimed while rubbing his knife and fork together.

Jay, Jocelyne, and Sally sat down at the table with us. Sally dished up a plate for me.

"This is chicken adobo; it is the national dish of the Philippines."

"What is in it?" I asked.

"Mostly chicken and vegetables. Just try it."

Sally put the white rice and a chicken leg from the pot on top of the plate. Scooping a ton of sauce on top of the rice made the rice watery. Adding a couple of egg rolls and a bun, she handed me the plate.

"Thank you so much," I replied graciously.

"It's our pleasure."

I patiently waited for everyone to get served when Jocelyne urged, "Eat! You don't want it to get cold."

When I dug into my first bite of chicken adobo, I was astounded. I'd never tasted anything quite like it.

Scrumdidilyumptious. The chicken was so soft it melted in my mouth. Surprisingly, the rice soaked in broth was paired perfectly with the chicken. This was the first of many wonderful days with Alon's family.

The happiness I saw and felt that day was inspiring. Papa was without his wife, the kids missing their mother, but they united, lifted, and strengthened each other.

From the moment I met them, I realized what it meant to have a functional family. I was jealous, and I wanted more. I wanted to *be* part of that family. I inserted myself as much as I could.

Several months later, I began to feel like a bit of a thorn in their side. They were always feeding me, and I couldn't pay for the food. I was incredibly grateful to them— not just for the food but for showing me that family could be amazing, loving, happy, supportive, and fun.

For the first time in my life, I finally had made connections that felt grounded, real, and healthy. I became best friends with Alon and was entrenched in his family. Making new friends at school was refreshing and a wonderful, unfamiliar experience.

Then one day toward the end of my eighth-grade year, out of the blue, Mom came home announcing, "We are moving to Maui."

Her words were a shot to my gut. My heart sank deep within me.

Snappishly choosing to move to Hawaii at the end of the school year wasn't good for Nile or for me. Nile was livid, to say the least. All we seemed to do was move from town to town, never staying in one place long enough to make friends. And now we were moving across an ocean?

Refusing to move to Hawaii, Nile gave our mother an ultimatum: either he was getting emancipated and would live on his own, or we would remain in California, specifically Sun Valley. Nile was unwilling to change schools again when he was finally starting to make strong connections.

Succumbing, Mom agreed to let him live on his own at sixteen years old. Nile and my mother spent many weekends looking at various apartments. Not many people were willing to rent to a sixteen-year-old while the parents lived in another state, especially to a teenager who wasn't emancipated. When he finally found a studio apartment close by North Hollywood High School, Nile moved in a few months later. Mom had everything set up in her name: utility bills, expenses, and rent. She required only three things of my brother in exchange: he must continue going to school and get good grades. Also, no drugs or alcohol. Nile was only sixteen, and I thought it a pretty sweet deal for him.

Beyond missing all my newfound friends, contemplating the thought of living without Nile was heartbreaking. For the first time in my existence on this earth, I would be separated from my brother. I was saddened and anxious, maybe even a bit panicked. It wasn't like we were just moving a town away; it would be a five-hour plane ride if I wanted to see my brother.

That summer, while Mom was preparing for our big move to Hawaii, she was home more often than not. One afternoon, my mother came home looking like a wreck.

"What's going on, Mom?" I asked.

"I'm exhausted, and I have been searching and searching and, well, sit down. We need to talk." She sounded desperate.

Curious, I headed to the dining room. Seated at our solid oak, maple-colored, oval dining table, I asked, "What's up?"

"I want to talk to you about something, and I am not quite sure how to begin."

"Mom, enough with the mystery. Just tell me."

"Okay, here goes… Before I married your father, when I was eighteen years old, I got pregnant."

I was shocked.

"What!? What are you talking about, Mom?" I demanded. "Did you have an abortion? Do I have an older brother?" I was a dramatic kid at thirteen and badgered her with questions.

"Just calm down," my mother said. "I will tell you everything." She took a breath before continuing. "When I was seventeen, I met your father. Things progressed quickly with us, and I really wanted to get out of where I was living with my mother and siblings. I had way too much responsibility and needed to make a life for myself. I ended up with your father, and I got pregnant."

"But, Mom, what happened to the baby?"

"I'm getting there," she replied impatiently. "Just hold on. I have never told you this before. I wanted you to know the truth, but I didn't feel like you were old enough or mature enough. But now, I think you are ready for it."

"Which is?" I insisted.

"Do you want to hear the story or not?" Mom gave me *that look.* I shut my mouth and listened. She continued. "As I was saying, I think you are old enough to know the truth now."

"The truth about what?" I wasn't very good at waiting patiently.

"About your father. He wasn't a very nice person."

"Um, duh… Like, where is he?" I gestured around, as if he might suddenly materialize in our home to prove me wrong.

"Beyond that, he did extremely hurtful things to me. When I was pregnant with your brother, we wanted to get married and start our lives together as a family. However, your father, being Middle Eastern, was very misogynistic. He was insistent that if I wanted to marry him, I would have to give up my baby for adoption. I never wanted to do it, but I was in a position where I couldn't care for myself. If I couldn't take care of myself, how was I going to take care of a baby all alone? Your father left me with no other choice. He told me specifically, 'It's him or me.' I did so many things to miscarry. I went horseback riding, I drank like a fish, and I even thought about trying to get him out with a vacuum at some point."

"MOM!" I yelled in astonishment.

"Well, my heart was broken. I didn't want to give my firstborn away. I just wanted to die if I couldn't have my baby. I had my first baby boy on August 22, 1963. In my mind, I named him Eugene, because that was the worst possible name I could think of. I did anything and everything to distance and separate myself from him mentally. I knew I wasn't going to be allowed to keep him."

I reached out for her hand. "Mom, that's horrible. I'm so sorry."

"It was the hardest thing I ever had to do in my life. I painstakingly went through nine months of pregnancy, knowing the entire time I wasn't going to be able to keep the incredible human being that was growing in my body. It was a dream turned into a nightmare. After hours of agonizing labor, I wasn't even allowed to hold my baby. It broke my heart, and I don't think it has ever mended. I couldn't even look at him. The adoption was prearranged, so the doctor took him before I could peek at his beautiful little face."

I handed my mom a tissue to wipe the tears streaming down her face. "I don't know what to say. I'm so, so, so sorry. How old is he now? Do you think it is possible to find him?"

Then I realized what day it was, and why she had been crying all day. We were having this conversation on August 22, 1984—his twenty-first birthday.

Finding out about my brother was a blessing for me. I longed for an older brother I could be close with. Nile and I had drifted further and further apart by this point, and I fantasized about how amazing it would be to have another older brother.

From that point forward, whenever going into a grocery store, I would always take an extra moment of the cashier's time.

"Excuse me," I'd say. "I'm looking for a guy that looks like me, but older. He's my brother, and I don't know what he looks like exactly, but I know he looks like me. I know because my other brother and I look very much alike. If you see someone that looks like me, could you please tell me the next time I come?"

Everyone I asked thought I was the sweetest thing. I wasn't trying to be sweet—I was on a quest. I really wanted to find my brother, and instinctively, I knew he was close.

A few weeks after we had this conversation, we moved to Maui. I stopped asking about my brother at random places once we moved because I thought it pointless. Not only was my mother ripping me away from Nile and my newfound friends, but she was taking any opportunity I had to find my recently announced brother away from me as well.

Shortly after moving to Hawaii, I came home to find my mom sitting at the dining room table staring at a large envelope.

"Hi, Mom," I called, bouncing in the door. I didn't get a reply, so I repeated, "Hi, Mom." Nothing. "Mom," I said, coming closer and increasing the volume of my voice. "Are you okay? What's going on?"

I looked at the manila envelope in her hand and noticed the return address was from a private detective in Los Angeles.

"Mom, what's that?" I inquired cautiously.

Looking up at me with tears in her eyes, she divulged, "Your brother… It's your brother. I found him."

"What?!" I exclaimed. "Really?! That is awesome, Mom!"

"Don't get too excited," she warned. "It's just the first step. I don't even know if he wants to meet me."

"Come on, Mom, why wouldn't he? You gave birth to him."

"Yes, honey, but it is more complicated than that. We will see. I am going to write him a letter and hope he replies."

"I hope so, Mommy. I would love to have another brother."

Wrapping my arms around her back, I crossed them over her heart and whispered in her ear, "I love you, Mommy. I'm going to the beach."

A few years later, back in California and living in Newbury Park, my mother received a letter from the son she'd been forced to give up. My brother, Patrick, was a successful businessman who grew up only a few towns away from where we were living. Our homes were only about a twenty-minute car ride away from each other. When my mother found him, he was living in Van Nuys, CA, less than six miles from where we lived in Sun Valley. Apparently, my intuition was correct; he had been close.

My mother replied to Patrick with a letter, telling him about Nile and me and that we wanted to meet our older brother. She proclaimed how elated she would be to meet her firstborn son, if he was open to it, of course. Patrick replied, and a meeting was set up on Mother's Day, 1985.

Mom was a nervous wreck. I don't think I'd ever seen her like that before. I was overjoyed and a bit anxious, uncertain if he would like me or how he felt about us. Everything was up for speculation until the moment we finally met him.

Travelling up and over the hills of the 101 freeway, we reached the restaurant on Ventura Boulevard. We were all nervous, but Mom was sweating bullets.

I gave her a hug. "Mom, it's going to be okay. He is going to love us."

As we strolled toward the restaurant, I held my mother's hand in solidarity. A tall, dark man paced back and forth along the sidewalk adjacent to the restaurant. *Could that be him?* I squeezed my mom's hand. We knew it was absolutely him. Before us stood her firstborn son and my eldest brother, Patrick.

Time moved in slow motion when Mom called out, "Patrick?"

He turned around, and a giant smile spread across his face. She ran to him as if she had known him his entire life, throwing her arms around him and kissing his cheeks like there was no tomorrow. He appeared a bit uncomfortable yet elated to meet his birth mother.

"Wow, that was some greeting!" he exclaimed with a smile.

"I'm sorry, I am just so over the moon to meet you," my mother replied.

"Well, I'm over the moon to meet you as well, Laurie," he replied as he hugged her.

Patrick stood about six feet tall and was the spitting image of my brother and me combined, with a little bit of extra love around the belly. He had a receding hairline, and the hair he had left on his head was the same color as ours. I distinctively recall the gaudy gold watch he wore upon his wrist, nestled in a thick bush of long, dark arm hair.

I stood next to my mother and waited until she introduced us: "This is your sister, Delicia."

"It is so nice to meet you. I have been looking for you for years now," I quickly interjected.

"Really? That is cool."

Mom pulled Nile in close. "This is your brother, Nile."

Patrick, grasping Nile's hand, replied, "It's so nice to meet you."

Tugging on Patrick as if he were five, Mom asserted, "Let's go eat."

Patrick and I immediately clicked, never running out of things to discuss that day, discovering we had the same sense of humor and enjoyed a lot of the same things. Patrick seemed genuinely interested in getting to know me, which felt really good. I was enamored with the thought of having a brother who actually liked me and, perhaps, would like to learn more about me.

Nile was eighteen, out on his own, and uninterested in getting to know me as an adult. He was only involved when he was forced to be, on family occasions and holidays.

Patrick and I got to know each other over the years. We discovered that we enjoyed each other's company very much and we had a lot of fun together. Patrick was a poker dealer, and I was infatuated with poker yet intimidated by it. I constantly badgered him to teach me to play.

"Poker isn't a woman's game," Patrick would proclaim.

"That is dumb. Why do you say that?"

"It's such an awful environment with all the smoke and alcohol and gross guys everywhere."

"Whatever, you chauvinist," I'd tease.

We'd both laugh. He got my humor, and I got his. I desperately missed the relationship with my brother Nile, so it was incredible to have a brother I could laugh and hang out with again.

Driving was a big deal as a teenager. Getting your license at sixteen was a privilege, and my mother made certain I knew that.

My sixteenth birthday was coming up, and the only thing I wanted was my driver's license. My mother made it clear that if I didn't maintain a C in all my classes, I wouldn't be allowed to attempt to get my license until the following January when grades came out again. To a fifteen-year-old, going on sixteen, that seemed like forever. Being on track to finish geometry with an F meant summer school and no license.

Mr. Nelson, my geometry teacher, was about five foot tall and a surfer from Ventura. Every morning before school, he would surf. He constantly compared geometry to riding a wave.

Everything about him screamed *brah,* from the way he talked— "Dude, you should really get a grip and learn to study, man"—to the way he dressed in his Hawaiian shirts and Bermuda shorts with Birkenstocks.

I couldn't say if he was a good teacher or not because either I just really didn't get geometry, or he didn't know how to teach me in a way I understood it. Mom knew how much I struggled in that class.

She made a deal with me. "I will let you get your driver's license on your sixteenth birthday *if* you pass all your classes with at least a C."

"But, Mom, you know how bad I am doing in geometry."

"Well, that will be motivation for you, won't it?"

"But Mom ..." I protested.

"But, Mom, nothing. You get at least all Cs—no Ds or Fs—and you can get your driver's license on your birthday. If you don't, then you will have to wait until the end of next semester. Driving is a privilege."

Knowing that meant I would miss three whole months of summertime driving, I agreed. "Okay, Mom, you got a deal."

Studying even harder than before, asking for help from a counselor, and asking Mr. Nelson to meet with me still didn't help me grasp geometry. Even with all that, I was at a loss; it was Greek to me.

The process of getting a license was quite complicated. First, there was driver's education and passing a written learner's permit test. In addition, you had to have six months of practice under your belt, so I planned accordingly.

I spent many weeks that summer doing driver's education. When September 6, 1986, rolled around, I was ready. Mom drove me to the DMV so I could take the written test. Passing the first time around, I was delighted to check this off my list.

"Hey, Mom, I passed! Can I drive?"

Chuckling, she said, "Get in ... the passenger side."

Having my permit allowed me to practice driving for several months. First in the empty school parking lot, then on the residential side streets. Eventually, I moved on to main streets and finally graduated to the freeway. It was only a few months before I was comfortable behind the wheel.

The majority of my friends didn't have cars. Newbury Park was quite boring, and we always wanted to go to LA or Ventura but never had a way to get there, other than our friend Cindi. I'd been working at Taco Bell since I was fifteen, and every penny I earned that I didn't spend on weed I was saving to buy my first beater.

Mr. Nelson knew how hard I'd worked in his class, managing to bring my F grade up to a D. Knowing I needed a C if I wanted to get my license on my birthday, I strived for more. Having dreamt about this for a long time, I did whatever it took to get that C in geometry. Being able to drive meant one thing to me: freedom. I could go anywhere, do anything, whenever I wanted, without having to rely on anybody else.

December rolled around, and I knew this was my last chance to get my grade up. During the final, I was so nervous. Everything hinged on this one test. Having done my best, I hoped and prayed over the weekend that I'd passed.

Monday was dead silent in class.

"Why is everyone so quiet?" Mr. Nelson shouted as he came into the classroom. "Come on, dudes, liven up. It's not that bad. Life is a party, man." Moving to the front of the classroom, he reached into his briefcase, pulling out a stack of papers.

Oh God, this is it, I thought. Wandering around the room, Mr. Nelson dropped the graded tests face down on each individual desk. He gave me a disparaging look while laying down my test. Slowly raising one corner while lowering my head on the table, I peeked to see what the grade was. I saw red writing but couldn't make out my grade. Turning it over, I saw a giant red D. I felt defeated. I'd tried so hard; there was nothing else I could have done. In addition to being a terrible test taker, I sucked at geometry.

At this point, all I could do was plead to his humanity. Staying after class, I approached Mr. Nelson. I learned from a rather young age that in order to get people to do what you want, you have to mirror them.

"Mr. Nelson, can I like talk to you, dude?" I asked.

"Totally," he responded.

"Hey, man, you know I have been trying like so totally hard in this class, and I don't understand how I got a D on this test."

"Because, dude, you got the answers wrong," he joked in his best Spicoli voice.

"Come on, Mr. Nelson, you know how hard I tried. I can't get a D. I just can't."

"Why, brah? What's the issue?"

"I made a deal with my mom that if I got a C in every class, I could get my license on my sixteenth birthday this upcoming March. This is the one class I haven't been able to do that. Dude, please, I have tried so hard."

"Well, it certainly wasn't for lack of effort, that is for sure. Not sure I can help you but let me re-grade your test and see what I can do."

"Please, Mr. Nelson, you would be my hero, literally."

"Have a good holiday," he said, dismissing me.

"Thanks, Mr. Nelson, you too. I hope you catch some sick waves, dude."

"Thanks, li'l lady."

The last time I remembered wishing or hoping for something so hard had been the night the ambulance drove away with my mother after her suicide attempt. I checked the mailbox daily, anticipating my report card. It felt like weeks turned into months waiting for this piece of paper that would determine my life for the next year.

In mid-January, having already started the new semester in school, it finally came. A little white, flimsy piece of paper with four perforations, one on each end. Tearing off those perforated edges felt like it took an eternity. I delicately opened the paper, and my eyes scanned down the grades past everything until my fourth-period class—geometry. I scanned to the right, my heart palpitating like it was going to pop out of my chest. Catching a glimpse of my grade, my mouth dropped to the floor when I saw C– in light gray lettering, I literally jumped for joy. Waiting for my mother to come home that day was torturous.

The minute I heard her car in the driveway, I ran outside, report card in hand, screaming, "Mom, Mom, look! I got a C minus! I passed!"

"Good job, baby!" she congratulated me. "I knew you could do it. Now you just have to keep practicing so you can pass the instructor's test."

"Thanks so much, Mommy, for helping me. I really appreciate it."

I practiced as much as my mother would let me for the next month and a half until I felt quite comfortable. I was even good at parallel parking. When I made my appointment at the DMV in Thousand Oaks, I was overjoyed. I made sure to schedule my appointment for the exact date I wanted, March 6, 1987. I didn't want to wait a single day longer than I had to. I didn't have a car yet, but that was the next step. The day of my appointment, I was unwaveringly confident I would pass.

On our way to the DMV, I was nervous but certain. The DMV was packed with people. Mom made me grab a number from the little red plastic number machine. When I heard 15C in the distance, I checked my number, and my hands began to sweat. Giving my mom a kiss, I stated, "That's me. Here I go."

She cried out, "Good luck, honey!" as I walked away.

Mom met me around back with the instructor. Clipboard in hand and a serious look on his face, he watched as I entered the vehicle. I wanted this so badly, I wasn't about to let him make me nervous. I chauffeured the instructor around for about fifteen minutes before heading back to the DMV.

Anticipating I had passed but afraid to ask, I waited for the instructor to speak.

Finally, he said, “Wow, I’m impressed. Not that many people are that comfortable on their first try. You passed. Congratulations.”

Mom was waiting for me with a big smile on her face when we got back.

“Did you pass, honey? Did you pass?” she asked with glee.

I wanted to trick her, but I didn’t want to lie.

Looking at her with a sad face, I pretended in a mumble, “Yeah, I passed.”

“What?” she asked, shocked at what she thought I’d said.

Raising my head slowly, I couldn’t help the huge grin on my face when I yelled, “Yes, I passed!” Elated, I gave her the biggest hug. “Thank you, Mommy, thank you for helping me.”

“Congratulations, honey!” Handing me the keys, she continued. “Now, you can drive.”

My dream car had always been a triple-white Super Beetle convertible—white interior, white paint, and white convertible top. Whenever I saw one, from the time I was ten years old, I would blow it a kiss. I wasn’t convinced it would be my first car, but I knew one day I would be so lucky as to own a triple-white convertible Volkswagen. On our way back to our condo complex, all I could think about was how much money I would need to save for my car.

Mom prepared a special birthday dinner. She always let me pick what I wanted for my birthday dinner, and this year I picked my favorite: lasagna.

I was still on a high from getting my license earlier that day. There was nothing else I needed; my birthday was turning out magnificently. At dinner, Mom handed me a card. As I opened the card, a folded piece of paper fell out. Unraveling it, I noticed it was some sort of contract.

As I read the contract, I was confused. I looked at my mother in bewilderment.

“Just read it,” she demanded.

I began to read out loud. “‘Number one, I promise to be home no later than two a.m.’ Huh?” I was confused at what I was getting myself into by reciting these lines.

"Keep going," she said.

Every line required an initial at the end.

"Here's a pen," she stated, holding it out to me. "You can sign as you go."

Reaching for the pen, I murmured, "Okay." I initialed next to the first line.

"'Number two, I promise not to drink, do drugs, and operate a vehicle.' Okay," I agreed, initialing the box next to it. There were many rules, and I was curious.

"Mom, why are you having me sign all of this? You know I don't do any of these things anyway."

"Just sign it," she demanded impatiently.

"Okay, geez." I initialed each of the various rules on down the list. After signing everything, I handed it to my mother. "Here you go," I said.

"Thank you," she said, snatching it back and reviewing it to make certain I'd signed everything.

"Come here," she beckoned. I saw now she had a handkerchief in her hand. "Turn around." Turning me so that I faced the front door, she wrapped the handkerchief around my eyes.

"What are we doing, Mommy?" I asked.

"Just wait," she responded quickly. "Can you see?"

I could feel the air moving in front of me like she was waving her hand, but I couldn't see anything.

"No, I can't see," I replied.

"Okay, come on," she said, grabbing my arm with both of her hands. Carefully, she led me out the front door.

"Wait. Hold on. Step down. One more step."

Relying completely on my mother's guidance as I had the majority of my life, I put complete trust in her.

"Okay, now, walk this way," she instructed, leading me fifty steps or so. Stopping, she asked, "Are you ready?"

"Yeah, of course, Mom," I replied eagerly. "What's happening?"

Hopeful, I suspected perhaps that my mom had gotten me a car. This was, of course, a giant speculation since I knew my mother didn't have that kind of money.

When she removed the handkerchief from my eyes, I was in shock. A white Volkswagen Beetle with a giant pink bow on top of a sunroof sat before me.

Dumfounded, when I finally found my voice, I asked Mom with tears in my eyes, "Is this for me?"

"It's yours, honey. Happy birthday. I want you to know that I am so proud of you and so proud of the woman you are becoming. I'm sorry I couldn't afford the convertible version for you, but I got one with a sunroof. It was the closest I could do."

"Oh my God, Mom, are you for real? Seriously? Oh my God! Wow, thank you so much!" I professed my heartfelt gratitude with tears streaming down my cheeks.

"Check it out, honey," she said, handing me the keys.

"No way!" I cried out, still in complete disbelief.

I ran my hand over the shiny white paint job, then hopped inside, looking around. It had black leather interior seats and a stick shift with a wooden knob; even the glove box had a little lock on it. Opening the sunroof and lifting my hands to the sky, I cried out in jubilation. Freedom was just around the corner.

I was super grateful to have a car that was cute as a button, but it was, admittedly, not the greatest car in the world, mechanically. It was a fantastic first car, teaching me many lessons, including how to fix a vehicle. Seven times out of ten my friends would line up around the back while I was in the driver's seat, everyone pushing until my bug had enough speed to pop the clutch. Then they'd run to jump in once it finally started.

A couple times that little bug endangered my life. Luckily, I was able to get out of those situations.

One time, on my way to the Valley, while powering down the grade, my brakes unexpectedly stopped working.

Mom bought this car not knowing it had retread tires on it. The retread came off and whipped around the tire. When I heard a noise and immediately attempted to switch lanes, I realized my brakes were not working at all; when I pushed my foot on the brake, it went all the way to the floor, but my car wasn't slowing down. Being a new driver and alone in the car, I needed to think fast.

Something came over me. Feeling like my brain left my body, I knew what to do automatically. Calmly, I pulled over lane by lane. Downshifting, I merged slowly from the fast into the slow lane until I was able to reach the emergency lane. The road flattened enough, and the car began to slow. I pulled the emergency brake and finally came to a slow, rolling stop, unbelievably, without any damage to myself, the car, or anybody else around me. I was just sixteen years old. At the time, I didn't think about it, but now I know my angels were looking out for me that day.

I have a lot of fond memories of my first car, the greatest being of the gift itself. Even though my mom didn't have money, she went above and beyond to make my birthday unforgettable. It wasn't just the car but the thought behind the car that truly mattered to me. When I saw that car with the big pink bow on top, I felt so much love. I thought the best present I ever got was this car. Ultimately, the love I felt that day was the real gift.

Things like this are what made my mother so incredibly special to me.

Although the first words out of my mother's mouth were, "She's ugly," we had a bond that could never be broken and became extremely close from the first breath I took. Of course, we had our issues—especially when I was a crazy teenager—but my mother and I loved each other more than words could express.

People always ask me why I don't blame my mother for more things that happened to me. My mother was my everything, my shining star in a world filled with black holes. My mother was the one who fought to get us back from Baghdad. If I hadn't come home from Iraq, I don't know where my life would be. I probably wouldn't have one.

My mother did her best with the tools she had available. She put a lot of effort into raising us, even though she never had good role models herself. She didn't do everything right, nor did she do everything wrong. My mom was the strongest figure in my life, my confidante, my rock, and the one person I knew I could count on. She was the one who would love me unconditionally until the day one of us died.

THE NIGHT STALKER

It was a balmy Southern California night; we had what we called "earthquake weather." It was eighty-plus degrees. The air felt wet and warm—muggy. Sleeping with the windows open, everyone in the house was hoping and praying "the big one" wasn't about to hit. Though part of me thought it ridiculous when people would say, "California is going to fall into the ocean someday," it was something I'd heard my entire life. Part of me worried it just might be plausible.

We were living in Sun Valley, a small town in the San Fernando Valley. Our house was a three-bedroom with a small front yard and a backyard with a pool.

Drying off after swimming all day, I came through the sliding glass door into the living room from the backyard. Exhausted, I laid down on the couch.

Mom called out from the kitchen, "Delicia, you better not be on the couch in your wet bathing suit. You need to get changed and come eat dinner."

Between the hot sun, swimming, and finishing up my mom's stuffed bell peppers, I was ready to watch some *Happy Days* and do a whole lot of nothing before going to bed. I headed to the TV and turned the big round knob on the television set before settling into the couch. As I watched Richie, Potsie, Fonzie, and the whole gang, my eyes got heavy, and before I knew it, I passed out on the couch. Mom must have seen how tired I was, and rather than waking me and making me head to my room, she covered me with a blanket.

That night was a particularly dark evening; the moon was only about a quarter full. A sliver of light shone through the sliding glass door. It was light enough to see, but there were mostly shadows.

Something caused me to wake. Abruptly opening my eyes, I saw the figure of a naked man standing in front of me. *Was I dreaming?* My body froze. I stopped breathing, or at least it felt like I did. Pretending to be sleeping, I stayed as frozen and stiff as possible, my eyes open just a slit.

Before me stood a tall, lanky, brown, naked man. He hovered over me while his hand slowly stroked his erect penis. Making out only his silhouette, I could tell he was about six feet tall, brown, possibly of Latin descent. His hair looked like a bowl cut and was noticeably curly. I lay petrified while he stared at me and fondled himself. I couldn't breathe. I hoped that if I pretended to be asleep, he would leave. This method had worked with my molesters in the past, and I prayed it would be my saving grace.

Turning around very slowly, he continued caressing himself as he strolled toward the sliding glass door. Turning his head in a very distinctive manner, he looked back at me as he walked. I felt a chill up my spine. He repeatedly looked back and forth between me and the door as he slowly made his way out, all the while continuing to stroke himself. I hoped with every fiber of my being that he would keep walking.

The second I could no longer see him, I jumped off the couch and ran as fast as I could into my mother's room. Jumping on the bed, I screamed, "Mom, someone is jacking off in the living room!"

By this time, my mother was already living with Ron, who she had met merely a few months prior. Before the divorce was final with Joshua, my mom had started dating Ron. He was an ex-football player and stood six foot four and weighed about three hundred fifty pounds, most of which was muscle. It took both of my hands to wrap around half of his bicep. In my mind, if anyone could get this guy, it would be Ron. Darting up, he ran out of the room, down the hallway, and through the living room into the backyard.

By the time Ron got up and out, nobody was around. The strange man had completely disappeared. We were uncertain how he'd vanished so quickly. At approximately three in the morning, we contacted the local police to report the incident.

A few days passed. I was playing on the front lawn with a couple of my friends from the neighborhood when a peculiar man passed by. I tried to ignore him and not make eye contact as he slowly and methodically turned his head to look at me, exactly as the naked man had a few nights earlier. But this time, I got a good look at him and felt a chill go up my spine.

When Mom got home, I described him to her in detail and explained I believed he was the same person.

In June of 1984, the same month this man came into my home, a man broke into the home of seventy-nine-year-old Jennie Vincow in Glassell Park, where he found her sleeping. He raped her, then stabbed her to death.

After Jennie, a spree of killings began to terrorize Southern California. For the next fourteen months, we watched murder after murder on the news. It wasn't until August of 1985 that these killings would be linked to a serial killer dubbed the Night Stalker.

The city was in a panic. People were so terrified that gun sales went crazy, and many folks slept with baseball bats to protect themselves. I, too, slept with my baseball bat right by my side.

I often wondered if the strange man who had stood over me in my living room that same month that Jennie was murdered was the Night Stalker.

It wasn't until a sketch was released on the news that my terrifying suspicions became a reality. Gawking at the television, I screamed.

"Look, Mom, the Night Stalker!" I cried. But it was my next statement that got her attention. "Mom, that looks like the guy who came into the house and jacked off."

From just a sketch, I couldn't be 100 percent certain, but I had a horrible feeling in my gut that I had once been mere inches from this merciless man.

On August 31, 1985, the Night Stalker, Richard Ramirez, was captured by citizens on the streets of East Los Angeles. A sinking feeling engulfed my body when I saw his face plastered all over the evening news. The same feeling I felt the first time I was molested at seven—utter disgust—washed over my entire body. I knew as soon as I saw his face—this was the naked man who had stood over me in my living room.

Several months before that night, just prior to my thirteenth birthday, I had cut my hair short. It was so short that I looked like a boy. I've always wondered if this could have been my saving grace. I will never know, but what I do know is that I thank God, the universe, my angels, and all the stars above that he did not take my life that balmy evening in June 1984.

GOING TO A GO-GO

By December of 1979, my brother was a pre-teen. Marvin, Nile's Big Brother, was into the ska scene and had recently gone to see Madness at the Whiskey-A-Go-Go on Sunset. The opening band was an all-girl punk band Marvin thought were pretty far-out. A friend gave him a bootleg copy of the demo from a live show the prior year. Marvin shared his copy with Nile the next time they saw each other. Nile thought they were okay but wasn't really that into them. On the other hand, he knew that *I* would absolutely love them.

One evening, when Mom was actually home having dinner with us, Nile punched me jokingly in the arm, as he often did. "Hey, Delicia. Marvin gave me some music, and I think you will love it. Mom, is it okay if she comes to my room for a while so we can listen to it?"

"Sure, of course," Mom replied.

I was jazzed whenever Nile wanted to share his music with me, so without question, I complied.

Parking myself on the wooden edge of his waterbed, half my butt rested on the wavy, dark blue vinyl while the water made a slight wave motion underneath me. Nile, standing next to his stereo in his Members Only jacket, excitedly removed a cassette tape.

"Marvin just discovered this band; I think you might like 'em."

It was a black cassette with a white sticker across the top third portion. Written in black Sharpie on the label were the words: "The Go-Go's, Whiskey, 10/4/78."

He popped the cassette tape into his stereo and pressed play. I heard the guitar strum and the drumbeat start: *bump, bump, bump, bump...* I felt my heart thump with the beat.

I was hardly able to understand the words, the tape was so muffled. The beat made my pulse race and my hands sweat, and I felt this incredible sensation to get up, dance, and jump around. I could barely contain myself.

"Who is this?" I called out as I shot up from my seat and began dancing around the room like a crazed octopus.

"It's a band called The Go-Go's, all girls," he replied over the music.

"WHAT?! WOW!"

I hadn't really heard punk music before. Something in it made the blood course through my veins like a jolt of lightning. Obsessed with the fact that they were all girls and how much their music rocked, I couldn't wait to hear more. I listened to that cassette tape until I wore it out.

By mid-year 1980, about a year or so after Nile played me their music for the first time, The Go-Go's were already on the rise to fame, scheduled to open for Madness on a world tour that summer. They were no longer playing small clubs.

When their first single, "Our Lips Are Sealed," was released in the mid-spring of 1981, it was practically an overnight success, hitting the *Billboard*'s Top 100 list within the first couple weeks of its release. The Go-Go's became a household name. Having loved them for over two years by this point, I followed them closely. I filled myself with as much knowledge as I could about the band, the music, the scene, and everything in between. In my opinion, they were the greatest band to ever walk the face of the planet.

Knowing their full ten-song album was scheduled to be released in July of that year, I watched the newspaper, magazines, and billboards. Fastidiously, I combed through every copy of *Bop* magazine looking for any mention of The Go-Go's. I finally saw it: an ad for *Beauty and the Beat,* The Go-Go's full album, which was scheduled to be released July 8, 1981. I counted the days until it came out and was the first in line at the record store the morning The Go-Go's premiere album was released. I'd saved all my allowance that summer so I could buy the album the minute it came out.

That July morning was like Christmas for me, only better. I could hardly sleep the night before. At six a.m., I was wide awake. Tower Records wouldn't open for another three hours.

Throwing off the covers, I ran to my closet, clutching my pink ceramic piggy bank. This was before some genius thought of putting a hole in the bottom of the pig so you could retrieve what you had been saving. I knew the time had come to, literally, break the bank.

I looked at my cute little pink pig that had been holding my money for all those months, knowing the big day was finally here. I took my piggy bank to the back stairs— "Thank you, little piggy"—and grinned, holding it in the air to get one last look at him.

I smashed that pig into hundreds of pieces, and the money I'd saved fell onto the concrete steps along with chunks and broken pieces of pink ceramic pig—there laid tiny folded-up dollar bills, quarters, pennies, dimes, and nickels. Sorting and separating the remains of my pig and money, I added it all up and headed back inside.

Before leaving, I knew I needed to sweep up what was left of the ceramic shards so nobody would get hurt. It was getting close to nine, and I was determined to be the first in line. I walked as fast as I could—sometimes even breaking into a jog—to Tower Records.

Rushing down the street and a few blocks over to Lankershim, I turned left and huffed a few more blocks to the giant record store. I peered inside the window, hopeful I could get someone to let me in early. The employees very intentionally ignored the impatient ten-year-old at the door. I watched the big round clock on the wall intently as the large hand moved in circles, minute by minute getting closer to nine. When the large hand hit the twelve, I knew it was time. I held my breath in anticipation as I watched the guy walking toward the door.

Familiar with my excitement, he queried, "Waiting for something special?"

Ducking under his arm, I ran past him into the store, shouting, "Yep!"

I ran straight to the punk section but couldn't find The Go-Go's.

Anxiously, I asked the person behind the counter, "Do you have the new Go-Go's album?"

"Who?" the apathetic teen replied.

"The Go-Go's, they are new." My desperation was barely concealed.

"Oh, we have all of our latest music there." The employee pointed toward the new music section I could see from across the store.

As I approached that section, there it was in all its glory. My heart skipped a beat when I saw the album cover. My hands shook with excitement.

Finding my treasure, I ran to the cashier, carefully placing the album on the counter. I emptied my pockets, putting the crumpled dollar bills and my change on top of the album, along with a few pieces of lint. The store clerk sorted through it, smiling half-cocked at me, as if he saw a little bit of himself the first time *he* bought his favorite band's album. Handing me back a few dollars and some change, he put the album into a thin paper sack.

"Thank you so much!" I ran out the door and all the way home. I couldn't wait to play my new record.

I ran into my brother's room just as he was waking up; I could hardly contain my excitement. "Look, look, look at what I got!" I shouted.

He swiped the album from my hand and insisted, "Let's play it."

He took out the vinyl record and handed me the album cover. I stared at the cover for a long while, taking in every splash of color, every pixel of the photos. All five girls had towels wrapped around their bodies and heads. The head towels were folded like turbans to keep their hair up. I committed every inch of that album cover to memory while I rocked my body back and forth, making waves on my brother's waterbed. Tapping my feet to the beat of the music, I eagerly awaited the next song. "Tonight" played while I adored the back side of the light pink and baby blue album cover. Each member of the band was featured in their own photo, all posing in a bathtub. This was a bit radical for the times, but so was an all-girl punk band.

"These guys are rad!" I cried out.

"I knew you would like them."

"Like them? Like, oh my God, they're so bitchin'."

Upon closer examination of the album cover, my eye was directed to an odd spot on one of the girls. *What the heck?* I thought. Squinting and peering closer at the album cover, I started to chuckle.

"What's so funny?" asked Nile.

"Look, is this her nipple?" I pointed to the picture in the lower left-hand corner while handing him the album cover.

"Far out, you're right, that is nip. Rock 'n' roll, man."

Crackin' up, we continued listening.

I was always keen to see how an album cover fit with the music it held. Taking out the inner paper sleeve where the album rested was the most exciting part to me. Printed on the inner album cover were the words to every song. That day, I'd stared so long at the front and back cover that by the time I opened it up, we were already on the fourth or fifth song. I quickly found my place so I could sing along.

At that moment, my brother demanded, "Okay, that's enough. Get out of my room." Teenage boys could be so moody and unpredictable—especially teenage brothers. One moment we were having a blast, listening to my new album; the next I was just his annoying little sister invading his space again.

"No, please, please, please, Nile," I begged. "I *need* to hear the rest of this album."

"No, I want my room back."

"Please, Mom won't let me listen on her record player, and they are like so totally rad. Please, just let me listen to the album."

"Okay, but I'm going inside," he conceded. "Just finish the album, then come get me."

This was the best of both worlds: listening to the album in my big brother's room, by myself. I dreamed of having this room as my own, but Mom would never let me since it was separate from the house. The double standard of what was okay for my brother but not for me was often frustrating. Whenever I posed the question of why, I was told, "Because he is a boy." There was a lot of that growing up.

Taking advantage, I enjoyed every minute of my time alone in that garage room. I pried myself up off the waterbed when it came time to flip the album to the B side. I never sat back down again. I spent the next twenty-ish minutes dancing, spinning, jumping, stomping, pumping, and gyrating my little ten-year-old self into a Go-Go's frenzy.

Following that day, life would never be the same for me again. My life is full of many turning points, days and moments that separate the "before" and "after." That day was one of the good ones.

From the moment my brother played me the first beat of The Go-Go's bootleg cassette tape, I was hooked. Becoming a household name within the first year of their album release was quite an accomplishment for the group. Their second single, "We Got the Beat," soared to the number one spot in *Billboard*'s music charts. It didn't take long before The Go-Go's were headlining sold-out stadium shows. This all-girl punk/rock/pop band was the first of its kind, and they were taking America by storm.

By September 1981, everyone in the neighborhood knew how much I loved The Go-Go's. When Isaac showed up with tickets for the first ever headlining Go-Go's tour, I was beside myself. He purchased the tickets about a month before the show and gave them to me for safekeeping.

I felt like I couldn't breathe for that entire month. Awaiting my first Go-Go's show was like waiting for my wedding day or my first child, one of those grand life events every little kid dreams of. They'd toured with Madness in prior years, but this time it was all about them. No longer the opening band, they'd graduated to larger forums.

October 9, 1981, finally arrived. Isaac knocked on the door, and Mom let him in.

"I want her back by midnight," she said sternly.

"No problem," he replied.

I ran to my white-and-pink jewelry box, where I kept the tickets, and opened the box. A little ballet dancer on a spring popped up and spun while music played. I reached in and took out the bottom of the jewelry box. I wasn't about to lose these tickets, so I kept them in this secret compartment, the most private and safe place I could find. Holding them to the light in my room, I read, "The Greek Theatre Welcomes: The Go-Go's." I couldn't help but smile ear to ear.

As we took the winding road to the Greek Theatre, we passed crowds of people dressed in the coolest outfits. Nothing like the DEVO crowd. These fans had large blue mohawks and wore tattered jeans with chains hanging from them, ripped T-shirts, and giant black combat boots. Many girls dressed like The Go-Go's themselves; some even had towels wrapped around their heads just like the album cover.

Being ushered into the parking lot with lines of other cars felt exhilarating. Although I had been to see DEVO a few years prior, this was *my* real first concert, the one I was dying to see. Practically bursting from the inside with anticipation, I saw the entrance in the distance. During our long, meandering walk down the sidewalk filled with crowds of people, I gazed in amazement at my surroundings.

Large chain-link fences surrounded the theater, and security was posted at every gate, the security guards wearing sunshine yellow coats. We handed our tickets to the guard, and he ripped them in half. As the paper tore, I felt my heart break a little. I thought to myself, *He just ruined my golden ticket.* I carefully placed the ripped ticket in my pocket, hoping it wouldn't be damaged further, and I thought perhaps I could tape it back together.

We headed into the gates and through the food court, only stopping briefly so Isaac could buy me a Coke. General admission at the Greek was either in the pit at the very front next to the stage or on the lawn as far back as possible. Both Isaac and my mother were uncomfortable with the thought of me being in the pit, so our tickets were for the lawn.

Although we showed up relatively early, there were still what felt like millions of people in front of us. Ending up in the very last row on the lawn, I was the farthest away from the stage anyone could ever be without going outside of the theater to join the mountain lions. That didn't matter to me. I couldn't see anything and everyone below us looked like ants, which didn't matter to me, either. What mattered was that I could hear them, and more importantly, I could feel them in my heart, body, spirit, and soul.

At thirteen, I had already loved The Go-Go's for almost five years. Having seen them play three years prior at the Greek Theatre, I was looking forward to their upcoming summer tour, hoping to catch them again in Los Angeles.

The Bangles' first album came out in May of 1984, and I can't recall how I was introduced to them, but I absolutely loved them. Their music was very similar to and, at the same time, very different from The Go-Go's, but I knew I'd found my second favorite band from about the third chord into the album.

My biweekly issue of *Bop* came in the mail. Flipping through the magazine, I came across an ad that jumped off the page at me. I about fell over when I saw that The Bangles would be opening for The Go-Go's at Caesar's Palace in Las Vegas.

I was beyond thrilled at the idea of my two favorite bands playing together. Looking at the dates, I discovered The Bangles weren't opening for them any other show of the tour. The Go-Go's were scheduled to come to Los Angeles, but the Vegas stop with The Bangles was before that.

Figuring out a way to get to Las Vegas to see my two favorite bands together was a must.

My uncle lived there, so I came up with a great idea: I would ask my mom if I could visit him, and while I was there, I could go see the show. I doubted she would be open to it since I was only thirteen, but I figured it was worth the try. It was The Go-Go's *and* The Bangles!

Mom happened to be home that day. Having sold the bar a few months before moving to Hawaii, she was home way more often.

Running into the kitchen with the magazine, I shouted, "Mom, Mom, look! The Go-Go's are coming, The Go-Go's are coming!"

"Oh? That's great, honey," she replied.

Reading off the dates and where they were going, I announced, "Mom, look, they're going to Las Vegas. Do you think I could go visit Uncle Rolf and see them?"

"I don't know, honey. It seems like it would be really complicated. How would you get there? Aren't they playing anywhere around here?"

"Yes, but you could take me and visit your brother."

"No, thank you, and I have to work. Not to mention, I don't like Vegas."

"I could take the bus," I offered.

"By yourself?" she snarked in a tone that implied, *No way, little girl.*

"Please, Mom," I pleaded. "My other favorite band, The Bangles, are opening for them, and it looks like this will be the only show they are playing together. Please, Mamma, please, please, please, Mom, please." I'd already made up my mind to be relentless in this task.

"Okay!" she said, finally. "Enough! I guess I could call him and see what he thinks about it."

"Yes, please, Mom, call him. This is going to be so awesome!"

"Okay, but you could only go for a few days, and he would have to go to the show with you."

"Yes, let's ask him, Mom, please," I begged. At that point, I'd agree to any terms just to get to the Vegas show.

Picking up the phone, she dialed her brother's number. I watched as she pushed each numerical button, knowing that with each press, I was closer to seeing The Go-Go's and The Bangles together. It would be a dream come true for me.

"Hi, Rolf?" she greeted her brother, then got straight down to business. "Delicia's two favorite bands are going to be playing in Las Vegas—The Go-Go's and The Bangles—and Delicia really, really wants to go. Do you think you would be willing to go with her?"

I put my head close to my mom's, listening for his answer and waiting with bated breath.

"Sure, I could do that," he replied. "Does that mean I get a visit from my Sugar Babes?"

Uncle Rolf always called me "Sugar Babes" as far back as I can remember. I often contemplated where the nickname came from—probably the Elton John song. He was the first person other than my mother to give me a nickname, and I really liked it a lot. Knowing how much my uncle adored me felt incredible because I didn't feel adored by many people.

"Would you like to talk to her?" asked my mother.

I was extra excited as she handed me the phone. "Hi, Uncle Rolf."

"Hi, Sugar Babes, how are you?"

"I'm good. This is totally rad. I'm super excited. So, it's okay if I come visit you? We can go see The Go-Go's?"

"Sure, Sugar Babes, that sounds great. Put your mom back on so we can figure out the details."

I handed the phone back to my mom and spun in joyful circles all the way to my room. I couldn't believe it. I was going to see The Go-Go's and The Bangles together in Las Vegas. As an added bonus, I got to visit my uncle. I couldn't believe my plan had worked.

I counted the days for two months until the concert. I was nervous but excited about taking my first Greyhound bus, alone, from North Hollywood. Though the anticipation of the concert had been taking up most of my thoughts in those two months, my nerves finally got the best of me while heading toward the Greyhound station. I was second-guessing the decision to go to Las Vegas by myself.

"Mom, are you sure this is a good idea? I've never been on a bus alone, and it's such a long ride," I questioned. Mom ignored my growing concern.

Upon arriving at the station, Mom purchased my ticket and walked me to the bus. "Wait here for a second," she said as she headed toward the large Greyhound bus marked *Las Vegas*.

"Okay," she said when she returned. "I talked to the driver, and he promised to keep an eye on you. Don't worry, Uncle Rolf will be there when you get off the bus."

Hesitantly, I climbed aboard. Seeing the faces of the people I would be sharing this five-and-a-half-hour journey with calmed my nerves a bit. *They don't look so bad,* I thought.

I worked my way toward the back of the bus so I could be near the restroom. Finding a seat, I waved goodbye to my mother out the window. Having driven with my mother to Vegas on several occasions, I knew how long this ride was, so I settled in.

On our way to Vegas, we stopped at Victorville, hitting up the famous McDonald's located inside of a decommissioned train. Mom, Nile, and I always stopped at this McDonald's whenever we traveled to Vegas, so it comforted me to know that we were going in the right direction.

I was hungry and happy we were finally at Mickey D's. I ordered a Big Mac, fries, and a Coke with the money Mom gave me, and I felt responsible.

My initial anxiety shifted, and this trip was starting to make me feel very grown-up.

When the bus pulled into the Las Vegas terminal, I spotted my uncle. He stood right next to the door of the bus. Upon my exit, we shared a big hug.

"Hi, Sugar Babes, are you ready for a fun time?" he asked.

"I'm so excited, Uncle Rolf."

Smiling, he eagerly stated, "Let's get this adventure started, shall we?"

I couldn't help but notice the people and the excitement on the strip in Las Vegas, even during the day. We travelled on the freeway until we reached his apartment in North Las Vegas.

Uncle Rolf lived in a one-bedroom apartment with a pool. I loved swimming, so I was hoping I'd get a chance to swim during my visit. It wasn't until our house in Sun Valley that we had our own pool. Before that, David, Isaac's son, and I went to the public pool at North Hollywood Park. Sharing with a hundred other kids and a massive amount of urine in the pool was the norm there. It always made me uncomfortable but was my only option, so I got over it.

My uncle made the couch up for me so I would have a comfortable place to sleep. After having dinner together and watching TV, I settled in for the night. Drifting off to sleep was easy, and I must have been asleep only a few hours when I was startled awake by the sound of what I thought was a bear.

Groggy and disoriented, I found myself thinking, *How can there be a bear in Las Vegas?* I'd never heard such strange animal sounds inside anyone's house before, and I was terrified. I lay on the couch for several minutes trying to discern what the noise was. Finally, recognizing the sound was coming from the back of the apartment, I reluctantly went to investigate.

Quietly sneaking down the hall, peering into the bedroom, I heard the noise getting significantly louder. I saw my uncle sleeping with his mouth agape. *What the heck?* I thought. I'd heard snoring before, but nothing that sounded like this. It was like a vicious animal wanting to rip something to shreds in the woods. Realizing—loud as it was—that it was just my uncle Rolf snoring, my fear lessened. I returned to the couch, attempting to sleep, but the noise was so intense I couldn't sleep one wink that night.

Having been diagnosed with ulcerative colitis, my uncle had everything except a portion of his small intestine removed. From the time he was seventeen, he had a colostomy bag. Everyone in the family knew and accepted it. I never thought about his colostomy bag until the next morning.

"Hey, Sugar Babes, do you wanna watch me change my bag?"

In my mind, I was thinking, *No, thank you, I really don't want to watch you change your bag*. However, I was staying at his house. Wanting to be polite, I muttered awkwardly, "Sure?"

Proceeding toward the restroom, he motioned with his hand: *Come with me.*

Reluctantly, I followed. Rolf stood inside the restroom, while I stood in the hallway, holding on to the side of the doorframe for dear life, as if my death grip would save me from this vile demonstration to which no thirteen-year-old should be subject.

He lifted his shirt. I winced, hoping he didn't perceive my distress. I didn't want to be insensitive or hurt his feelings, but this really wasn't anything I desired or needed to witness. I saw what looked like a plastic bag attached to his stomach that appeared to be filled with poop.

I questioned hesitantly, "What is that?"

"It's my colostomy bag. This is where I poop," he said matter-of-factly.

I threw up in my mouth a little, thinking, *Oh God, please, please, please don't ever let me have to poop in a bag. That is so disgusting.*

The only words I could muster were, "Huh, it looks weird."

"I know, Sugar Babes, but that is just part of me. You know I was sick for a long time, right? To be honest with you, I have wanted to commit suicide over this bag so many times, it's not even funny. I have lost so many girlfriends and so many people think it is the most disgusting thing they have ever seen. It's hard, Sugar Babes, but it saved my life, so what can I do? I shit in a bag."

"I know, Uncle Rolf. I'm sorry all that happened to you." Hearing this confession, I felt a little guilty for my disgust.

Opening boxes with the necessary medical supplies and lining them up along the sink, he stated, "It's important to keep everything clean."

I watched as he painstakingly cut a perfect circle in the bag, then applied some paste to the top of it and plopped it on his belly.

"There, now I have to hold it for a while and let it adhere to my skin."

"That's it?" I asked.

"Yep, that's it."

"Huh, cool," I said, still a little unsure about why I had to witness this. Maybe Uncle Rolf thought it was a good lesson? Or maybe he just wanted someone to talk to while he performed this every day, depressing routine. Whatever the reason, I was glad it was over. "Can I go watch TV now?" I asked.

He smiled as I moseyed back into the living room.

I felt odd and awkward in this very strange situation; it was almost the same feeling as when I was molested the first time, like I was trying to be polite but was unable to leave. I felt so uncomfortable and really just wanted to go to the concert.

Pacing the floor practically all afternoon, my heart palpitating, I stared at our tickets: "Caesar's Palace Presents: The Go-Go's with Special Guests The Bangles, August 15, 1984."

The moment I had waited for for so long was about to finally arrive.

"Uncle Rolf, I'm ready to go," I called.

I heard moaning coming from the bathroom and thought, *Uh-oh.*

"Is everything okay?" I yelled from the living room.

"Yes, Sugar Babes, I'll be out in a minute," my uncle replied.

Whew, I wasn't about to miss this concert for anything.

I was getting worried as time passed; I thought we might be late. Knowing he wasn't feeling well, the only thing I could do was pace in the living room.

He finally emerged from the restroom, profusely sweating, after what seemed like an eternity. I hoped the concert would be getting a late start.

When we got in the car, my uncle muttered, "Hey, Sugar Babes, I'm not feeling well. Do you mind if you go solo?"

"No, that is fine, Uncle Rolf," I said, though I knew my mother would not like this.

"Are you sure, Sugar Babes? I could do my best, but I'm just not feeling well."

"No problem, I don't want you going if you don't feel well. You can just drop me off, and we can pick a place for you to pick me up later. Is that okay?"

"Sure, Sugar Babes, that is perfect. Thanks for understanding."

"Of course. I hope you feel better."

Once we hit Vegas, my hands were sweating, and my pulse was racing. I couldn't remember ever being this anxious about anything in my life. The strip was lit up like the world's largest Christmas tree. Vegas was so bitchin' at night. I could see Caesar's Palace in the distance as we inched closer and closer; every second felt like an hour to me. In front of me, I saw a giant marquee that read in gargantuan letters, "Tonight: The Go-Go's with Special Guest The Bangles." My heart skipped a beat. I couldn't believe I was finally there!

Having lived in Vegas for an awfully long time, my uncle was familiar with the area. There were what looked like thousands of people lined up to enter.

Veering to a secret entrance at the back of Caesar's, he pointed. "Go in here, Sugar Babes, turn left, and the entrance to the theater is right there."

"Thanks, Uncle Rolf. Will you pick me up right here?"

"Yes, right here, eleven p.m. exactly."

"Okay, thanks, bye!" I waved with gusto.

I clutched my golden ticket while skipping into Caesar's Palace.

I found the theater very easily and gave my ticket to the person at the door. She began to tear my ticket.

"Please, don't rip it," I pled with a puppy-dog stare.

"I'm sorry I have to," she responded.

"Please, I have been waiting for this show for months. I'm thirteen and came here by myself from Los Angeles on a Greyhound bus specifically for this show. Please don't rip my ticket."

"Entrance number four," the nice lady said, smiling as she handed me back my untorn ticket.

I had saved every penny of my allowance so I could buy a T-shirt at the show. The shirts were so awesome and the sweatshirts even cooler, but I couldn't afford one of those.

"Can I help you?" a man with a little black apron said as he approached.

"Um, I'm just looking right now, thanks."

Seeing so many things I wanted—T-shirts, buttons, mugs, programs. I decided to take some time to think about it before choosing since I could only get one.

Finding entrance four, I proudly handed my ticket to the usher. Shining a light on my ticket, he illuminated my way down the stairs. He motioned with his arm to show me the row I was in. I was far from the stage, but the whole entire bottom section close to the stage was a general admission pit. My mom was not comfortable with me being in a crowd and was adamant that I had my own seat. She felt it was safer for me.

The lights dimmed and crowds rushed into the theater. My heart raced from adrenaline. The announcer came onstage introducing The Bangles. Susanna, Michael, Debbi, and Vicki came onstage. A few scattered people cheered, but everyone else chatted while enjoying their drinks, including the crowd around me. Putting my thumb and my index finger underneath my tongue, I let out the loudest whistle I could muster. Everyone around me turned and looked, but I didn't care.

The guy standing next to me said, "You must like them?"

"Yep," I exclaimed, smiling and dancing around with delight. "Like" was an understatement.

Knowing every beat and every word, I was in heaven watching them live and in person. The people around me were amused. Some were touched watching the passion in me, others were annoyed, but it didn't matter either way. I just wanted to be me, be free, and have fun.

During intermission I bought what I wanted from the merch booth—a T-shirt and a few buttons. Trying to buy my things and use the restroom at the same time was a bad idea. I learned quickly that you can't do both. Everyone was rushing back to their seats for the show while I stood forty people back in line for the restroom. Thinking, *Forget it, I am not missing one second of this show,* I ran and got back to my seat just before The Go-Go's took the stage.

Strobe lights began flashing, making the crowd go wild. The Go-Go's emerged onto the stage, one by one. The audience rose to their feet, cheering so loud the rumbling beneath me shook like a 9.0 earthquake. Bouncing, dancing, giggling, and smiling for the next seventy minutes or so, I had the most fun I'd had in a very long time. What others around me thought or said wasn't important. What was important was that I was determined to have a good time, and that's exactly what I did.

I never wanted the show to end, and I felt miserable when it did. Yet I knew the most amazing time in the world couldn't last forever.

Uncle Rolf picked me up. The entire ride home, I rambled incessantly about how great the show was. He was thrilled and happy to see me so ecstatic.

That night, I was still so stimulated from seeing both of my favorite bands, together, that it was extremely difficult for me to fall asleep. It took some time, but eventually I drifted off, only to be crudely awoken shortly thereafter in the middle of a nightmare. My uncle was rubbing his finger on my vagina. Waking up and coming to the realization of what was happening, I pretended to be asleep. I couldn't move or speak and tried not to breathe. I had been in situations like this many times before—many times more than any girl my age should be able to count; still, none was less terrifying than the last.

Molestation wasn't something I ever got used to, no matter how many times it happened. However, having been molested since the age of seven, I was well versed on how this was going to go.

I waited until he was done, all the while pretending to be asleep, frozen. Once he finally realized I wasn't going to wake up, he left. I clutched the blankets as if they were my teddy bear and sobbed myself to sleep—if you can even call it that. What thirteen-year-old girl should have to sleep with one eye open the entire night, in the supposed comfort of her own uncle's home?

How was it that little Delicia was never allowed any amazing moment in life without a monstrous occurrence that would balance it out?

When I woke up the next morning, I felt extremely uncomfortable. I tried to pretend as if nothing happened, knowing from previous experiences that if I acknowledged the abuse, it could be misconstrued as, "She must have enjoyed it." So, I kept quiet.

I finally got to swim that morning, but I couldn't wait for time to pass so I could go home. Frankly, following the prior night's molestation session, I was more than ready to leave.

Rolf cornered me near the diving board in the deep end while I swam. Since I swam almost every day of the summer and was a junior lifeguard, I was a great swimmer. Yet Rolf was acting as if I couldn't swim, making statements like, "Sugar Babes, let me hold you up, you're in the deep end," while forcefully holding my body next to the wall.

His fingers moved down my bathing suit bottoms and into my private area. I froze yet again, unable to speak or move. I wanted to say, "Stop," but nothing came out. I was riddled with fear as his erect penis grazed my thigh when, thankfully, something came over me. Finally, I found the strength from within to break the freeze and pushed with all my might, while screaming, "STOP IT!"

In that moment, he abruptly awoke from a dream state, like he was on another planet and had just landed back on Earth. Eagerly getting out of the pool, wrapping my towel around me, I marched back to the apartment, got dressed, and waited for him to come in.

"I'm ready to leave," I stated sternly when he did.

"But, Sugar Babes, it's not time to go yet."

"I said, I'm ready to leave. Either you take me now, or I call my mother."

That got his attention. He quickly responded, "Let's go."

The car ride back to the bus station was awkward. Few words were spoken, if any.

As we drove on the street near the station, I said, "Just drop me off here," and pointed to the front.

"Are you sure, Sugar Babes?"

"Don't call me that," I snapped back. "And yes, I'm sure."

I got out of the car, then poked my head in the window. With rage in my voice, I gave a curt, "Goodbye."

It was an undeniably final goodbye, and he knew it. I never wanted to see this man again in my life. At the moment he touched me whilst I slept, he went from being my endearing uncle to just another man whom I could not trust, and I had no desire to be around him ever again.

The bus ride home was excruciatingly long. Disgusting thoughts of him touching me ran through my mind, repeatedly. *Why do I freeze when things like this happen? What's wrong with me? Why don't I stop people from touching me? Especially when they touch me in ways that make me feel so uncomfortable.* I couldn't understand it.

At the North Hollywood bus station, Mom was waiting for me, smiling a huge grin. Clearly, she was ecstatic to see me.

She hugged me and asked, "Did you have fun, honey?"

"Yeah, Mom, it was awesome. The Go-Go's and The Bangles were amazing. Thank you for letting me go," I replied, and we headed home.

That trip had its highs and lows. This was the first and last time that The Bangles and the Go-Go's ever shared the same stage exclusively, and I was lucky enough to witness it. I wouldn't have traded that for anything in the world. I wondered how my life would have been different if I hadn't gone. Would it have really made a difference if I had had one less abuser in my life?

In my mind, I tried to separate the events. How could I forsake one of the best moments of my life to rid myself of one of the worst? By that point, I'd already endured so much abuse that this was simply "another one for the books." I would have regretted missing that concert for my entire life had I not gone. The memory of that concert alone has buoyed me through many more dark times.

Mother's Day, 1986

Nile was eighteen and living on his own once again. He had refined his taste, and we never knew what he might have in store for us whenever we met him for a meal. He always ate at only the fanciest restaurants.

When we arrived that day and saw Nile standing in front of the restaurant, he looked quite dashing in the white-collared suit he wore so well. I gave him a big hug, and he met me halfway with a one- armed, half-hearted hug. That was the best I could get out of my brother. Mom hugged and slathered him with kisses before strolling inside the restaurant.

In my family, we always loved a good brunch. This Mother's Day, we were at The Sagebrush Cantina in Calabasas. It was the halfway point between Los Angeles and Newbury Park and was always my family's favorite brunch restaurant.

I filled my plate with a mountain of peel-and-eat shrimp along with a heaping mound of crab legs; I couldn't wait to dig in. While I squeezed lemon after lemon onto my shrimp, my brother said, "Hey, I have a surprise for you today. After brunch, you are coming with me, and I'll drop you off later."

"Really? For me?" I asked in disbelief. "It's Mother's Day. Shouldn't the surprise be for Mom?"

"Shut up," he said, rolling his eyes before getting up for a second plate.

Nile had been working for Marvin as the vice president of his company since graduating from high school and was doing quite well for himself. Not knowing what he was planning, it was enough that I got to ride in his Porsche; I loved how fast it was. We hugged our mom and set out on our way.

"Where are we going?" I asked.

"Just wait," he said, pressing his foot on the gas. The Porsche peeled out, tires screeching.

"Holy crap!" I screamed as the G-force pushed my body backward.

"Oh please, that's nothing," he said, increasing the speed.

"Nile, come on, you are scaring me."

"Give me a break." He chuckled as he weaved in between cars on the 101 at what felt like eighty miles per hour.

I hunched down in my seat, reaching for the "oh shit" handle, closing my eyes, praying we would make it wherever we were going safely. I was nearly crapping my pants while my brother was amused by my fear.

Heading up and over Ventura Boulevard and continuing onto Highland, we reached Hollywood. I was extremely curious where the heck we were going. We pulled into a parking lot with a security station just past Sunset. Nile got out, whispered something into the security guard's ear, then got back into the car. The gate opened, and we entered. I waited in anticipation, yet nothing would be revealed.

I asked again, "What are we doing?"

"You'll see," Nile replied.

As we walked across the parking lot, I saw a short woman with long blonde hair. I had to do a double take because it looked just like Charlotte Caffey, the keyboardist from The Go-Go's. She was incredibly short, and I never imagined Charlotte would be that short, so I figured I was mistaken. We continued our journey through the parking lot into a building filled with corporate folks in power suits. We were in a large, dark studio with nothing but walls and a stage. I was thoroughly confused.

Nile instructed me, "Why don't you go sit down on the floor?"

"Huh? Sit on the floor?" What could I do but comply? "Okay," I relented and took a seat.

I sat anxiously on the floor, perplexed. My brother socialized, keeping his eye on me. I threw him a questioning look that he immediately understood; no words were necessary. He waved me off with his hand in a *just wait* kind of motion.

The woman I saw in the parking lot who looked like Charlotte Caffey walked into the building. Though I had been told to wait, I couldn't help myself. I jumped up and ran over to my brother, exclaiming, "Nile, that *really* looks like Charlotte Caffey from The Go-Go's. Do you think it's her?"

"I don't know," he said coyly, implying with a wily smile that he knew exactly who she was. Then he said, "Why don't you go ask?"

"No way, I'm too embarrassed."

"Just go back and sit and wait," he instructed.

"Whatever." I was growing impatient.

Knowing that The Go-Go's had broken up the previous year and Belinda was scheduled to release her first solo album in about a week made this even more mysterious. I was anxious and nervous imagining the possibilities of what this surprise could be.

I was the only person sitting in the middle of the floor; everybody else stood around me mingling. I felt super uncomfortable in social situations and would rather sit on the floor by myself anyway.

Lights flashed and everyone formed a semicircle around me and the stage. The lights came on, and hearing a beat of music, I knew it was Belinda Carlisle. My mind reeling, I put two and two together. Belinda emerged onstage singing.

Was I dreaming? Literally pinching myself, I looked at Nile and mouthed the words, "Oh my God."

He smiled, knowing he had just made one of my lifelong dreams come true.

As I remained on the floor, I felt like Belinda was singing to me and only me. I was in complete disbelief while at the same time trying so hard to enjoy the moment. The concert was over in a flash. Ecstatic, I ran up to my brother, throwing my arms around him. I could tell my embrace made him uncomfortable. It always stung, being hit with the reminder that we weren't as close as we had once been.

Excitedly, I asked, "Who are these people? How did you do this?"

Whispering, he snatched me to the side. "They are record execs, and this is a record release party for her upcoming *Belinda* album."

"WHAT?! HOW THE HECK?! THANK YOU!" I whisper-screamed. "Do you think I could meet her if I walked around the back?"

"We could try."

Peeking around the back of the building, I saw someone who looked like Mindy Cohn from *The Facts of Life.*

"Is that ... ?" I started, looking at my brother.

"Yes, looks like Mindy Cohn to me," he replied.

At that moment, Belinda Carlisle appeared, and she had many suits surrounding and congratulating her. I wormed my little fifteen-year-old self into the crowd of execs. I was so nervous, knowing I was about to meet my idol.

I'd dreamed about this moment for seven years but never thought it possible. My brother was making it happen for me, and I couldn't contain my excitement.

Delicia, you have to do this. Don't be nervous. She is just a person. Go, Delicia, go, I thought. Mustering up the energy, I tried to calm my nerves. My hands and head were dripping with sweat. My idol stood less than three feet from me, and I only had a few seconds to find the courage to introduce myself.

"This is it, Delicia. It's now or never," I mumbled under my breath.

As I approached Belinda Carlisle, I felt my brain leave my head and my body go on autopilot. I wasn't thinking or remembering, just a robot with only one line in my head: "Hi, I'm Delicia. It is so nice to meet you." *Don't mess this up,* I thought again.

Finding the strength from within, I marched right up to her. I gave a polite, "Excuse me," to Mindy Cohn as I brushed past, which, in itself, was like totally bitchin' because she was someone I grew up watching on television and really admired. But, in this moment, she was just another human being standing next to my idol. Once I was face-to-face with Belinda, my nerves went wild.

Reaching out my hand, I announced, "Hi, I'm Delicia."

Time stopped when Belinda reached her hand out for mine. I thought I was going to die right on the spot.

"I have loved you since I was eight," I confessed. It was not the line I had rehearsed, but it was the truth.

"Wow, it is so nice to meet you," she replied graciously.

"Can I please take a picture with you?" I asked.

"Sure." She reached her arm around my neck and pulled me close.

As soon as I heard the click of the camera, the spell was broken, and I was rushed out of the way by other people who came in to talk to her. I silently slipped away.

"Oh my God," I crooned to my brother. In tears, I couldn't stop thanking him and asking, "How in the world did you do this?"

Meeting my idol for the first time was one of the most glorious moments in my life. I have only my brother to thank for that. Nile has a challenging time showing me love, but going out of his way to do things like this lets me know he loves me. I feel it in every fiber of my being, which is something I have not felt from many people in this lifetime.

From the moment I heard the first beat of that album in 1979, I knew The Go-Go's were going to be a significant and poignant part of my life. I could have never imagined that, when Isaac took me to The Go-Go's show, it would be the first of forty-five times I'd see them live in my lifetime ... thus far.

ISLAND FEVER

You would think as a thirteen-year-old, moving to Maui would be exciting, but to me it was abysmal. I was moving, yet again, to someplace new and without my brother. Trying to make new friends in another new school. I was certain we wouldn't be staying long enough to keep any of the friends I did make, so why did it matter anyway?

Extraordinarily humid and hot, Hawaii was the most boring and dreadful place on the planet—at least, it felt that way to me as a teenager. No matter how hard I looked, there was absolutely nothing to do.

The small town of Kihei that Mom chose seemed to only have apartment complexes. Rows and rows of apartments lined the white sandy beach with coconut trees scattered about. The apartments were sandwiched between a busy tourist highway and a mountainside.

There were two theaters on the entire island that played the same movie for six months running. Hawaii was always about six months behind the mainland anyway. By the time the movies came to our island, they were already on video in the continental U.S.

High school in Maui was funny. Everyone talked in Pidgin, Hawaii's version of very broken English. The natives have very heavy accents, and it took me several months to understand them.

This was the first time in my life an opportunity presented itself to live with a female other than my mom. My mother's longtime boyfriend, Ron, had two daughters from a previous marriage. His youngest daughter, Holly, decided to come live with us in Maui. Holly was extremely tall, about six feet, and pasty white. She stood out like a sore thumb. For the first time in my life, I wasn't the one that the kids made fun of. I didn't relish it, though, and always defended her whenever people picked on her.

Taking the yellow school bus from in front of our apartment complex every day back and forth helped us make connections. Kids would sing The Go-Go's as I passed them—"We got the beat, we got the beat" or "Vacations [there is no *s*, people], all I ever wanted." After enduring hell at Oxnard Street Elementary School and being the kid whose mom taught special ed at junior high, this brand of "teasing" at Baldwin High School was a cakewalk for me.

Holly and I were part of the drama club. Within the first couple of weeks of living there, the club was planning a trip to a "secret" swimming hole. We were elated to hang with "locals only."

While packing our bags for the overnight camping trip, we could hardly contain our excitement. Making sure we had everything we needed, including a tiny first-aid kit, we waited by the side of the road in anticipation, duffel bags in hand, for the silver minivan to arrive. Throwing our bags in the back, we hopped in and off we went.

We were overjoyed to be doing something cool with people our own age. Singing camp songs along the way— "Ninety-nine bottles of beer on the wall, ninety-nine bottles of beer..."—we swayed in our seats as the van rocked and rolled down the dirt path.

Lush, green landscape surrounded every side of us as we trekked miles through the mist and fog. We finally saw a parking lot that was so tiny, it could only fit about three cars.

After stretching our legs and grabbing our bags, we set out for our adventure.

The terrain getting to our camp spot was pretty gnarly. We had to precariously balance our bodies as we clung to steep cliffs. I felt as though any second, I could plummet to my death.

Our small group hiked over the cliffs to a large, sprawling pasture of cows. We walked among them as if we were Joseph traveling with his herd of sheep. We finally reached our destination about a half hour later.

It felt like our own private paradise—a swimming hole below a cliff that stood about twenty feet high. Gorgeous coconut trees surrounded us, with giant fan leaves and the most flourishing landscape you can imagine. We pitched our tents next to the water's edge and changed into our swimsuits.

The other kids were running up to the top of the cliff and jumping in. Holly and I were afraid. I was petrified of heights, and neither of us had the nerve to do it. Fascinated, I stared in awe, watching the others jump into the water like it was nothing.

"Come on," said one of the kids, running out of the water from their last jump. "It's so much fun. You won't get hurt."

I watched as she ran back up the cliff for another jump. I was terrified, but it looked like so much fun, I really wanted to try it.

I mustered up the courage and climbed to the top of the cliff. I took one look from the edge down to the water and yelped, "Oh no, not for me!"

Happily walking back down, I crouched next to Holly by the water's edge. We sat and watched them jump over and over for an hour or so. Then I jumped up with vigor. "Oh, screw it, are you coming?" My resolve was crumbling, and I wanted Holly to come with me.

"No way, you go right ahead," she said with certainty.

I hiked back to the top while the kids cheered me on— "Come on, Delicia, you can do it. You won't get hurt. Just do it."

As I stood at the edge of that cliff looking down, my stomach dropped into my girl parts, and I thought, *There is no way I am jumping from this high.* My feet were tingling—I was frightened. Not the same fear as when the Night Stalker was in my living room or when Isaac molested me on so many occasions—this was petrifying yet exhilarating. *This* was the type of fear teenage girls were supposed to experience. It was a new feeling for me, and I was busy soaking it in when someone abruptly pushed my back. Free-falling twenty feet down a cliff, watching the water come closer and closer as I fell, I crumbled my body the best I could into a ball before hitting the water which felt like a thousand shards of glass stinging my backside. The pain was extraordinary. I found myself sinking farther and farther down, wondering, *How deep does this go? Am I going to drown? Am I going to come back up?* I went with the flow and let the water take me.

Finally, my head bobbed up to the top of the water, and I gasped for air. I felt the rush of adrenaline wash through my body, and my conscious mind finally realized I was safe. Hearing applause, I looked up.

Everyone on top of the cliff was cheering, clapping, and shouting, "You did it, yay, you did it!"

Getting out of the water as fast as I could, I went up to Holly, dripping cold water all over her. "Come on, it's so much fun. Come on, come do it with me."

"No, you go. I am good, really."

Running back up to the top of the cliff, passing everyone, I jumped in again. While falling, I heard cheering. This time I knew what to expect, so it was totally tubular. Jumping from that rock, over and over and over again, gave me confidence to face my fears.

This was something I hadn't ever done before, except maybe when I sang in German for my fourth-grade Christmas play. Feeling super proud of myself, I realized that I would have missed out on one of my fondest memories had I not faced my fears that day. That lesson would last a lifetime. That was, by far, the best day I recall while living in Maui.

My first encounter with marijuana was when I was eight years old. The kids in the neighborhood we grew up in were not that great. Someone was always getting into trouble with the law. My best friend's older brother, Jacob, was one of them. Drinking and smoking daily, he wasn't the best hangout friend to have. Jacob's dad, Bud, sold weed and always had plenty to go around.

One afternoon, I went to see if Jacob's sister, Jessica, was home. I crossed the street, walked down the alley, then knocked on the trailer door. Nobody answered. I headed through the gate, down the walkway, and to the side door of the house, where I knocked once again.

Jacob answered the door. "Hey, Delicia, Jess isn't home. Do you want to come hang out for a bit?"

"Do you know when she will be back?" I asked.

"No idea. Come on in, have a seat."

Jacob and I chatted for a bit and watched a little TV while waiting for Jessica to come home.

"Hey, I was just going to go get some weed from my dad and smoke it. Wanna come?" Jacob asked.

"No, thank you. I will just go home. Can you tell Jess I came by?"

"Sure," he said. "But why not come with me and try it? It's fun."

"I don't know, Jacob. I've never tried it before." Of course, I hadn't. I was *eight*. Then again, I wasn't exactly living the life of an average eight-year-old, either.

"Don't worry, just follow me."

Reluctantly, I followed Jacob out the door and waited outside by the trailer while he went in and stole some of his dad's stash.

When he came out of the trailer, Jacob exclaimed, "Okay, got it. Let's go."

We wandered down the alleyway until we found an almost empty carport. Deciding that was the perfect spot, we found a comfortable place to sit. There was an old beat-up car. Obviously, it hadn't been moved in quite some time, as it had a layer of dust an inch thick. A few engine parts lay strewn about. We ducked behind the dark blue, dusty Dodge Dart, making sure we hid in the corner so nobody saw us.

Jacob took a small pipe that had a screw-on metal bowl out of one pocket and a sandwich baggie he had filled with his dad's shake—leaves from the marijuana plant as opposed to the buds—out of his other pocket. Carefully, he pinched some out of the baggie and loaded the bowl, then held it to my mouth.

Instructing me just before he lit the lighter, he said, "You have to take a deep breath, hold it, and then let it out."

I sucked in the biggest breath, then blew it out, attempting to get the most lung capacity possible. Weed went flying everywhere.

Angrily, he shouted, "What are you doing?"

"You said to take a deep breath!" I said meekly, embarrassed.

Frustrated, he scooped up as much of the weed as he could. Then, using the edge of his finger, he picked up every speck, like a piece of tape plucking lint from a sweater. Salvaging most of it, he shoved it back into the pipe.

"You have to wait until I light it, then take a deep breath."

I watched and waited until the lighter hit the dark green leafy shake; I had no idea what a significant impact this brief moment in time would have on my life, and for such a profound period.

Frankly, I don't even remember getting high that day. Regardless, I knew weed was something I was going to try again.

Try again I did, again and again and again.

On many occasions, I've felt like marijuana has saved my life, although I would have preferred to wait until I was a bit older than eight to try it. Marijuana has been a significant influence in my life, both positive and negative, but overall, I view marijuana as an old, and sometimes lost, friend.

Maui initiated my daily weed-smoking ritual. The island was so incredibly boring, and weed was plentiful. I could find it anywhere. All I had to do was ask any local where I could find "pakalolo," and it would magically appear. Most days were spent hanging by myself on the beach, listening to music, and smoking a lot of weed.

The pot in North Hollywood wasn't nearly as strong as the weed in Maui. Maui brought about some extremely high times. I wasn't quite sure what was in the pakalolo in Hawaii, but I liked it.

A typical day coming home from school meant I would do my homework, then head off to the beach to get stoned. After feeling the buzz, I'd head straight for the balcony with my Walkman to listen to The Go-Go's for hours. Many times, Mom would have to come out the sliding glass door and tap the back of my head to get my attention.

"Tone it down. The entire apartment complex can hear you," she'd cry out.

"Was I singing out loud?" I would ask earnestly. Mom would just laugh.

It only took six months of living in this crazy boredom before I begged my mother to move back to California.

"Please, Mom, I am going crazy here. I really can't stand it much longer. I am so bored."

My mother wasn't even remotely interested in moving back to the mainland, but I was relentless. I pleaded with her on a daily basis, over and over, even turning on the waterworks, hoping she would see how extraordinarily bored I was. What a terrible place for a thirteen-year-old to live!

All I wanted was to be back in California. Several months of annoying her finally paid off, and Mom agreed. In December of that year, we moved to Newbury Park, CA.

COMING OUT

In the spring of 1983, when I was just twelve years old, I realized I was gay. I'd had several experiences with men by that time, although not by choice.

Arriving home from school this particular day, I settled in to watch *The Facts of Life*. Jo Polniaczek always had me a bit captivated, pondering thoughts a twelve-year-old shouldn't but often does: sex.

I spent a lot of time thinking about when my menial existence and sex would someday meet. How and when would I really "make love" for the first time instead of the constant molestation I endured? Who would it be with? What were my desires? It was a puzzle I couldn't quite figure out.

I was constantly trying to fit in, and I desperately tried liking boys. I proudly cut out centerfolds of C. Thomas Howell and Ricky Schroder and displayed them on my bedroom walls. Boys certainly intrigued me, yet I was also very attracted to girls, though I refused to admit it.

I often recall the truth-or-dare session that happened between me and my friends a couple years before moving to Sun Valley. Jessica, Yolanda, Angie, and I were bored hanging out one afternoon. One of us suggested we play truth or dare.

"Sure, sounds like fun!"

Positioning ourselves in a circle, making eye contact with one another, we began.

"I'll start," proclaimed Yolanda, always the leader of the group and the first one to jump in on anything. "Jess, truth or dare?"

"Dare," Jessica answered.

"Dare, wow, right away. Okay. I dare you to run across the street to old man Juarez's house and scream, 'Dirty old man,' and run away."

"Okay," Jessica stated without fear.

She ran across the street. We waited and watched, giggling.

She quietly moved past old man Juarez's house, poking her eyes just above the hedges, checking to see if anyone was home. We doubted she would do it.

When she reached the end of his house, she turned around and ran, screaming, "Dirty old man!"

Scurrying as if she were a matador being chased by bulls, she ran back across the street and inside the house. We all fell to the floor with laughter.

"Okay, okay, let's keep the game going," Yoli said. "Jessica, your turn to ask."

"Hmm, okay. Delicia, truth or dare?"

"Truth."

"Hmm... Who do you have a secret crush on?"

"Um, nobody," I quickly answered.

"That's boring," Jessica said.

The game went on for fifteen more minutes or so before it got a bit heated. As heated as a nine- or ten-year-old's game of truth or dare could be, anyway.

"Truth or dare?" asked Yolanda.

"To who?"

Looking around the room, Yoli pointed to me. "Delicia, truth or dare?"

"Dare."

"Hmm, I dare you to kiss me."

"What?" I asked with a furrowed brow, my voice rising about ten octaves.

Jessica and Angie were just as perplexed as me, looking at each other, heads tilted slightly sideways, each with one eyebrow cocked.

Yoli repeated, "I dare you to kiss me."

"Um, where?"

"On the lips."

Curious what it would be like to kiss a girl, I went for it. Giving her a quick peck, I backed up with vigor.

"That wasn't a real kiss," she blurted.

"I dare you to *really* kiss me."

"Like, *French* kiss?" I shrieked.

"Yep," she said with a huge smile.

Looking at her again, I asked, "Really?"

By this time, Jessica and Angie were into it as well, chanting, "Kiss her, kiss her, kiss her."

Leaning in, I gave Yolanda a kiss. She pulled me closer, kissing me gently, and she slowly stuck her tongue in my mouth. Shocked, I quickly recoiled.

"Okay, next," I said, trying to avert the situation.

"Angie, truth or dare?"

"Dare," she said.

"I dare you to go steal a joint from your mom so we can smoke it."

Yoli and Angie's mom always kept an ornate wooden box underneath their coffee table. It was filled with paraphernalia, weed, and all the fixins'. We always had fun if we dared sneak a little.

"Easy," she replied.

Stepping out to the living room where her mom kept her stash, she returned within minutes, joint in hand.

"My turn," Angie said.

"Delicia, truth or dare?"

"Dare," I answered.

"I dare you to kiss me," Angie said with a smile.

"What? Again? Oh my gosh ... okay," I said, leaning in to kiss her.

I was a little attracted to Angie. Therefore, this kiss was a bit sweeter and a little longer than the last. Yet it remained quite awkward.

"Oh damn, you are a good kisser," Angie professed.

"Why, thank you," I boasted while tugging at the collar of my shirt as if adjusting my tie.

"Jessica, truth or dare?"

"Truth," she replied.

"Hmm, okay, if you were to have sex with someone right now, who would it be?"

"Oh, I know, John Travolta. He is so dreamy."

"Okay, your turn, Jess."

"Delicia ... truth or dare?"

"Dare," I answered with hesitation.

"I dare you to kiss me."

"What? Again? Okay, but this is the last time."

Leaning in, I gave her a short kiss, relieved there was no tongue this time. Jessica was my best friend. I found it odd that all these girls wanted to kiss me.

Feeling super uncomfortable, I made an excuse to leave. "My mom needs me home for dinner, so I gotta go. See you tomorrow."

I ran out the door and home as fast as I could, my head spinning and confused. I wasn't supposed to be kissing girls; it didn't feel right to me—or did it?

Jess, Yoli, Angie, and I never spoke of that day again. We just went about our lives as if it never happened. We remained friends until I moved to Sun Valley, at which point we drifted apart.

After reminiscing, I was truly considering—was I gay? Did I like girls or not? There was so much confusion inside of me, and I was beginning to question if I would ever figure it out.

A flashback of Isaac staring at me while stroking his penis began to whirl like a hurricane in my mind. He was able to have an orgasm just by staring at me while he masturbated. When I was seven, this made me feel dirty and gross, but at twelve, it gave me an idea that might help solve my dilemma.

Entering my mother's room, I laid on her bed, staring at the ceiling. I was wondering if masturbating would solve my confusion. Recalling Mom's neck massager in her side drawer, I looked to see if it was there. At twelve, I didn't realize my mother probably masturbated with that same vibrator; I genuinely thought she used it as a massager. Although I had been "sexually active" for the last five years, I was still a very naïve twelve-year-old.

Gripping the long orange plastic handle, I plugged in the two-prong white cord, examining the massager closely. One side smooth and white, covered in a type of leather material. The other had orange bumps I thought were used to work the knots out of your neck. I turned the switch on, and my hand vibrated. The vibration was so strong it startled me, and I quickly turned it off.

There I was, in my mother's bed, thinking about using her neck massager in places she never needed to know about. It was a confusing mixture of excitement and terror, but not as confusing as the thoughts that had led me here. I really wanted to get to the bottom of this constant worry, and I thought this was as good an idea as any. I turned on the television to cover the noise in case somebody came home. The more I thought about it, the more I wanted to try it.

Placing the white, smooth side of the vibrator on top of my jeans, I turned it on. Just as I turned on the massager, lines appeared on the television, mimicking the sounds of the vibrator. When I turned it off, the lines disappeared. I turned it on again; the lines came back on the television. Shrugging my shoulders, I continued, trying to ignore the strange lines and vibration sounds on the television.

Feeling my body quiver and shake all the way to the top of my thighs when I turned the massager on, at first, felt odd. I was unsure if I liked it, but a few seconds later, the heat from the vibrator together with the pressure created a friction I'd never felt before.

Rubbing the massager in circles on top of my jeans wasn't quite enough for me. Turning off the massager and unzipping my pants, I removed them to the bottom half of my butt. Nervous that someone might come home, I wanted to be able to pull my pants up in a second and put the massager away, if need be.

Placing the massager on top of my underwear, I turned it on, and it pulsated. I put pressure on the massager with my right hand and began to make small circles, trying to have an orgasm without thinking, just feeling… it didn't work. I was really turned on but couldn't seem to have an orgasm. I wasn't sure if this was because pleasure wasn't something I normally associated with sex or if I was scared of being caught. Whatever the reason, it wasn't working. I decided to add an element of fantasy to see if that would help.

Wanting to experiment to find out if I liked girls or boys, I decided if I was able to have an orgasm thinking about boys, then I liked boys, if girls, then I liked girls.

I began to fantasize, thinking about boys. I thought about all of the cute boys I knew and about actors I found attractive. I imagined being with each one of them. I tried for what felt like hours, although it was probably more like twenty minutes.

Reluctantly, I decided to change tactics. Maybe neither option would work anyway. I began to fantasize about a girl I knew from school. Within seconds, I was squirming around on the bed, thrusting my hips to the ceiling. Screaming from pleasure for what felt like ten minutes, my mind reeling, I couldn't believe it.

Having accomplished the first real orgasm of my life, I turned off the vibrator, threw it down next to me, and with my two fists struck the bed as hard as I could and screamed out, "GOD DAMN IT, I KNEW IT!"

My heart was broken. I didn't want to like girls. I knew liking girls wasn't right or what I was supposed to do. I just wanted to be "normal" and like boys.

A few short weeks later, my neighbor's niece was visiting from Chicago. Having a pool in our backyard meant instant friends. This was no different for our neighbor's niece, Rebecca.

One July afternoon in 1983, the sun was so hot you couldn't stop the sweat from dripping down the sides of your face and into your ears. My eyelids were sweating. It was the kind of sweltering heat that is unbearable in the summertime. Boy, was I grateful we had a pool.

On my way to my room, I yelled out, "Mom, I'm going swimming."

"Okay," she replied, "just make sure you are done in time for dinner."

I ran past her cooking in the kitchen. I was already in my bathing suit with a towel wrapped around me when I said, "You got it, Mom."

Dashing toward the sliding glass door, I dropped my towel on the lounge chair as I dove headfirst into the pool, splashing around and swimming, alone. I was very much enjoying my pool time.

I loved swimming laps. Each lap, I would change up the stroke. I swam regular swimming strokes, backstroke, butterfly stroke, and sidestroke. Sometimes, I would hold my breath to get across the entire length of the pool without coming up for air.

Taking a deep breath, my body propelling slightly out of the water, I would thrust downward again, kicking my legs in a froglike motion, swimming deeper and faster. Three quarters of the way across the pool, my lungs ached. I opened my eyes under the water, checking how far the other side of the pool was; I thought I could make it. Kicking my legs even harder, I pushed the water back with all my might, my eyes remaining open, coming closer and closer to the wall, until finally I touched it.

My body surged as fast as possible to the top. I gasped for breath, feeling like a deflated balloon. I threw my arms on the hot concrete, water droplets splashing around me, cooling the sizzling ground beneath me.

I was trying to catch my breath when I heard, "Hi."

Turning around quickly in the water, I looked to see where the voice had come from—no one was there. Then, hearing laughter, I turned back around.

Peering over the fence was a girl I'd never seen in the neighborhood before.

"Hi, I'm Rebecca. I'm here visiting from Chicago."

I wasn't that great at hiding my facial expressions, and I hoped she couldn't discern that the only thing running through my mind was, *She is beautiful. Did God just send me an angel?*

"Hi, I'm Delicia. Do you want to come swimming?" I asked, attempting to keep a straight face.

Striking, she was mixed-race and had green eyes that could pierce your soul from twenty feet away, or however far "over the fence" was. Her hair was blonde, frizzy, and curly. She was much older than me, or so she appeared. Tongue-tied, I tried to act "normal."

"Sure," she said, "that sounds like fun." The lump in my throat grew larger when I heard her say, "Let me get my bathing suit on and I'll come right over."

"Okay, I'll let my mom know. Hey, what's your name again?"

"It's Rebecca. I'm their niece." she replied.

"Mom!" I shouted from the pool. "The neighbor's niece just poked her head over the fence. I invited her to come swimming."

"Okay, honey, I will show her to the pool when she comes."

We played in the pool for hours and were having a groovy time. I felt like I'd made a new friend. Mom noticed how much we clicked and invited her to eat with us. Turned out she was four years older than I was and already in high school. I was in awe—too bad she was only visiting for the summer.

Rebecca and I hung out frequently over the next few days. She invited me to spend the night over the weekend, and I was stoked. I'd never been invited to a sleepover before. Even though this was right next door, I was thrilled to bits.

Recognizing we were alone in the house, I inquired, "Where is everyone?"

"Oh, we have the place to ourselves tonight. They are all out."

"That's bitchin'," I responded, trying to remain casual and cool.

We headed to the living room, ordered pizza, and started to watch a movie. I was elated to have a friend to hang out with on the weekends since Alon was often busy with his family. She was older than me, cooler than me, and super pretty. Although I was still really infatuated and intimidated by her, hanging out for several days allowed my walls to come down. She seemed intimately close to me while watching that movie. I said nothing.

"Do you want to go watch a movie in my room?" she probed.

"Shouldn't we finish watching this one?"

"No, I have a better one in the room. It's a scary movie: *Werewolf of London*."

"Oh, I love scary movies, awesome."

When we got to the bedroom, I changed into pajamas.

Upon returning from her uncle's room, Rebecca had on a satin lavender nightgown. Desire loomed within me. I desperately wanted to touch the soft silk, maybe an innocent brush past her protruding nipple, but I couldn't muster up the courage. I tried not to stare as she reached around the TV, flipping a switch from TV to VCR. She then turned the VCR on and pushed play. We settled back on the bed. The movie began.

"Oh, it's in black and white?" I asked, surprised.

"Yeah, it's an old one," she replied.

After watching about twenty minutes of the movie, I was bored by it but didn't want to say anything.

Apparently detecting my boredom, Rebecca suddenly said, "I forgot, my uncle got something today and I want to show you." She jumped off the bed and ran out the door while I wondered what it could be.

She returned with a magazine in hand.

"Look," she said, jumping back on the bed.

Bracing her back against the headboard, she showed me the cover. It was a *Hustler* magazine, and some of the pictures were extremely risqué, even for me.

"Wow," I said timidly, "those are some pics."

"Aren't they nice?" she whispered, writhing her body, tilting her head back while showing me some cleavage.

I had crazy butterflies, and they weren't in my stomach. What was happening to me?

My body recoiled. "It's okay," she said. "They are just pictures."

Browsing through the magazine, I saw women spreading their labia and showing their private parts, up close and personal. It was something I'd never seen pictures of before, and it was making me feel very strange.

"Have you ever done anything with a woman?" she inquired.

"Umm," I answered uncomfortably. "Well…I played truth or dare once with a few of my girlfriends; they kept daring me to kiss them. At first, I thought it was bitchin' because they all said I was a good kisser, but then I got scared and ran away."

As we browsed through the magazine, her hand grazed my back. I thought, *Oh boy, what is happening?* I felt the panic set in and started to feel extremely uncomfortable. My body began to freeze, just as it had on so many occasions prior during times of molestation. She wasn't molesting me. *Was she?* It felt like a strange dichotomy from deep within my soul. I wasn't sure why I started to freeze and recoil when I was extremely attracted to her. I tried with all my might to push through these feelings and enjoy the situation, but my body was fighting me every step of the way.

She was sixteen. I was twelve. She was a woman and so much more experienced than I was. I knew that two women being together was not the societal norm. Was I reading the situation correctly? If I was, could I really do anything about it? Would my body let me enjoy a situation that had nothing but negative connotations for me?

"I have a boyfriend back in Chicago," she stated.

"Oh, you do? That's bitchin'," I said nervously, and she giggled.

"What's so funny?" I asked while tilting my head.

"You say bitchin' a lot. We don't say that back in Chicago," she explained.

"Really? What do you say?"

"Other things like fresh and dope."

"Huh, different. So, what is your boyfriend like?" I asked.

"He is so cute and really amazing," she said, somewhat dreamily. Then she paused, thoughtfully, before saying, "But there's just one problem."

"What's the problem?" I asked.

"He has never eaten me out before."

"What is that?" I asked with curiosity, although Isaac had taught me years earlier. I was ashamed of the abuse I had endured and wanted to seem more innocent.

Turning the page to the center spread, she opened one flap, then the next. The model was in a sexy lingerie piece with her fingers spreading her lips. Again, I felt the anguish of having to fight my own body and mind to try to make this situation pleasurable.

Rebecca pointing to it, motioned her fingertip around her girl parts in a circle while she said, "It's when a man takes his mouth and does this with his tongue to her clit."

My cheeks flushed. As many sexual encounters as I had in the past, nothing came close to feeling what I was feeling in this moment. The difference was the previous encounters had all been forced in one way or another. This was something it felt like I wanted, but did I *really*? My body was telling me otherwise with the reactions I was having to consciously fight off.

"What's a clit?" I asked naively.

Smiling, she pointed to the clitoris on the picture and said, "It's short for clitoris."

I felt flush. For the first time in my life, I was hot for someone, literally and figuratively. Was I starting to feel what pleasure from sex was supposed to feel like? These were feelings I hadn't encountered before with anyone else, and I wanted to explore them. However, the other part of me was petrified and shaking on the inside.

Shocked, I looked at her and asked, "What?"

"Yeah, we do everything else, but he has never done that to me. In fact, nobody has. I've always wondered what it felt like."

I knew what it felt like because Isaac had been doing that to me for years, but that was never even remotely enjoyable for me. I couldn't understand how at sixteen, she hadn't done that before. Yet another way my years of abuse had skewed the way I perceived what a "normal" childhood should look like.

I felt excitement and panic all at the same time. I had fantasized about being with a girl just a few weeks earlier, but could I do it?

Before I knew it, the words, "I'll do it," flew from my lips like bees from a hive that just got hit with a piñata stick.

My mind was reeling. I could feel my face flushing.

"You will?" she asked with excitement.

"Sure, why not?" I said like I'd done it a thousand times before. Somehow, I managed to push all of my yucky feelings around sex aside for the moment.

Leaning in, she kissed me. The butterflies in my stomach multiplied, wandering to my feet. Her hand drifted down to my A-cup breasts and fondled my nipples. Having never felt carnal or erotic, I was surprised and perplexed by the feelings I was having. Nervous, I ran my hand down and around her nipples. She moaned. This turned me on even more. Reaching my hand down, I felt her literal hotness. My finger circled as she writhed her hips, moaning even louder.

While nibbling on my ear, she whispered, "Will you eat me out?"

Sliding my body down hers, I kissed every part of her ever so gently, exploring her curvaceous body. By this time, the flashbacks of abuse had subsided, and I felt sensual unlike ever before.

As I moved downward, the nerves inside me were like a shock of electricity. Crazy thoughts ran through my mind. *What if I do it wrong? What if she doesn't like it? Oh, Delicia, just do it. How will you ever know if you like it if you don't try?* I was talking myself into it, but at the same time, I was completely uncertain.

Getting closer, I detected a strange scent. Trying to ignore it, I continued encircling her private area. The stench got stronger. I wondered if that's what it was supposed to smell like?

Continuing on my mission, I kissed the top and continued down the sides. The stench was getting more and more intense. I tried my best to ignore it, but it was overwhelming. No longer was I turned on. Trepidatious, I reached out my tongue to touch her clit, moving it around in a circle, like how she showed on the picture. I could only endure this for about five seconds before feeling like I was going to throw up. The smell and taste were far too foul for me.

Darting up, I ran to the bathroom. After vomiting, I remember desperately trying to wash my mouth out in the sink.

Sneaking out of the bathroom and gathering my things, I ran back home. I never saw or heard from Rebecca again. This experience, unfortunately, didn't make my confusion any clearer. I'd recently enjoyed orgasms thinking of women, not men. However, when the opportunity arose, it made me vomit. I had a lot of figuring out to do.

High school in California was much more difficult than in Hawaii. I was never a good student and not really that interested in school. I always felt behind, and I didn't put in a lot of effort. This was reflected in my grades.

Once I began making friends and people seemed to like me, my grades suffered even more. Having a social life didn't help my interest in academia. I was way more interested in socializing since that was something almost non-existent in my life before high school.

Pot was plentiful in Hawaii, and I made it my mission, upon landing in Newbury Park, to find weed. I knew that if I was able to find the smokers, I would be able to find someone who sold weed. Hanging out behind the library where everyone smoked cigarettes was my best bet. A few of my friends smoked, and even though the smell made me nauseous, whenever they asked me to go for a smoke break, I'd never turn them down.

After algebra one day, when I was fourteen, I headed to the back side of the library. Recognizing a few girls I had previously been introduced to and feeling confident, I interjected, "Hey, ladies."

Taking a long drag off her cigarette, Laurel blew smoke rings while exhaling. I secretly held my breath as the smoke seeped from her lips. Around the corner appeared the most stunningly beautiful girl I had ever seen. While I choked on the billowy cloud of smoke, she glanced toward us, making sure everything was okay.

Once my coughing fest stopped, I asked Laurel, "Who was *that*?"

"Who?" she replied, as if she hadn't even seen the stunningly spectacular, heart-palpitating beauty who just passed.

How could that be?

A few days later, while in the restroom, I heard the door creak. Suddenly everything was in slow motion. As I watched the door swing open, there she was again. I was stunned to see this one-in-a-million girl who took my breath away. I'd never felt the way she made me feel before. My heart was pounding, my palms were sweating, and I quickly became dizzy.

I'd thought of getting together with girls in the past, and the idea very much intrigued me. Although the experience in Sun Valley completely turned me off.

I was flustered while scooping up my books, a paper clip sticking slightly out of my mouth.

I motioned for her to take the paperclip out of my mouth while mumbling, "Paperclip," as best as possible.

Figuring out what I was asking her, she began moving toward me. My hands were sweating, and fear set in. I was scared I would drop the books or worse. I watched as she came closer, thinking she would grab the paper clip with her hand. Her face came closer and closer to mine. Closing my eyes, I felt her lips pluck the paper clip out of my mouth. I was astonished and embarrassed, certain my brown face must be red now if it hadn't been before.

I mumbled, "Thanks," under my breath while rushing out of the restroom.

I could hear the echo of her laugh along the bathroom corridor as I pushed the door with my shoulder and headed off to class.

The next time I saw her was on the quad, hanging out with a lot of the same people I did.

Approaching me with a smile, she asserted, "I think I saw you in the bathroom earlier?" Extending her hand, she continued, "Hi, I'm Cindi."

I replied timidly, "I'm Delicia. It is so nice to meet you. Oh, and thanks for your help earlier," I said with an adoring smile.

Giggling, she invited me to her house, and we were inseparable for many, many months. We became thick as thieves; we were best buds and hung out all the time. Every weekday we went to her house, watched the soap opera *Santa Barbara,* ate, and hung in her room.

The first time I saw her room, disappointment loomed. I had been secretly hoping she was interested in more than just being friends. Her walls displayed posters from all the teenybopper magazines, and they were all of boys.

Months later, we sat with our butts on the floor, resting our backs on the natural oak wood surrounding the box spring of her bed while listening to the newly released *Ready for the World* album.

Cindi was enjoying her gum when I inquired, "Can I have some gum?"

She chuckled and stuck the gum out of her mouth.

I tried to grab the gum with my fingers as she backed up, muttering, "Uh-uh."

"What?" I protested.

She only stared at me, gum sticking halfway out of her mouth, not saying a word.

I'd thought so many times of kissing her but was petrified. It had been two years since the Sun Valley experience, and I hadn't thought of being with anyone until meeting Cindi. Would I get scared away again? Would it be different now that I was older? Would I like it more because I felt so much for her? I would never know until I tried.

Thinking, *Here's my chance,* I went in for the gum. Shyly snatching some with my lips, I quickly backed away. Cindi never let go. She came toward me again, got about a quarter of an inch from my lips, and withdrew. Knowing it was my turn, I moved closer, coming about an eighth of an inch from her lips. Millimeter by millimeter, our lips grew closer and closer until we finally kissed.

WOWIE! *!*$*!&$&!!! Fireworks exploded around us...for real! My mind left my body and ejected my soul into a universe where I felt love in every crevice, seeping like molten lava. My heart was aflutter. Was this love? Could I actually be in love at fourteen?

Cindi's parents had been planning a long summer trip to Canada. By summertime, I was fifteen, and Cindi was sixteen. Cindi and I had recently started our flourishing relationship, and neither of us wanted to spend time apart from each other. Since we were best friends, our parents didn't think much of it when we begged for me to go along on the trip with them.

At first, we had nothing but fun. Going on a trip to Canada with her parents was awesome, until it wasn't.

Our first stop on the way was Las Vegas. Staying in a campsite in her parents' large motor home, we slept in the front, where the table turned into a bed. Her mother and father slept in the back of the trailer in a private room.

Since we weren't of legal gambling age, we hung out at Circus Circus. Cindi and I wanted to veer off from her parents and were given a time and place to meet back up with them. This was long before cell phones, so you always had to pick a place and time to meet. If you weren't there, whoever you were supposed to meet would get worried, especially if kids were involved.

We were enjoying playing a few games when I saw a water shooting game. I was really good at them.

I exclaimed, "Hey, let's go over here. I wanna win you a bear."

"Yeah, right, you can't win me one of those giant bears," she challenged.

"Watch me."

Grasping the dirty metal gun, I placed my quarters on the hard enamel. I aimed my gun at the clown's mouth so that when the bell went off, my finger was already full force on the trigger.

Shooting out a stream of water directly into the mouth of the clown, I knew the trick to winning was holding it steady. I won.

"No way, I can't believe you won," she said, giggling.

"Just for you, my lady. Go ahead and pick your prize," I stated with pride. Smiling and giving me a kiss on the cheek, she picked her giant bear.

As we descended down the spiral walkway leading from the top level of games to the bottom, Cindi pushed me against the railing and kissed me passionately. I was a bit taken aback and embarrassed, as I wasn't one for public affection. Uncomfortable, I pushed her off and scolded, "Not here."

Kissing my neck, she pleaded, "Come on."

I quickly backed up as we heard the laughter of people approaching, but she leaned in and kissed me again passionately once they passed.

"No, come on, not here." I began walking up the spiral runway when Cindi scowled.

Pouting, she accused, "You don't love me."

"I do, I just don't want to kiss you right here," I reasoned.

Standing with her lip out like a puffer fish who lost its best friend, she waited for a kiss.

"Oh geez, if I kiss you here, can we go?" A bashful smile lit up her face as I planted one on her.

"Okay, we can go." She grabbed my hand, and we skipped down the spiral together. That was the night Cindi asked me to be her girlfriend.

After we'd been "officially" together for a few weeks, I felt safe and comfortable with Cindi. I was falling in love for the first time in my life. I was elated to have someone I could share intimacy and feel safe with. It was something I'd never had before. I'd experienced sex without love and love without sex, but I'd never felt comfortable with anyone enough to experience sex and love together, until now.

In Montana, the bugs were biting Cindi badly. Her parents had long gone to sleep, and Cindi was feeling frisky.

"No," I snapped, "your parents just went to bed. I don't trust it."

Cindi was a bit of an exhibitionist, insisting, "We can be quiet, and they will never know."

As she kissed my lips, neck, shoulders, and breasts, I couldn't resist. Completely forgetting that her parents were in the same space, things progressed. In the thrusts of passionate lovemaking, we completely lost track of the world around us.

Just as I was about to have an orgasm, her mother yelled, "Cindi, why is the motorhome shaking? Are your feet itching again?"

"Yeah, Mom, really bad," Cindi replied without removing her fingers from my wet vagina. Smirking, she put her head under the covers, sucking on my nipple with her fingers still inside me.

"I can't," I said, pushing her off me.

"Why? She will never know."

"Are you kidding? She already does… How embarrassing."

As we resumed our trip into Canada, it became obvious her mother knew something was going on between us. This was made clear when her parents cut the trip short. We only spent a single night in Canada before turning around. We began traveling home without making any stops, other than to sleep.

The day after we returned, her mother called my mother and claimed, "Your daughter turned my daughter into a lesbian."

My mother's response was, "What if *your* daughter turned *my* daughter into a lesbian?" Cindi's mother didn't get the response she wanted, and that conversation didn't last long.

The following morning, my mother asked bluntly, just before taking me to school, "Are you a lesbian?"

I answered quickly and definitively, "Yes, please take me to school."

The ride to school that day was silent. My mother was clearly trying not to show her emotion while tears welled up in her eyes. She appeared incredibly angry and hurt.

My mother had stressed my entire life that people were people, and that all people should be accepted as they were. I was extremely puzzled as to why she was so distraught over my coming out to her as gay. I thought it would be super easy for her, considering what she had instilled in me growing up.

I was heartbroken, thinking that being who I was upset my mother so much, especially since, at the time, one of her best friends, Stephanie, was a lesbian. Not to mention, growing up, another of her best friends, Effron, was flamboyantly gay.

When Mom came home from work that day, we talked.

"Mom, I felt terrible that you were so sad this morning."

"I'm sorry," she responded, and for a moment I was hopeful this conversation was headed in a more positive direction. But then she said, "I had some time to think about it, and I spoke to Stephanie. She said it's just a phase."

"Mom, it's not a phase. I have known since I was twelve."

"How could you have known since you were twelve?"

"I just did. There is a specific day that I knew. It was when we lived in Sun Valley."

"How?" she shrieked as her voice rose several octaves.

"I don't know, Mom. I just know that is who I am. I don't want to be this way, I didn't choose it, but that is who I am."

"I hope it is just a phase. Not because I care if you are gay, but it is a really hard lifestyle and isn't accepted in this world, and I don't want you to have to live a life that is that hard."

"It's okay, Mom. It is what it is, and I am who I am."

"I know but..."

Storming off to my room, I shouted, "But nothing! I can't do anything to change it!"

Later that night, Mom came to my room.

Wrapping her arms around me, she affirmed, "Delicia, I love you, regardless of if you love men, women, or cats. I don't care. As long as you are happy, that is all that matters to me."

Throwing myself into her arms, I wept.

Cindi and I both came out in high school, which really seemed to cause a ruckus in 1985. Cindi and I had been "best friends" for a while and decided it was time to let the world know about it.

After a night of passionate teenage lovemaking, there were several hickeys that ended up on my neck as well as hers. Cindi's were very noticeable since her skin was paler than mine. The next morning before class, we were hanging out behind the library smoking.

Cindi took a drag off her cigarette. A friend of hers approached us.

"Hi, guys, can I bum a cig off you?" the girl asked, not taking notice of the obvious hickeys.

"Sure, here you go." Cindi handed her a cigarette, arching her neck slightly, as if to show it off.

Cocking her head a bit, her friend suddenly screeched, "What in the world are those?" She pointed to Cindi's neck.

Cindi just gave me a coy smile and giggled.

Her friend quickly put two and two together. "Hey, you two have only been hanging out with each other. What the heck is that? Are you two… EEEEW-WWW, that's disgusting."

She stormed off yelling, "Dykes!"

Cindi chuckled to herself and threw her cigarette on the ground. She grabbed my hand, and we walked through the crowded hallway of smokers as they stared us down like we were maggots crawling on an old, dead animal.

Bellows of "fucking dykes" echoed the hallways as we proudly walked hand in hand to our classes.

I felt in my bones that it was necessary for us to come out in high school. I knew if we didn't make it normal, it would never be considered as such.

Enduring many years of teasing from this moment onward, I grew thick skin. The skateboarders were the absolute worst. Some of them were okay, but others were just horrific. One was particularly awful—Kip. There wasn't a time I could remember that Kip didn't pass me in the halls without shouting, "Dyke," "Muff diver," or some other derogatory term.

It wasn't until almost the end of twelfth grade, long after Cindi and I had broken up, that I finally stood up for myself.

A popular hangout spot for the skateboarders was in front of the cafeteria. My friends and I would hang on the quad or outside of school normally, but one day I had to pass the cafeteria to get to my car. Passing the large group of rowdy skateboarders, I heard in the distance, "Fucking dyke."

I slowly turned around, shouting, "Who said that?"

Surrounded by friends hanging on the short brick wall attached to the outside of the cafeteria, Kip looked directly at me, stating, "I did. What are you going to do about it?" while puffing out his chest.

Strutting slowly and methodically toward him without saying a word, I came within one inch of his face. "That's right, and I get more pussy than you do!"

Turning purple, he blushed while everyone around him started laughing and teasing him. "Aw, she told you."

"Ha, ha, you dumbass. She's probably right, too."

I smiled all the way to my car, feeling the pride of standing up for myself, though I wasn't happy he was getting teased. I was, however, elated that he never said another word to me ever again.

Coming out in high school is something I am extremely proud of, and I knew it was necessary. Regardless of the incessant teasing, I had to help pave the way for the kids behind me to make it a bit more normalized so they, hopefully, wouldn't have to endure what I did.

LONELINESS AVERTED

Wanting to find the safest place she could when we moved back to California, my mother chose Newbury Park. Just north of Los Angeles lies Ventura County. Within Ventura County, Thousand Oaks is one of the safest places in the nation. Our new town was a suburb of Thousand Oaks.

Moving here was truly a joy for me. Anywhere away from boring Hawaii would have been fine with me. Transplanting was always hard, but by this point in my life, I was used to it. I had relocated ten times, and I was only fourteen. Would this be it? The place we finally stayed long enough for me to make friends?

Mom promised me this time we'd stay until I graduated, and I was hell-bent on holding her to that, knowing I would never have friends if I didn't stay in one place long enough to sneeze.

I was anxious and excited on the plane ride back to California and looking forward to seeing this new "super safe" neighborhood that Mom found. Landing at LAX, we took a taxi to a nearby hotel. Our belongings were shipped from Hawaii, and Mom had already secured a condo for us, so the following day we were on our way.

How far was it? What would the kids be like? Would I make friends? How long would this one last? So many questions ran through my mind.

The drive felt like forever as we passed the Getty Villa along the coastline of Highway 1 and up into the rolling hills of Agoura.

Growing impatient, I asked, "How far is this place?"

"Not much farther," Mom replied.

Finally reaching our destination, the first thing I surmised was this was an extremely white town. Growing up in and around North Hollywood and just landing from Hawaii, where the population was extremely diverse, it felt uncomfortable.

Our condo was perfect. My room even had a balcony that overlooked the small, private, residential street.

I probably spent all of ten minutes in the house before dashing out the door shouting, "Bye, Mom."

"Wait, wait, wait. Where do you think you are going, young lady?" she asked.

"I just want to wander around the neighborhood a little."

"Be back before dinner. I will order pizza around six," she relented.

I stepped outside and spotted a garage across the street. The door was open with loud punk music playing. Sneaking over to investigate, I heard, "Why can't I get just one kiss, why can't I get just one kiss..." The Violent Femmes got louder and louder as I approached. The closer I got, the more my heart raced with delight. I loved the Violent Femmes, and not many people knew who they were, especially in Hawaii.

Seeing this girl spinning and dancing around in the garage, whipping her hair around, enjoying every minute of life, my heart leaped with joy. Perhaps I'd found my first friend here?

"March, turn down that nonsensical music! It is time to come inside," a voice hollered from somewhere inside the house.

I sauntered past the garage as she turned down the music, and we caught a glimpse of each other. She seemed as curious as me.

The following day, hearing music again, I decided to introduce myself. Meandering across the street, I heard the Sex Pistols playing, loud. I thought, *This girl is bitchin'! I have to get to know her*. Another punk fan living right across the street—I had a good feeling about this place. Hoping she was friendly, I continued. The music was blaring, and again, this black-haired, free-spirited kid was dancing and whirling in circles with her arms out to the sky. She spun her head around, catching a glimpse of me watching her, and she almost tripped on her own shoe while trying to stop.

"Hi, I'm March," she said, beaming a smile, her silver braces sparkling in the sun.

"Hi, I'm Delicia. We just moved here from Maui."

"Maui? Wow, that is cool. It's so nice to meet you." Reaching her hand out to shake mine, she asked with gusto, "Do you like punk?"

"Like it? I love it! What do you think drew me over here?"

March was my first friend in Newbury Park. That December, while school was on break, we sat up for hours listening to punk music either in her room, garage, or my room, depending on which parent had the most patience that particular day.

I started at Newbury Park High School mid-semester in January of 1985. Everyone else had already had six months to get to know each other. This made it much more difficult to make friends. March attended NPHS for the first semester as well as junior high school in Newbury Park, so she already knew a lot of people. The first day of school wasn't so bad thanks to March.

Being queer myself, I was always drawn to others like me. I don't necessarily mean gay. Don't get me wrong, some were absolutely gay, myself included. Others were just odd or different. We shared the same energy; we were connected. During lunch, a group of us hung out on the lawn just outside of school at the park next door.

Others probably referred to us as misfits, but I'd say we were more like eccentric bohemians. Some had hair in various shades from pink and green to rainbow. Others had spiked mohawks that stood two feet tall. In our group, it didn't matter the color of your skin, if you were large or small, straight or gay, a punker or a hessian, average or a genius or even a dirty hippie; we loved and accepted each other for who we were. My friends and I definitely enjoyed letting our freak flag fly.

Living in Newbury Park wasn't quite as boring as Hawaii, but it still felt like there was never anything to do. The people were cool, but the town itself was uneventful. It felt as though I had moved from dull, beautiful Maui to dreary, white-tract-home capital of the world.

As I'd always done growing up, I'd often wander around our neighborhood exploring.

One day, I ventured next door to a large apartment complex. It was drab, kind of like the new town we had moved to—all the same color, all the same style: mahogany brown wood with tan stucco.

At least in Hawaii the ocean was right next to us. Here, it was all so plain. As I romped about the complex, I observed a young man petting and cuddling a cat sitting on the sidewalk. He was so into this cuddle session, he didn't notice me approaching.

"Hi," I said with a smile.

Startled, he quickly lifted his head and, seeing me standing over him, pushed his wide-brimmed glasses up onto his nose so they fit flush against his face. "Hi."

He had a perfectly shaped face and blue eyes like sapphires that could penetrate your soul. I was a bit taken aback. He was the spitting image of Boy George.

During my years in junior high school, Boy George overtook Belinda Carlisle and The Go-Go's as my idol for a brief stint. Daily, I'd wear a trench coat to school with literally hundreds of Boy George and Culture Club buttons proudly showing off my love for them.

"Whoa, has anyone ever told you that you look just like Boy George?" I couldn't stop myself from asking.

"All the time." He chuckled. Extending his hand out, he introduced himself. "Hi, I'm Jason."

I shook his hand firmly and replied, "I'm Delicia. It's nice to meet you. What's your cat's name?"

"Fluffy," he said, stroking the light gray, silvery coat. "Did you just move here? I haven't seen you before."

"Yep, we just moved the other week from Hawaii."

"Hawaii! Wow, well, aloha!"

"Yeah, it wasn't all that, trust me." I was getting a bit tired of having to explain this to everyone who thought Hawaii must have been amazing.

"What do you mean? I can imagine it must have been dreamy," he replied in a melodic tone.

"It was really boring, actually."

"Really?" He seemed to consider this for a moment, then moved on. "Huh. Do you want to hang out?"

"Sure, that sounds like fun."

As we embarked through the maze of apartments while Jason held Fluffy in his arms, I noticed how similar each building looked and doubted I would ever find my way out.

When we reached his apartment, Jason removed his combat boots, stating, "My dad says shoes off in the house."

"Okay, not a problem." I slipped off my Vans.

We headed into the living room, and I saw a man in the kitchen.

"This is my dad, John," Jason introduced us.

John was a handsome man and looked very much like Jason. They had the same receding hairline and the same piercing eyes.

"It's nice to meet you. You got a name?" John asked.

"It's Delicia."

"Well, son, it's about time you picked up one of the pretty ones."

Jason just laughed.

John was a butcher and loved his guns. Guns were proudly displayed throughout the apartment in various cases.

Taking in the scene, I proclaimed, "Boy, you have got a lot of guns."

John growled, trying to be serious while mocking, "It's our right to bear arms in this country."

A half-cocked smile appeared as he spoke. It being the first time I'd met John, I couldn't discern if he was being serious or not. I hadn't been around many guns in my life, and it made me a little uncomfortable.

Observing my distress, John teased, "Don't worry, I don't use them... unless I have to."

Jason and I became the best of friends. Turned out, John liked me a lot as well.

Jason had a moped, which was his main mode of transportation. The bus system in Newbury Park was minuscule at best. Sometimes we had to wait hours for the bus. Even though I knew my mother was vehemently opposed to it, I would hop on the back of Jason's scooter, and we would putter around town. It was dangerous for me if I got caught; therefore, Jason and I were always super careful.

One afternoon, he picked me up from where I was working at Taco Bell to give me a ride home. Jumping on the back of the scooter, I thought nothing of it. I smiled as we rode and chatted while the wind blew my hair all over my face. Jason always wore a helmet, but I didn't have one. There was never a passenger helmet available.

Up and over the freeway bridge we went. While passing the gas station, I saw a gold Toyota van. As luck would have it, the very tall, silver-haired man standing next to that van happened to be Ron, my mother's fiancé.

Shouting, "Oh shit," I buried my head sideways behind Jason's back.

Riding on the back of the scooter, I peeked with one eye open. Ron stared directly at me, shaking his head.

Asking Jason to drop me off at the street, I really hoped I hadn't been spotted on the scooter. In my heart, I knew I was doomed.

"Thanks, J, see you tomorrow," I said, thinking to myself, *Shit, time to face the music.*

Ron was six foot four and weighed about four hundred pounds, most of it muscle or "sleeping muscle" as he used to call it. He had been a "professional" football player in college.

I began freaking out a little, knowing he had seen me. I silently creaked open the front door. Ron uttered from the living room, "I'm not going to tell your mother that I saw you."

"What?" I asked, startled.

"You heard me," he replied.

"Really? Thank you so much." Relief surged through me.

"But don't let me catch you on that scooter again. You know how your mother feels about two-wheeled vehicles."

"I know, thank you so much, Ron." This was one of the only times I felt bonded with my mother's fiancé.

Jason was always bringing me to cool parties around the neighborhood. One Saturday night, he took me to a friend's house in Thousand Oaks, where a rager was happening. At that party, I met Tommy, who would turn out to be just like a brother to me.

But Tommy and I didn't hang out much at that point. Mostly, we saw each other at parties. He was a few years older than me and didn't go to our school. I would say we were more like acquaintances, not so much friends, at first. Living in an incredibly small town, queer folk often frequenting the same places, we all knew each other.

We were crazy kids. My friend Michelle was a caregiver for Roy, an elderly gentleman in his mid-eighties. She cooked his meals, kept him company, bathed him, etcetera. Roy was much older than anyone I knew, making him seem ancient to me. I recall Roy peeing himself on several occasions and Michelle cleaning him up. Roy's house was in an area of Newbury Park everyone called "white watts."

Roy didn't have family, at least not that we knew of—none that we saw, anyway. His eyes were the sweetest blue, but they were always tinged with a hint of sadness. My heart ached wondering where it all came from.

Roy was an alcoholic who was always so drunk he didn't want to think or talk about the past or his family. Whenever I inquired, he refused to discuss it.

People often frequented the house to party and keep him company. Usually, Roy would buy alcohol for everyone, all of whom were under the legal drinking age. Inviting people over to party was a weekly occurrence, and Roy was fine with it. The way he saw it, kids were going to drink anyway, and in his mind, he was creating a safe place. He could either be having fun with a bunch of drunk kids or sitting there alone in his urine-soaked pants.

Always looking forward to partying at Roy's, we counted the days until the next one. One night, Tommy brought his younger sister, Gertrude, with him. Gertrude and I bonded immediately. We felt an instant pull toward each other, like an energy magnet. We exchanged numbers, and she called me later that night.

After talking for hours about life and everything under the sun, I heard a man's voice with a heavy Mexican accent screaming in the background. "Gertrude, if you don't shut that fucking baby up, I'm going to throw it out the goddamn window!"

Concerned, I quickly asked, "Who's that and what baby?"

"Oh, I have a one-month-old baby," she responded casually.

"You do? How old are you?" I asked in bewilderment. I was truly shocked.

"I'm fifteen, same as you," she responded.

"Whoa."

"I know. It's a long story, but yeah, I have a baby. And that's my dad. He is yelling because I am on the phone and the baby is crying."

"Do you have to go?" I asked. This whole situation was strange to me. I couldn't imagine having a baby at my age.

"No, I have time."

Over the next three hours or so of our call, I would find out that her parents never educated her about sex. She was being earnest when she'd told me, "I really didn't know how people got pregnant." Somehow, she managed to hide it from her mother and father until the baby was ready to pop out.

I had found a new friend, and we bonded so well. This was a rare occurrence in my life. I was ecstatic. I ended that first phone conversation with an "I love you," which are words I don't throw around lightly. I was even thrilled about the baby, Zachary, and excited for the opportunity to meet him.

After that first long phone call, I was at their house almost every day. I even helped raise Zachary for the first few years, until I moved out on my own at seventeen.

Gertrude and Tommy also had a little brother, Bruce. Bruce was a wild kid.

When we were teenagers, we sniffed amyl nitrate, otherwise known as Phuck. When we sniffed the bottle, we'd get dizzy and fall over. Looking back, it's strange to think we actually liked this as kids, but being legal and available at any liquor store, it was an uncomplicated way to get high.

I was hanging out with Gertrude in her room on the day two-year-old Bruce came in and began immediately climbing up the bookshelf.

"Bruce, what are you doing?" Gertrude asked.

"Phuck," the toddler wailed.

Shocked, I blurted out, "What did he just say?"

Bruce continued climbing the bookshelf, and Gertrude said nothing. When he reached the top, he snatched the bottle of Phuck. I was in a state of disbelief.

Jumping off the bed, Gertrude took the bottle away from him.

Bruce started wailing and screaming, "Gimme Phuck! I want Phuck." I couldn't believe my eyes.

Another day, I was awakened from sleep by Bruce standing in front of me with a large knife. My eyes bulged while I tried to stay calm. I whispered, "Bruce, what are you doing?"

He replied in a gruff two-year-old voice, "I'm Conan, the fucking barbarian."

"You shouldn't be playing with knives," I chided while retrieving it from his hand. I tried my hardest not to laugh while returning it to the kitchen.

One day, when Zachary was about two months old, Gertrude and I were sleeping when he began crying. I'd never encountered a baby before and had no idea what to do. The closest I'd come were my dolls when I was younger.

Gertrude nudged me while I slept and groaned, "Your baby is crying."

"*My* baby?" I stressed.

"Yeah, go feed him," she moaned while rolling back over to sleep.

Amused, I tended to his needs. He was such an adorable baby. When I tossed him up in the air, he would get the most enchanting, magical smile. Every time I saw it, my heart burst with joy. Helping to raise Zachary for the first few years of his life was a true gift.

Another party at Roy's was on the horizon. As always, we were looking forward to the prospect of a night of drinking without the worry of getting home safely. My condo was within walking distance, and tottering home after a few too many drinks was never a problem.

Taking shots of tequila and conversing among friends was a terrific way to spend a Saturday night at fifteen, if we weren't hanging in LA. There were about twenty people at Roy's that night.

The phone rang, and Michelle picked it up. When we overheard her shouting to whoever was on the other end, someone turned the music down.

"No, no, I don't think so. I haven't seen her. Okay, bye," Michelle said as she hung up the phone.

"Delicia, that was your mother," she announced.

Infuriated, I asked, "What? How did she get this phone number?"

"Uh, she said she couldn't find you. She talked to Gertrude's mom, and apparently, they think you are running away."

"Huh?" I was truly perplexed. Where on earth had this come from? Sure, I'd been spending a lot of time at Gertrude's, but just because I hadn't been home every minute didn't mean I was *running away*. But then I was a bit tipsy. Urging Gertrude, I announced, "Well, if they think we are running away, then fuck it, let's run away."

"Really?" she questioned as if I wasn't serious.

"Yeah, really. Fuck them, let's stay here. Roy, can we stay with you?"

Snickering, he grinned. "Anytime."

Minds made up, we continued to party. Around nine thirty p.m., there was a loud knock on the door. It was my mother. I snatched Gertrude and pulled her into the bedroom. We listened intently with the door closed. I heard my mom fuming, "Where is my daughter?"

"She's not here," Michelle answered.

"I know she is here; you are lying!" my mother said with spite.

Mom had a thing for witches. I never understood it, but she had, literally, thousands of witches. They were everywhere. You couldn't come into our house without seeing a witch in every nook or cranny. Kitchen witches hung from every possible space around our fluorescent ceiling lights. There must have been one hundred witches hanging in our kitchen alone.

I never thought much of my mother's witch fetish, until that fateful night at Roy's. When I heard my mother scream, "I'm a witch, and if my daughter isn't home by ten p.m., I am going to burn this fucking house down," at the top of her lungs from the living room, I was mortified.

After waiting for my mother to leave, Gertrude and I slowly came out of the bedroom. Concerned, Tommy stated, "You better go home."

"Fuck her. She can't treat me like that. If she thinks I'm running away, then that's exactly what I will do. Come on, Gertrude, let's go."

"I'm gonna go home," she replied.

"Suit yourself. I'm outta here."

Though I'd actually had no intention of running away, I was embarrassed while at the same time petrified of my mother. I didn't want to go home. On numerous occasions, my mother had flown into a rage and struck both myself as well as my brother, and with the fury I'd witnessed in her that night, it appeared to be one of those times. I knew she had gone off the deep end, and frankly, I was terrified.

I remained hiding in the room until I thought it safe, then returned to the living room where a handful of people were still hanging out and partying. Paranoid, I kept looking out the windows every few seconds.

Peeking out the tiny curtain that hung on the front window, I saw my mother marching up the street. *Shit,* I thought, *what can I do?* I ran to the bedroom and shut the door.

I heard my mother scream once again, "Where is she? I just saw her in the window. Where is my daughter?"

"She's still not here," Michelle replied calmly.

"Fine, I'm calling the police."

As my mother stormed off, I knew she wasn't kidding. Sneaking out the bedroom window, I ran through the back of the apartment complex.

Each building had a laundry room attached to its carport that served every four apartments. Inside each was a folding table and one stackable washer/dryer. I ran several buildings down, thinking I'd found the perfect hiding spot.

Crouching so I couldn't be seen from the street, I hid in a panic, hoping the police wouldn't find me. I hid for hours. Every now and then, I would see a spotlight and hear the CB radio of a cop car outside the room.

I returned around four a.m. and entered the same window I'd snuck out of earlier that night. The house was empty. I was confused. Unbeknownst to me, the police had shown up at Roy's house and arrested everyone who was there, including Tommy, Michelle, and Roy.

I headed to the front door and peeked out the window again. This time I saw my mother. Recognizing me, she marched up the street. *Fuck,* I thought. Locking the front door, I headed back into the bedroom, opened the wooden sliding door to the closet, and stepped inside.

The closet was filled with urine-soaked clothes. Gagging, I knew there was no other option. I couldn't sneak back outside because my mother was there. I crouched down and hid in that closet for what felt like an hour before hearing my mother's voice again.

"I know she is in there. I saw her with my own eyes," she insisted.

"Ma'am, are you sure?" a deep voice asked.

"I'm 100 percent certain she is in there."

"Ma'am, we already arrested everyone that was inside earlier."

Another voice interjected, "Officer, I saw someone break in at around four this morning."

"Stand back, ma'am," replied the officer.

Hearing the crashing of glass, I knew I was done for.

The officer came through the broken window. I heard him instruct, "Ma'am, I need to search the house. Please wait for me outside." When he opened the closet door, he saw me crouched down among the pee-soaked clothes. Reaching out his hand to help me, he instructed, "You're going home."

"Uh-uh, no way," I uttered in fear.

"Why don't you want to go home?" he inquired earnestly.

"Um, duh. Just look at her. She is crazy. She told all my friends she was going to burn this house down."

"You have to go home."

"No, please, don't make me go with her," I begged the officer.

"Wait here," he commanded, then headed out the front door to talk with my mother. Returning, he took handcuffs out of his pocket.

"Um, what are you doing?" I demanded.

"I'm sorry, young lady, but your mother has requested that I arrest you."

"What?" This was getting ridiculous.

"Your mother told me to arrest you. Put your hands behind your back."

"Why am I being arrested?"

"For running away." Placing the handcuffs on me without reading me my Miranda rights, he walked me to the cruiser.

As I got in the back seat of the cop car, I gave my mother the nastiest look I could. At that moment, I loathed her.

That night, I slept with my hands cuffed behind my back, head on a table in a holding cell.

The next afternoon when my mother picked me up from the station, I was still fuming.

Mortified, I thought I could never face my friends again. Her demand for my arrest, the threats she made, and her actions shamed me to my core. This was one of the most embarrassing moments of my life, and I wanted to die. My mother was always projecting her problems onto her children.

The car ride home was silent, until I realized we weren't going home.

"Where are we going?" I asked.

"I am taking you to a boarding house in Pasadena. I can't handle you any longer."

"What are you talking about, Mom?" I was suddenly outraged and panicked. "I am a good kid; I do hardly anything wrong. I even have a job, and most kids don't think about that at fifteen."

The conversation escalated to the point that I tried jumping out of the car on the freeway. Opening the passenger door while moving sixty miles per hour wasn't a good idea, I quickly found out. Not caring if I lived or died by the end of the conversation, I seized my mother's purse and emptied all her medication bottles into my hand.

"Here, Mom, are you happy now? I want to die because of you, and I want you to watch it happen."

She just laughed.

Swallowing pills, I choked on some as they went down my throat.

A moment passed as she began to realize I wasn't kidding. Then she became hysterical. Frantically driving to the emergency room, she screamed on arrival, "My daughter just attempted suicide!"

As a teenager, you have a bit more of a voice than a kid, so the doctors and nurses took the time to hear *my* version of the story, which was a welcome change.

In the end, they determined I was just a frustrated teenager and not genuinely suicidal. The suggestion from the medical team was for me to live with someone else for a while. I knew this wasn't an option as I hadn't had a father for the last ten years.

My mother and I eventually figured it out, but our relationship was never the same. The trust was lost on so many levels it would be impossible to repair, or so I thought. The energy between my mother and I felt fractured. The intense bond we had previously had been broken. I felt like she didn't know who I really was, and it didn't seem like she wanted to. At this moment, my mother was lumped in with all the others that made me feel "less than," unworthy, and unwanted in this world. It felt like she would never trust me and didn't believe in me. That was truly heartbreaking for me since my mother's opinion meant everything to me. I felt shunned on many levels by my mother. I started to shrivel internally like a raisin in the sun, my depression began to worsen, and a lot of the time I felt dead inside. The warmth and love I felt from her began to feel cold and unwelcoming. It was very awkward for the next several months between us.

Since the relationship with my mother was tense, I spent most of my time at Gertrude's house bonding with her mother, Lucy. She was a second mom to me. Thomas Senior, their dad, was a very abusive and violent man, but I became as close as a stranger could be with him.

Gertrude, Tommy, Lucy, Zachary, Bruce, and Thomas Senior were like family to me, and I consider Tommy, Gertrude, and Bruce my siblings and Lucy my "Mamma Lucy."

From tenth grade onward at Newbury Park High School, students didn't have to stay on campus for lunch. Hearing the chime of the lunch bell ring, we couldn't wait to get off campus. Our group would meet on a patch of grass just to the left of Borchard Park, near the tennis courts. I loved rap and hip-hop, specifically the Beastie Boys, and almost daily when I arrived at our little patch of wonderland, my friends would be waiting.

LR, otherwise known as "The Green Goddess," would often color her hair various shades of green. Her house was green, her clothes were green, everything about her screamed green, so the nickname was quite fitting. Linda was a blonde-haired beauty with the brains to boot. Laurel was in a league of her own and wore one side of her bangs cut to the length of her chin. The other side was cut short enough to show off the intricate sketches she drew daily of spiderwebs and other macabre shapes on her face. Kevin dressed in combat boots and chains draped from his pockets. His hair stood about two feet tall with giant spiked sections forming a single line mohawk across his scalp. Altogether, there was a group of about ten to fifteen of us who would hang out at lunch on a daily basis.

Among this group were two girls who were part of my history. One happened to attend Oxnard Street School and remembered me from my third-grade class. The other, Annie, was my friend from Camp Fox who was so dear to me. We had lost touch throughout our teenage years and ran back into each other in Newbury Park. Coincidences like this always reminded me of what a small world we live in.

Approaching the group, I'd holler, "What's the time?"

Everyone would shout back, "It's time to get ill."

I'd usually take a spot next to LR so we could begin chatting. One day, I caught a glimpse of a super-cute blonde guy coming around the corner. I hadn't seen him before and was curious. His hair was totally New Wave, short on one side and spiked high on the other. His infectious smile made me want to know him.

He knelt next to me and stated, "Hi, I'm Marc, and this is my friend Jeremy."

"Hi, I'm Delicia. Nice to meet you."

We chatted for a while about Hawaii and how I came to be in Newbury Park when Marc changed the conversation.

"Hey, we are going to get burritos at Manny's and then smoke a bowl," he said. "Wanna come?"

"Awesome! You don't have to ask me twice," I responded. I was thinking, *Wow, I finally found my stoner friends.*

Manny's was a taqueria across the street from the school that everyone frequented for burritos at lunchtime. If not Manny's, there was an Italian restaurant on the corner of the strip mall that had lunch specials for the kids. We grabbed our burritos wrapped in aluminum foil so they would stay hot—they felt like they weighed two pounds each—we jumped in Jeremy's car and journeyed into the neighborhood hills where we found a safe place to smoke.

We shared a bowl of weed, discussing life, death, and what felt like everything in between. We were pretty certain we had missed our afternoon classes, but time slows down when you are stoned, so who knew for sure?

When we drove past the park into the parking lot, everyone was gone. Knowing we were late, we quickly parked and ran our separate ways to our classrooms.

Smoking out with Marc and Jeremy that day was the start of an amazing journey and beautiful friendships lasting many years to come.

Jason was part of our close-knit group of friends. He was extremely effeminate and endured constant teasing. He allowed me to embrace my "gayness," introducing me to West Hollywood, bars, parties, and events. He was the world's greatest queen mentor. I was his "li'l girl" who he wanted "to corrupt."

Cindi and I remained good friends after our breakup and hung out quite often. Cindi was one of the first to get her license as well as a car, a Ford Falcon convertible that shifted using the lever next to the steering wheel. She was always referring to the gear shift as a "three-on-the-tree." Nobody could drive that car, except for Laurel, who was a genius. Cindi was normally the designated driver since she didn't want anyone else driving her classic.

Underground clubs were a big deal when I was in high school. Jason had connections in LA and was always able to find out where these clandestine clubs were. Packing into Cindi's car on weekends, Jason, Marc, Tommy, Cindi, and I would escape to Los Angeles, seeking out the underground clubs.

I was fifteen when I started clubbing. The Saturday before we were going to an underground club for my first time, Jason decided it was necessary for me to have a fake ID.

We agreed to meet so he could help me.

"Bring your old ID," he said.

"Sure, I just got a new permit, so I have an old ID I can bring."

"Perfect, that's all you need, and I will take care of the rest."

I showed up, old ID in hand. Jason laid everything out on his living room coffee table: a pair of scissors, some tape, an ID that didn't belong to me, a pen, and a magnifying glass.

"What is all this stuff?"

"Just wait, you'll see. You will be able to get into any bar in Gay Town with this."

"That would be cool, but I'm only fifteen. I doubt they will let me in."

"You never know until you try," he stated with a coy smile. "Now, where is your old ID?"

I handed him my ID. He cut the photo of my face ever so carefully and pasted the cutout picture on top of the "borrowed" ID while cutting that same template out of the other ID. Flipping them over, he married them together, then taped the back, hoping it would hold together.

"Okay, where is your wallet?"

I snickered. "What? That will never work. You just cut out my picture and taped it on a new ID!" I shook my head in astonishment.

"Just wait, snotty girl," he said, grabbing my wallet from my backpack. "Watch this."

Placing the taped-together ID into my license window in my wallet and shoving some various cards and paperwork behind it actually made it look real. I would be in trouble if anyone ever asked me to pull it out, but I figured, *What's the worst that could happen? Having to make another one?* I was willing to chance it.

The following Saturday, the only thing Jason had was an address to find the secret club. Getting dressed up to the nines was always special for me. Piling into Cindi's Ford Falcon, we headed to Los Angeles. It was a scavenger hunt finding our final destination. We pulled out the Thomas Maps from Cindi's dark blue, metal glove box, found the coordinates, and set out to locate the club.

Life felt miraculous adventuring down La Cienega with the convertible top down, wind blowing in our faces.

Noticing the street we'd been searching for, Marc hollered, "Cindi, there it is! Turn here."

She turned the corner in a quiet, wealthy neighborhood, and we saw what appeared to be someone in a unicorn outfit.

"Do you think that is what we are looking for?" Cindi asked.

"I dunno," said Jason. "Let's ask."

Cindi pulled over near the man standing on the corner dressed in the white unicorn outfit. His feet were covered in white, shaggy-haired hooves, and he had a rainbow horn in the middle of his head. Jason rolled the window down to ask for directions.

"Excuse me, Mr. Unicorn, can you give us directions?"

The man just stood there staring at us in his unicorn outfit, and all of us in the car tried our best not to laugh when Jason blurted out, "Dirty pictures," in a deep voice.

The man turned toward us, rearing his head while kicking, and trotted to our car. He handed Jason a paper, then quickly skipped away.

"Thanks," Jason muttered, and we veered away, guffawing.

"Let's see, where do we need to go?" Jason read the next set of instructions as Cindi slowly proceeded.

"Tell me where I am going," Cindi asked anxiously.

"Hold on, just pull over and we can figure it out."

Pulling out the Thomas guide again, we found our next stop along this quest. Though we were skeptical it would be the final destination, we continued south on La Cienega to the 10 East toward downtown Los Angeles.

We parked on the street while searching for the address of the hidden location and saw lights. Large bubbles filled the air, the kind where you use two pieces of rope so you can make them as grand as you want. Music was blaring.

"That must be it!" Jason shouted as we swerved in that direction.

A line of people stood waiting for something. Not certain if we were on the right track or not, but figuring, *What the heck?* we stood in line. We waited for over fifteen minutes before finally reaching what looked like a valet.

"What's the secret word?" he inquired.

"Huh? Nobody gave us a secret word," Jason responded.

"Check the paper," the guy stated in a monotone voice.

We looked at the paper we got from the unicorn man. It had a word on it: moonflower.

"Moonflower," Jason nervously shouted at the man.

"Here is your next clue." He handed us dayglow bracelets with writing on them, another piece of evidence we had to decipher to figure out our next steps.

Following the clue led us to a small warehouse in downtown Los Angeles, where we finally reached our destination. I was extremely nervous about using my fake ID for the first time, but the guard let us in without asking to see our identification. The club was, literally, underground. We entered from steps descending into what felt like the abyss of Los Angeles.

It was as if someone took the coolest bathroom artwork and made an exhibit out of it. The black lights everywhere made the art on the walls glow. Other than the artwork and the dark purple hue from the lights that illuminated the room, it was pitch-black. In order to see us, the bartender had to wear special glasses and seek out patrons by their dayglow bracelets. It seemed like this was a modern-day speakeasy; it was all very clandestine.

Advancing to the bar for drinks, I nervously approached the bartender, still wondering if he was going to card me. "Can we get some screwdrivers, please?" I asked.

"Sure, how many?"

Counting to make sure I wasn't missing anyone, I replied, "Four, please."

"Coming right up."

Not two minutes later, he came back with a small brown plastic tray filled with tiny paper cups, the size of a small shot glass.

"What are those?" Jason scoffed.

"They're your drinks," the bartender responded.

"Whatever, you're kidding, right? That is like a sip."

"Listen, honey, you get what you get."

We all laughed while raising our tiny cups high in the air as we cheered: "To Dirty Pictures!"

Numerous drinks later, we were feeling surprisingly good. I veered off from my friends and curiously wandered around. I almost immediately wished I hadn't. There were places inside with people doing things I wasn't interested in witnessing. Mostly sex, and a lot of it. I wasn't a sexual person. Especially after what I'd experienced thus far in my lifetime.

Finding my way back to my friends and the dance floor, I exclaimed, "Oh my God, you guys, you have to go check this place out. There are rooms with people doing crazy things."

"Rooms, what rooms?" Marc and Jason took off in a hurry.

A few minutes later, Marc ran back, shouting, "Oh my God, girl, you were right. This place is crazy."

"Crazy cool," Cindi said as we danced the night away.

Jason was my portal to this incredible time in my life. I wouldn't have been introduced to the world of West Hollywood, or "Gay Town" as we called it, had it not been for him, especially at the ripe young age of fifteen.

My friends and I were diligent workers in high school, mostly to fund our drug or drinking habits. Marc, like myself, worked as soon as the state allowed it. He worked at a clothing store called Marshall's at the time, handling inventory as well as janitorial work.

My mom had sold the bar before moving. She also spent all her savings moving the family to Hawaii. Therefore, when we moved back to California, we were, once again, living hand-to-mouth. Mom was back to square one with Los Angeles Unified School District and had to start climbing up the salary chain all over again.

Always trying to earn my own keep, I avoided asking my mom for anything. My first job, after working some painting jobs with my future stepfather, was at Taco Bell. Brown polyester was my daily uniform. I mainly worked so I had money to spend on weed; I never thought about buying nice outfits or makeup for myself. That just wasn't my thing.

One day, while doing my homework, I heard something being thrown onto my balcony from the street. I was almost hit by a pebble as I opened my sliding glass door to see what the ruckus was about. I looked down and saw Marc standing next to his Toyota truck with two giant trash bags in hand.

"Marc, what are you doing? Why didn't you just come to the front door?"

"I'm scared of your mom."

I grumbled back, "Oh brother, don't be silly. What's in the bags? I'll come down."

Marc was standing at the door with two large trash bags and a heartwarming smile. He announced, "I got you some clothes."

My mother emerged from the kitchen, asking, "What's all the commotion? Who's at the door?"

"Marc brought me some clothes," I replied.

"Why are they in trash bags?" my mother inquired, giving him a concerned look.

"Oh Mom, whatever. Come on, Marc, let's go upstairs."

Marc opened the bags and dumped out what looked like a couple of years' worth of clothes onto my bed.

"Check these out. They threw all of these away, and I went dumpster diving for you."

"Wow, thanks, Marc. That is awesome!"

I had fun trying on clothes for what felt like hours. I was grateful to have a friend like Marc. This bond of friendship was something that came rarely in my life; however, it seemed like I was making quite a few friendship bonds in our newfound town.

Babysitting was the thing to do to make money when I was a teen. I was fourteen when I started. By the time I was sixteen, several people knew I was available to help. One evening, a neighbor of ours about six townhouses down needed a sitter for their twelve-year-old son, Sam.

I recalled Marc had recently switched jobs and was working at the local pizza place. Deciding to order pizza and knowing he would hook us up, I ordered from there.

"Amici's Pizza. Will this be for dine-in, delivery, or carryout?"

"Marc, is that you?"

"Hey, girl."

"Hey, I'm babysitting and wanted to order a pizza."

"Right on, what can I get for you?"

"Let's do a cheese pizza."

"You want a small, right?"

"Do you think that will be enough for two of us?"

"Don't worry, I got you, girl. I'll deliver it myself."

While Sam and I watched TV, hungrily awaiting our pizza, Marc apparently got lost on the way. Since it was so close to my house, he reluctantly decided to stop there and ask my mom where I was babysitting. She pointed the house out to him, and a minute later, we finally had our pizza.

When the doorbell rang, both Sam and I raced to answer.

"Finally," I said, exasperated.

"Sorry, I got lost," Marc explained. "But your mom told me where you were. Here, I made it a large instead of a small."

"Oh, cool. Thank you, you're the best, Marc!"

"No problem," he said. "I better get back to work."

Marc left, never having stepped a foot inside—what you'd expect from a typical pizza delivery—and Sam and I sat down to enjoy our pizza. Soon, we heard a pounding on the door.

I was concerned because I wasn't expecting anyone, and it was the kind of knock the police make, loud and scary. Running to the door and standing on my tippy toes, I peered out the peephole. On the other side stood my mother, looking infuriated while fidgeting and pacing.

Perplexed, I opened the door, not thinking anything of it.

"What's up, Mom?" I asked.

"Come outside," she demanded with rage in her voice.

"Why? I'm babysitting."

Lowering her voice, she hissed, "Get your ass out here, now!"

I complied, and we stood in the middle of the driveway, in broad daylight where the entire neighborhood could witness what was about to happen.

"What's up, Mom?" I asked suspiciously. I didn't like where this was heading.

"How dare you," she said with disgust.

"How dare I *what*?" I asked with sincere confusion.

"How dare you invite your friends over while you are babysitting? That is so irresponsible of you."

"What?" I asked with an annoyed tone. "What are you talking about? I ordered us a pizza for dinner."

"You ordered a pizza, yeah, right. You just wanted to have your friend over and shirk your responsibility."

"Mom, what are you talking about? I ordered a pizza. Marc works at the pizza place. That's it."

"Don't you lie to me, young lady."

"Mom, I swear, I just ordered a pizza. What is wrong with you? Did you have a hard day at work?" I figured there must be a reason for this insane outburst.

"Don't you talk to me like that!" she ordered.

"Like what?" I asked, even more bewildered. I was suddenly outraged. "Would it make you happy to hit me, Mom? Is that what you want? I did nothing wrong. What is your problem?"

"Don't you ever talk to me like that!" she shouted again.

"Oh, Jesus, come on. Mom, I ordered a freakin' pizza!"

"Don't lie to me."

"What is with you today? Really, would it make you feel better to hit me? Go ahead, hit me, why don't you? Hit me, here is my face, hit me!"

Suddenly, I felt a heavy-handed slap across my face. I stood still, trying to recover from the sting. Before I could compose myself, there was another slap, and then another, and another. The hitting continued until I was crouched down in the driveway in front of the garage door in a fetal position, attempting to protect my body from her wrath.

My mind flashed back to when my mother was attacking my brother in Sun Valley. Nile huddled on my bed in the same fetal position.

I looked up at my mother from the ground and snarked, "Are you done? Do you feel better now?" I was holding back my tears.

My mother left, and it took me a few minutes to compose myself. Wiping the tears from my eyes and putting a smile on my face, I staggered back into the house where Sam was happily watching TV and eating his pizza. *Thank goodness,* I thought, *I am so glad he didn't see that.*

When I came home that evening, I was furious with my mother. I had absolutely nothing to say to her. I went straight for the stairs. As I climbed them, I heard her call my name from the living room.

"Delicia," a somber voice beckoned.

"What?" I sassed back.

"Please come here," she asked, kindness in her voice.

"I don't really want to talk to you right now," I barked back.

"Just come here, please. I have something to say to you."

She was sitting in complete darkness. Upon hearing me enter, she turned on the light next to the table and quietly instructed, "Please have a seat."

I took a seat on the recliner Ron normally claimed as his own.

"I'm sorry. I will never strike you again." My mother got straight to the point.

"Mom, that was so not cool. I didn't do anything wrong, nothing! All I did was order a pizza for me and the kid I was babysitting. You made me look like a fool and humiliated me in front of the entire neighborhood."

"I know, and I am so sorry and embarrassed. I really shouldn't have hit you. I promise you—I give you my word—that will be the last time I ever strike you in your life."

Thankfully, my mother wasn't lying, and that night was the last time she ever hit me.

Weekends in high school were even more amazing once I had my own car and license. Unless you were a surfer or liked to shop at the mall, there wasn't much to do around town. Neither activity was of any interest to my friends and me. Partying in LA and living large was more our style.

Griffith Park, located in the heart of Los Feliz, is known for its amazing hiking, concerts at the Greek Theatre, the Griffith Observatory, and many other incredible ways to pass your time. One less known fact about Griffith Park is that it used to be a hookup place for gay men. The trails were one of the few safe places where they wouldn't be harassed or arrested.

On Memorial Day of 1968, there was a "gay-in" hosted in Griffith Park. It was a call to action for gay rights and against homophobia. Hundreds gathered on the lawn to protest in peace. This was two years before the first Gay Pride parade took place in 1970. The spot where the gay-in happened remained a gathering place for many years. On Sundays, gays and lesbians from all over Los Angeles and the Greater Los Angeles area would meet up, party, socialize, and look for hookups.

A friend told us about these parties happening every Sunday, so we decided to check it out. The parking lot felt like a little gay Grateful Dead show. Cars were parked along the sides of the fence, forming a circle approximately a quarter mile round. Most people had awnings set up to save their skin from the scorching sun, and others hung out in their folding chairs, drinking, smoking, and listening to music. Groups of people walked the circle, stopping to socialize with others along the way. I wondered if this was what it was like to live in the sixties.

I was never a big drinker and usually was the designated driver. I smoked weed a lot but always felt like I was fine within an hour or so of smoking. I saved up a bunch of money from working at Taco Bell, and I was dying to purchase my very own bong.

I knew this was illegal since I wasn't eighteen, but I thought since my ID worked at bars, it would be easier at a smoke shop. I checked out the glass bongs lining the shelves on the wall. Knowing I only had twenty-five dollars to spend, I diverted my attention to the less expensive section.

There it was—the most beautiful bong I'd ever seen. Tan and chestnut brown, made of glazed ceramic in the shape of a Baja Bug—VW Bugs that were popular in the '70s and '80s. They had an oversized, extraordinarily loud muffler pointing out the back and were normally off-road vehicles with monster truck tires.

The bong's muffler was where you inhaled, the down stem stuck out the hood of the bug, which was where you put the weed. I had to have it as my very own.

"How much is this one?" I asked, pointing to the Baja Bug in the case.

"That one is cute, huh?"

"Super, I want it."

"Nineteen ninety-nine," he said.

"I will take it," I replied, grinning from ear to ear.

While carefully wrapping the bong in several layers of newspaper and a black plastic bag, he requested my ID. I flashed it to him and quickly closed my wallet. Barely looking at it, he finished wrapping the bong and rang up my purchase. Fetching a crumpled twenty-dollar bill and a five from my pocket, I straightened them out as best as possible and handed my cash to the cashier. I carried that bag to my car as if I had found a hidden buried treasure. I carefully placed it in my front trunk, surrounded by T-shirts, sweatshirts, blankets, and anything else I could find to make sure it remained safe and unbroken.

The following Sunday, upon our arrival at Griffith Park, I noticed it seemed busier than usual. Marc, Jason, Cindi, and I had been going for a few weekends by now and had met some regulars. Identifying a truck I hadn't seen before near the entrance, I couldn't help but notice the blonde-haired beauty leaning against it. I was a bit taken aback.

Making "the circle" was the thing to do, checking everyone out along the way. Everyone shared everything. If you brought weed, you were expected to share with everyone. Carefully removing my new Baja Bug bong out of my trunk, I placed it on the little makeshift table we set up. After we plopped down our lounge chairs, I grabbed my lighter and baggie of weed. I was ready to go. I proudly displayed my new bong for everyone to see. After smoking a bowl for courage, I asked, "Hey, Marc, will you circle around with me? There was a really cute girl I saw on the way in."

"Heck yeah, let's go."

I made it a mission to find out who this incredible woman was. As we paced the circle, I spotted her smiling and drinking a beer, having fun with her friends, and I pinched Marc as we passed.

"Look, over there, at the blonde… I want to meet her," I told him.

"Let's go, girl," Marc said, tugging me along.

"No." I yanked him back toward me.

"Why, girl? It's time for you to meet someone."

"No, not right now… Just wait."

"Okay, but you are never going to meet anyone if you don't say hi."

"I know, just stop."

As we returned to our spot, I went over and over in my head what I would say to her. Nervous as ever, I decided to smoke another bowl out of my extremely cute bong.

While finishing my bowl, I saw her again. This time, she and her friend were walking the circle. They were heading straight for us. My hands started sweating and panic set in the closer they came.

The guy with the gorgeous blonde walked directly up to Marc and said "Hey, I'm David." Apparently, he had been checking Marc out, but we were completely clueless. "This is my friend Penny."

I looked at Penny, and my heart melted. I thought, *This is it, I've met my match.* Her eyes were like crystal blue diamonds that sparkled in the sun. Mystical music should have been playing in the background when she stuck her hand out to shake mine. I blurted out the first words that popped into my head. "Hi, I'm Delicia. Want to smoke out of my bug bong?" I stared hopefully into her eyes.

"No, I'm good. Maybe some other time. It looks like fun, though." She smiled.

David and Penny hung out at our area for quite some time, and we got to know each other. We spent some time over at their spot as well, mingling with their friends.

As the weeks passed, we became closer and closer with Penny and David.

One Sunday, Penny and David invited us to go back to their place in Seal Beach. I was sixteen at the time, as was Marc. Cindi and Jason were both eighteen, but Penny and David were much older than we were by about five years. They lived on their own in a little apartment.

Penny and I had been dating for about a month, and instead of heading to Griffith Park, we wanted to go to the beach. There were several rocks, and in between the rocks were small pools of saltwater. On the sides of the rocks were mussels, sea anemones, and other small creatures. Bending down, looking closely at the animals in the tide pool, Penny stuck the tip of her finger toward one of them when it closed on her fingertip. She jumped back with a little shriek, startled. At the time, Natalie Cole's "Jump Start" was a popular song. One line in the song says, "Don't step on me now." Penny and I put our toes in the sea anemones, singing, "Don't step on me now," while playing.

Cracking up, we journeyed off the rocks onto the sand. Penny lay atop my body, passionately kissing me. The waves crashing about ten feet from us; it was one of the most romantic moments of my life.

Penny lifted her head, looking me lovingly in the eyes, and said, "God, you are so beautiful, but you are so young."

"Get off of me," I suddenly demanded, pushing her off. Fuming, I went storming down the beach, Penny chasing behind.

"Delicia, listen, I like you a lot, but we are just at different places in our lives. I want to be friends and hang out, but I just don't think we should be more than friends."

Extremely hurt, I felt unloved and unwanted, yet again. However, I knew from an incredibly early age that relationships were important, especially those where I felt a true connection.

Having a long time to think about our conversation on my two-hour journey home, I made up my mind. I liked Penny. Our friendship was important to me, and I wanted to stay friends with her. As much as it hurt, I knew that was my only choice; she was special, and I wasn't about to let her go.

By my junior year in high school, I had experimented with almost every drug known to man. Newbury Park was a very boring town, and the kids who weren't involved with extracurricular activities were lured in an alternative direction. Drugs were plentiful and easy to find. At this time in my life, I'd promised myself never to try heroin. I knew what an addictive personality I had and seemed to mask my pain from the trauma I had endured with weed as often as I could possibly partake. In addition to heroin, I also made a promise to myself never to try meth or PCP. A promise to myself wasn't something I took lightly.

The lunch bell rang one April day in 1987. Figuring it was a regular day, I ventured out to our normal lunch spot. For whatever reason, nobody was around. *Perhaps I was early?* I decided to beat the crowds and head to Manny's for my burrito. Crossing the street and moving through the parking lot, I ran into a friend of mine, Mike, standing outside his car, smoking a cigarette.

"Hi, Mike," I said with a smile.

"Hey, Delicia, how's it going?" he replied.

"Great. Hey, can I bum a cigarette?" I asked politely. This was during the brief stint in my life when I was smoking to be cool and with the "in" crowd. In reality, I loathed everything about cigarettes but was getting used to the stench and horrific taste. In fact, I smoked often enough that the nicotine addiction was setting in.

"Here, why don't you take a drag off of mine? I don't have any more," he stated as he handed me his cigarette.

Thinking nothing of it, I took a hit, then another and another. I noticed the filter from the cigarette was gone and was quite curious.

"Why did you remove the filter?" I inquired.

"Oh, it's dusted," he responded.

My mind went into a tailspin. "DUSTED?" I questioned, knowing that this only meant one thing in my teenage vocabulary: The cigarette was dipped in liquid PCP. "What? You are kidding me, right?"

"No, you just smoked PCP." He laughed so loud it bellowed across the parking lot.

Slapping him with an open hand as hard as I could across his cheek, I screamed in his face, "I told myself I would never do that, you asshole!"

"Well, it's done now," he mocked.

Quickly realizing that I was in a heaping pile of trouble, I knew I had to skip lunch and get back to the park as soon as I possibly could before it hit me. I was alone and had no idea how my body would react to this drug.

After this, there are only flashes of memories throughout the rest of the day. Time escaped me, and there was no familiarity with my surroundings whatsoever. It was as if I were an infant in a world I was seeing for the first time, even though these were roads I'd been down hundreds of times.

I managed to get myself to the park across the street; however, upon arrival, I realized the park was empty. I couldn't think or see straight, so I plopped down on the lawn. Feeling the slightly wet grass beneath me, I sat in wonderment for a few moments, hopeful that I would be rescued.

While sitting alone on the lawn, I felt as if I were melding with the earth, my body hot molten lava that could mold and shape with the piles of fresh-smelling dirt beneath me. While rolling in circles, I somehow managed to work my way to the concrete sidewalk. Feeling like if I pushed hard enough, I could become one with the concrete, I was withering my way along the sidewalk when Kevin, my friend with a spiked mohawk, appeared out of nowhere.

"Kevin, my hero." The words barely slurred from my lips as I lay upon the patch of earth I was so trying to become a part of.

Seeing the condition I was in, Kevin became quite concerned. "Whoa, what happened to you?" he asked with a worried tone.

"PCP" was all I could get out of my mouth.

"What?! You did PCP? With whom?" he questioned with a bit of disapproval in his voice.

"Mike, parking lot, cigarette." It was becoming almost impossible for me to complete a sentence.

"Oh my God, let's get you home." Pulling me up and off the sidewalk, he carried me to his car.

Kevin had no idea where I lived, and there was no chance of me conveying directions. My legs were limp and felt completely unusable. "Gertrude" was the only word that came out of my mouth. I knew I could never go home in this condition; if my mother were there, I would literally be dead. I needed to get to Gertrude's house so she could take care of me until I sobered up enough to go home.

Luckily, Kevin was accompanied by Laurel, who lived around the corner from Gertrude, so she was able to show him the way. As we pulled up to Gertrude's house, we saw the garage was open. Her dad, Thomas, was standing inside, and as we approached, he walked to the car.

"Hello, Thomas. Is Gertrude home?" I tried my best to complete the sentence and sound sober, but my words slurred so badly he hardly understood what I was asking.

"What, are you fucking drunk?" he roared, slurring his own words in a drunken manner. "It's the middle of the day, you fucking loser kids. What the fuck is wrong with you kids these days? Pinche puta." With that, he headed back to the garage.

"Gertrude?" I managed to get out one more time.

"That fucking bitch never came home last night. I have no idea where that whore is."

"Wow, he is a ray of sunshine," Kevin commented as we drove off in search of Gertrude.

We drove around the neighborhood for what felt like hours, trying to find her. Kevin was relentless and insistent on keeping me safe. Eventually, we ventured to the back of Jason's apartment complex, hoping that if we couldn't find Gertrude, perhaps Jason could help me. Turning the corner, Kevin noticed Gertrude was there, hanging out in the carport with a few of her friends. He called out to her and motioned for her to approach the vehicle.

Gertrude and Kevin did not know each other, and she was very hesitant to approach the car. Once she saw me passed out in the passenger side, her concern grew.

"What happened to her?" she asked Kevin.

"She smoked PCP by accident."

"What?!" Her response was an echo of what Kevin's reaction had been when he'd found me: shock. "I will take care of her. Thanks for getting her to me safely."

"No problem," Kevin said as he helped her get me out of the car.

"Oh, Gertrude, I found you." I sighed with relief as if I had just found my savior.

"Come on, let's get you home." She started walking me toward the condo complex where I lived.

"No way—my mom might be home. I can't go home like this," I replied as best as I could.

"What am I supposed to do with you?" she asked. "Come on, let's go."

Not having control over my actions or feelings, I knew my only option was to do what she said.

Within thirty minutes, she walked me a block and a half home. Luckily, when we arrived, my mother's car was not there.

"Quick—before she gets home, help me to my room."

Gertrude guided me up to bed, and I slept the rest of the evening, avoiding my mother.

I'd broken a promise to myself, but not by choice. Taking any drug, without knowledge of doing so, is something that can affect your psyche on such a deep and frightening level. You would think that after an occurrence such as this, drugs would be the last thing I would ever want to do again. However, that wouldn't be the case.

In mid-1988, I was a senior, and Grad Nite at Magic Mountain was fast approaching. It was another magical moment Marc and I would spend together. Well, it should have been a magical moment, anyway. Marc was in eleventh grade and was my partner of choice for all senior events; he always graciously complied.

Everyone filtered onto three big yellow school buses to head to the park, chaos ensuing with so many seniors so close to graduation in the same place. This was just one of our Grad Nites—the big one was at the end of the year: an all-nighter at Disneyland. You had to pass all your classes to have the privilege of going.

Ninja was a brand-new roller coaster that had just opened weeks before we were scheduled to arrive. It was always so exciting when a new roller coaster opened. The lines were hours long. Marc and I agreed to ride a less-crowded roller coaster before getting in line for Ninja.

We rode a few before deciding that we really wanted to wait for Ninja. We had been standing in line for about an hour when Marc removed a pack of cigarettes from inside his light blue Levi jean jacket.

"You can't smoke here," I cautioned.

"Girl, they aren't cigarettes."

"Is that weed?" I asked.

"It's not just weed. It's good weed. Look, I got two joints. We can smoke them just before we get to the ride and then get on super stoned."

"Dude, yes, that sounds awesome. Let's do it."

Marc and I each had our own joint. Waiting to light up until we thought it was just the right timing, we started smoking them, and everyone was staring at us while whispering. We felt like we were racing to finish them before we got to the front of the line. Neither of us cared that people were staring, which is a big part of what attracted me to Marc in the first place. He is who he is, unapologetically.

We were getting high as kites waiting for Ninja. One minute, I was smoking my joint, anxiously nearing the entrance; the next minute, about twelve people had formed a circle and were looking down on me. My brain was foggy, and I lay on the floor mystified.

Marc reached down to pick me up as a stranger next to him helped. Marc quickly asked, "Are you okay?"

"Yeah, why?" I asked as if nothing happened.

Amused, he said, "Girl, you passed out… hard."

"My head hurts. What are you talking about? I'm dizzy."

"Yeah, you hit your head, really hard. Let's go find the first-aid station."

"No, Marc, we waited so long in this stupid line." My words slurred as if I was drunk. "We have to go on the ride."

"Um, you aren't going on any ride. We are going to the infirmary."

As we waited for the nurse, Marc told me the story of what happened.

"It was crazy. One minute you were smoking the joint and the next minute you turned to me, stuck your gum out of your mouth, and said, 'Take my gum.' I took it out of your mouth, and you turned around and went face-first onto the floor. Then you rolled over and were going into convulsions. Scary, girl."

"Shit, really? How fucking strong was that weed?"

"Not that strong. I just think you smoked it too fast."

"Damn it, and we waited all that time for the ride. I'm sorry, Marc."

"It's okay, don't worry. We are going to sit in here all night if we have to until you feel better."

"I'm so sorry. Let me see if I can get up now." I stood up, immediately lost my balance, and collapsed on the cot.

"Listen, sit down. I love you. Don't worry about it. I want to make sure you are okay."

From our first smoke-out session with Jeremy in the hills of Newbury Park, Marc and I have remained close. We have made so many magical—and some crazy—memories together. One of the fondest memories for me was going to my senior prom.

Never having felt "wanted" by people, it was no surprise to me that I was single when my senior prom rolled around. Determined not to miss this once-in-a-lifetime opportunity, I thought carefully about who I would ask. The choice was clear and easy for me: Marc. Marc and I had been close for years. I considered him one of my best friends. In addition, he was extraordinarily handsome. The time had come to muster up the courage to ask.

While hanging out at lunch one day, Marc approached with that infectious smile of his.

"Hey, ladies, what's happening for lunch?"

"Hi, Marc," everyone yelled back.

Parking it next to me on the grass, Marc gave me a big hug.

"Hey, Marc?"

"Yeah?"

"I wanted to ask you something."

"Ask me." He chuckled.

"You know prom is coming up?"

"Are you asking me to go to prom with you?" he insinuated.

"Kind of, yeah, I guess. Yes, I'm asking you to go to prom with me."

"Oh, hell yes, girl, let's get this party started. Of course, I will go to prom with you. Jeremy, do you want to go with us?"

"Heck yeah. Maybe I can ask April," Jeremy replied. "We could go in on a limo. This is going to be awesome."

Prom night arrived, and the limo pulled up outside my driveway. Feeling as unloved as I have in my life, I had visions of the *Carrie* prom scene running through my mind. Although I knew Marc would never do that to me, I had been abandoned, disillusioned, and disappointed by so many people I'd loved, these thoughts were always in the back of my mind, no matter how much I thought people cared.

Mom answered the door, yelling with glee, "Delicia, your prom date is here!"

I descended down the stairs in my white spaghetti strap dress with my hair beautifully done, and I watched Marc's face as his mouth hung agape. He hadn't ever seen me in makeup before that day. I had always been a real natural girl and didn't like "painting my face." Having a boutonniere ready for him in the fridge, Ron fetched it for me. Marc was in a tux and looked dashing. I had the most amazing prom date one could ever ask for, and I was beaming with pride. There would be no pig blood involved tonight, thank goodness.

"Hi, Marc," I said, dashing down the stairs the best I could in the pumps I was wearing.

"Wow, you look amazing."

Smiling, we gave each other a big hug. Then he revealed a beautiful corsage in a plastic box. "Here, this is for you."

"What? Wow, you didn't have to do that."

"Girl, it's your prom. Of course, I did. Here, let me put it on." Carefully, he placed the corsage onto my wrist. "Come on, let's go."

"Bye, Mom." I waved as Marc and I dashed out the door.

"Bye, Mrs. Niami," Marc said.

"Bring my baby home safely. You kids be home by three a.m., okay?"

"You got it. Thanks, Mom. Bye."

We got into the limo, joining Jeremy and April, and the party got underway. Marc removed a flask from his pocket and started pouring shots for everyone. The limo driver didn't seem to care that we were underage. Putting up the partition, we clanked our shot glasses together and toasted our beautiful friendship.

Marc withdrew a folded piece of paper from his pocket and carefully opened it. Seeing it was filled with cocaine was exhilarating. Having done coke a few times before, I recalled how much I liked it. We divided up lines in the back of the limo, and I snorted several while cruising down the 101 freeway to our high school prom.

Dancing the night away, taking pictures, we did all the prom things one did—except for sleeping together afterward, of course. We knew that wasn't happening, since Marc and I were both gay.

Over the years of knowing Marc's family, including his parents and sister, Genevieve, they became extremely special to me. They have always included me as if I was their own, even inviting me to family events. Knowing my mother was absent most of the time, they would often invite me to dinner at their home so I wouldn't have to cook for myself. It is truly inspirational for me to encounter families such as Marc's.

They were always incredibly wonderful and kind to one another. Of course, they had their issues, but on the surface, they were the perfect "American" family. Feeling loved and included, I wanted to spend every extra minute I could with them. They were the functional family I'd always desired.

Besides hanging in Los Angeles at the gay bars most weekends, a lot of my friends really liked the Grateful Dead. They traveled around to many of their shows when the band was in California, and some even toured with the Dead across state lines. This obsession began for many of us in high school. My Deadhead friends were a crossover from our lunchtime group. I wasn't really into the music of the Grateful Dead so much as a teenager, but I loved the experience of going to the parking lot at a Dead show. I'd done a lot of drugs in high school and experimented with almost every drug known to man. There were a few drugs I'd yet to try that I wanted to, like acid and peyote. Dead shows were the

Willy Wonka factory for drugs, so I knew if I could get acid anywhere, it would be there.

These shows were Burning Man before Burning Man. Half-naked girls spun in circles on top of cars painted with daisies. Rows and rows of cars were lined up next to each other, a party at every car. Everyone was incredibly high, sharing everything with anybody.

Deadheads roamed around the parking lots, stoned out of their minds, holding up one finger imploring, "I need a miracle." This meant that they were hoping someone would gift them a ticket to the show. I never needed a ticket to get in. The drum solo would make me pass out and I'd usually sleep through the shows, so I figured I should spend my money on drugs instead.

Roaming the parking lot searching for drugs was my insane idea of fun at Dead shows. I had never done acid before and always wanted to do it, and I figured there was no better time than the present. The same Michelle that took care of Roy was the queen of acid. She would take sheets of acid at a time and could still be normal like any other day. It mind-boggled us that she had such a high tolerance.

When we found out that the Grateful Dead were going to be playing at the Ventura Fairgrounds that summer, we made plans to go. Linda, Marc, Jason, and I hopped in Linda's VW Karmann Ghia. Looking for a good time, we cruised north from Newbury Park down the grade past Camarillo, Oxnard, and finally into Ventura.

We arrived at the parking lot; there were hundreds of cars and camper vans, old VW buses with music blaring in the background, everyone dancing and socializing.

Turning to Linda, I proclaimed, "I think I want to try acid today."

"Really? Fun," she replied.

"Where can I find some?"

"Anywhere here, really."

We chuckled as we kicked off our magical journey.

Linda and Marc had tickets to get inside, but per the norm, I opted to hang in the parking lot. I knew a bunch of our friends were going to be there, and Jason didn't have a ticket, either. We planned on hanging out and listening to the music from outside the show.

Marc and Linda met up with our friend LR, and they headed inside. Jason and I were strolling along when we happened upon some of his friends.

Politely introducing us, he inquired, "Hey, she is looking for some acid. Do you know where we can score?"

"Groovy, dude, come with me," his friend said.

The fringes of his leather jacket shimmied as he roamed about. He had an afro and round rim glasses that sat perched atop the tip of his nose. We followed him to an old dark-blue VW bus. Inside was a small kitchen with a bed and a table. He jumped in the bus, then came back a few seconds later with what looked like a sheet of paper in hand. Ripping off five tiny squares, he handed them to Jason.

"Don't keep that in your hand for too long, man. The acid will seep into the pores in your skin," he said in a slow, hippie drawl. "Did you know that your skin is like the biggest orifice in your body? It's like super porous, dude. The sun awaits. I must seek my master."

Jason and I looked at the five tiny squares, quickly popping two each onto our tongues.

Several hours passed, and I wasn't feeling much of anything, unsure if it was because of the opium I'd smoked earlier with some hippies in the parking lot. Perhaps it was just bad acid? Immobilized against a chain-link fence, covered in blankets while drifting in and out of consciousness, I was super stoned from the opium but wanted to feel the effects of the acid.

The universe gave me a sign when Michelle suddenly approached me. Noticing I was a little out of it, she questioned, "Hey, Delicia, are you okay?"

"Yeah, man, I am just tired. I smoked some opium, and this drum solo, you know, always makes me want to sleep. Hey, Michelle?"

"Yeah?"

"I really wanted to do acid today, and I took a couple of hits, but I don't feel anything."

"Open your mouth."

"Why?"

"Just open your mouth," she instructed again.

Opening my mouth, I pretended she was a doctor and said with my tongue sticking out, "Ah."

Before I could put my tongue back into my mouth, she slapped something on it.

"What is it? What is it?" I mumbled with my tongue sticking out of my mouth.

"Green gel," she replied.

"What? Get it off, get it off," I begged.

"Too late, have fun." She sauntered away with a shit-eating grin.

Fuck, I thought. *Well, I'm going to feel this.* Green gel was a type of super-strong, fast-acting acid that wasn't for the faint of heart. I already knew I was in for a wild ride.

Wild ride it was. Most of the night was a blur. I do remember having a blast, but not much else. Jason and I had lost each other. I think he ended up leaving with LR, but I couldn't recall as I was abnormally high. A few hours passed when Michelle came back to check on me. Having acquired prism glasses while in the show and seeing how high I was, she put them on my face. The rest of the night was spent staring at the pretty rainbow lights, tilting my head from left to right, back and forth, and in circles, making patterns with the lights.

When the time came to leave, Linda and Marc sought me out. Eventually they found me and Michelle staring at headlights. We'd made a friend who was indulging us, flashing his lights to the music as Michelle and I rocked out with the rainbow lights, dancing and spinning in circles.

The last thing I remember was tripping in the front seat of the Karmann Ghia while sober Linda drove up the Camarillo grade. I was flying high on acid, but I was extremely grateful and happy that my friends were so trustworthy and always made sure I got home safely—the majority of them anyway.

Less than six months after moving to Newbury Park, towards the end of tenth grade, I was greeted by my mother with yet another surprise that nearly killed me.

"Hi, Mom," I shouted as I bounced in the door.

"Hi, honey, I have something to tell you."

"What is it, Mom?"

"Sit down," she said in an almost somber voice.

"What, Mom? What is it?"

"I hate to have to tell you this, but we have to move again."

"WHAT?!?! No, absolutely not!" I shouted with rage in my voice. "You PROMISED me! You PROMISED that we would stay until I graduated, and I'm sorry, but I refuse to move again. It is not fair to me, and I am standing my ground. I am finally starting to make friends and connections. NO, absolutely not!" I screamed again in her face.

"Wow, I didn't realize you would take it so hard," she replied.

"Think about it, Mom. How many times have we moved? How many times have I had to make new friends or at least attempt to make new friends? No fucking way—you promised me." I never cursed in front of my mother, and she was a bit shocked.

"Don't you speak that way in front of me."

"I'm sorry, Mom, but my answer is no. I will be homeless on the street before I allow you to move from here. Well, you can go, but I'm staying here," I demanded and stormed off to my room.

That was the end of the discussion, and we did not move again.

Standing my ground, insisting that my mother keep her promise to stay in the same town until I graduated high school, was the smartest and best thing I ever did for myself. The people and friends I met while living in Newbury Park became my family. They were so much more than just friends. My friends have been more my family than my own on so many occasions, I call them my "framily." I can't imagine what my life would have been like if I had kowtowed when my mother demanded that we move less than six months after relocating to Newbury Park.

MY FIRST DRUNKEN BLACKOUT

In May 1988, a month or so before graduation, Gertrude invited me to go to a party with her. I wasn't much of a drinker, but when I did drink, I thought I could hold my alcohol well. By then, I smoked weed regularly and sometimes partook in drinking with my friends as well as dabbling in mushrooms, LSD, and other drugs.

I didn't get to go to many hometown parties, so I was skeptical. Being known as the school lesbian, I was constantly teased. Embracing my gayness wasn't a cool thing to do in 1988. Most of my weekend nights were spent in LA at the bars, not around town at the lame football player parties.

The night of the party, I got dressed up, even wearing makeup. I had been out and open about my sexuality for many years at this point. Many kids still teased me incessantly, but I grew thick skin. I'd picked out my best-looking jeans and a blouse, which was nicer than the normal T-shirt I wore, and I thought I was looking pretty cute.

I jumped in my 1972 VW Super Beetle, hoping it would start. There were so many times my friends had to push my car to get it going. Knowing I was meeting Gertrude at her house in fifteen minutes, I put the key in the ignition and prayed.

"Please, God." I closed my eyes and turned the key. Nothing. "Come on, not tonight... please," I begged aloud, turning the key again while pumping the gas. The car spat a few backfires out the tailpipe and finally turned over. *Yes!* I thought, and off I went to pick up Gertrude.

I propelled up Ventu Parkway into the rolling hills. The houses were sparse, each house a half mile from the next. I came to a stop in front of the small stucco home, beeping from the car, hoping she would hear. I had no desire to deal with Thomas Senior today, because I never knew if he would be in a good mood or not. Gertrude came out after a few minutes, looking amazing. Gertrude and Brian were newly dating, so she was dressed to the nines. Having casually invited him, she wasn't sure he would show but was hopeful.

Brushing off the dust on the seat so it wouldn't get her pants dirty, Gertrude got into the bug, and off we went, through the hills and valleys of Thousand Oaks. Gertrude directed me since I wasn't familiar with this part of town.

We pulled up to a rundown house with a couch and a keg on the lawn and knew this was it. Large red cups were plunked atop for people to help themselves. The same cups were strewn throughout the lawn. Between the trash and empty cigarette packs, we found our way inside the house. *What a dump,* I thought.

"Come on," said Gertrude, grabbing me by the hand and pulling me into the crowded, smoky house. "Let's get a drink."

"I'm not so sure. I have to drive."

"Just have one drink, lady," Gertrude implored.

Parties and crowds of people made me nervous.

Figuring I should have a drink so I could deal with the jocks at the party, I suggested, "Let's get a Sex on the Beach."

There was a bar and bartender set up in the backyard, and Gertrude left to get us drinks. We were sipping our cocktails when she spotted Brian. She looked at me with puppy dog eyes, pleading to leave me alone so she could hang out with him.

Hesitantly, I said, "Go ahead." I moved like a sloth toward the house, searching for the nearest couch to hide out on.

I sipped on my Sex on the Beach, wishing I had gone to LA instead. If I had known I would be at a big party, alone, I would have never gone. I went mostly because Gertrude needed my support as a friend.

I imbibed a few more drinks while feeling timid and alone. While working on my fourth drink, I decided I wanted a beer from the keg. I wobbled to the front lawn, removed a cup from the top, and attempted to pour some, but it wasn't working.

A really drunk jock appeared from behind me and said, "You gotta pump it... like this." He gyrated as he demonstrated.

Chuckling, I pumped the handle, and finally beer came out, but it was so foamy, I gave up. I let the foam settle and was able to drink it after a few minutes. Somehow, from there I began drinking whatever anyone poured into my cup for the next hour or so, and I became more and more inebriated without even realizing it.

Someone came around with a bottle of champagne, pouring it into everyone's cup. It didn't matter what was in your cup; you were getting champagne. Feeling a bit tipsy and nauseous, I wanted to leave. I got up to search for Gertrude and realized I was way more wasted than I thought. I couldn't walk. My only choice was to stay put until she found me. I continued sipping whatever happened to be in the cup in front of me, not knowing if it was mine or not and, frankly, not caring.

What felt like hours later, I was awakened by Gertrude shaking me. Finally, she found me and was trying to get me to leave. Attempting to stand, I immediately fell backward onto the couch.

Slurring, I muttered, "I feel nauseous."

"Oh boy," Gertrude responded. "I can't drive."

Gertrude didn't have a license, so she retrieved Brian to help. Once she found him, they headed outside to get me. They attempted to pick up my drunk, dead-weight body. It took a mountain of effort, doing everything in my power to lift my arm up to the sky, my hand held high, pleading, "Help me up."

Gertrude clutched one hand and Brian the other, and they helped me to the bathroom. I stumbled in. Luckily, the light was already on. Looking in the mirror, I was horrified. I looked as terrible as I felt. My face showed signs of crying the entire night through, yet I didn't recall crying. The room was starting to spin, and I held on to the walls as I found my way to the toilet.

I knelt on the cold bathroom floor. All I wanted to do was lay my head down on the porcelain toilet seat. Ah, the cold felt so good. I laid my cheek on the toilet, not caring that my hair was getting soaked in urine. Staring at the water swirling in the toilet, I gagged, my stomach cramping.

I attempted to swallow, but the lump in my throat wouldn't comply. I couldn't keep it down and began to vomit. Hearing me from outside the door, Gertrude came in and held my hair back as I threw up what felt like the last year's worth of food.

I looked up at Gertrude, drool and vomit dripping down one side of my face, and murmured, "There is no way I can drive."

"I know," she reassured me. "Brian is going to give you a ride home."

"Oh, thank you," I slurred while reaching out my hand.

"Let's wash off your face," Gertrude proclaimed while wetting a paper towel and proceeding to wipe throw-up from my face and hair.

"Okay, let's get out of here." Brian and Gertrude held me up as we stumbled to the car.

Brian had a small Honda CVCC, one of the little round ones, so I would have had to squeeze in the back seat. We all knew that wasn't happening. Gertrude got in the back while I slumped into the front, trying to show Brian the way to my house. Realistically, I couldn't show anybody anything at that moment because as soon as I was seated, I passed out. Brian buckled me in and off we went. Thank goodness, Gertrude knew the way to my house.

Shortly thereafter, I was awakened by Brian shaking me and screaming in my face, "Delicia, wake up, Delicia, wake up!"

Coming to, I muttered, "Where are we?"

"We got a flat tire. We are waiting for AAA to come."

"Why did you wake me up then?"

"My friends are here. They are going to take you home."

"But they don't know where I live."

"Gertrude told them. Don't worry. I know the driver. He will get you home safely."

Helping me up, he practically carried me to the truck and helped me into the front seat. He strapped me in, then looked at the driver and said, "There you go." I drifted back to sleep.

I began coming into consciousness, feeling my body being pounded, a heavy weight on top of me, and the vinyl seat of the truck rubbing against my skin. I opened my eyes slowly, dazed and perplexed as to what the commotion was about. Still in a fog, it took me a few seconds to focus.

Seeing a bare chest on top of me, I began feeling immense pain penetrating deep inside of me. Like a peeled tomato rubbing against a cheese grater, I felt raw. My legs were outside the passenger door. The driver, who was supposed to get me home safely, was raping me. Sobering up instantaneously, I pushed him with all my might, screaming at the top of my lungs, "Get off of me, you motherfucker!"

Running as fast as I could away from the truck, I realized I had no idea where we were. I looked around frantically, trying to get my bearings.

He hollered, "Come back."

I saw a shadowy figure running toward me and another standing up in the back of the bed of the truck.

"Come back. I'll take you home!" he shouted.

"Where the fuck are we, you asshole?" I screamed back at him from the other side of the parking lot. I couldn't see anything but a few streetlights, doors, and a vacant lot.

"Just come back. I promise I will take you home," he bellowed from the middle of the parking lot.

I decided I better trust that he would take me home. I had no clue where we were or how far from home I was. Returning to the truck, I painstakingly got in the passenger seat. Looking him directly in the eye, I fumed with rage, "Take me home."

Turned out, we were less than a block from where I lived.

The time was around two-forty in the morning. I would often come home this late, so my mother wouldn't think anything of it. Normally, I would go straight to bed. Making my way upstairs, I turned down the hall and headed straight for the bathroom.

It was a horrific feeling, not knowing exactly what happened. Drunk and blacked out in the truck, I woke up to a stranger fucking me in a parking lot, my legs hanging out the passenger door with another stranger watching from the bed of the truck.

The only thing running through my mind was, *How did this happen?* I got in the shower, the water as hot as I could stand; I hoped it would wash away the abhorrence and filth from my body.

"Delicia?" I heard my mother call from the hallway.

"Yeah, Mom?"

"What in the world are you doing? It's three a.m."

"Showering," I replied.

"Why in the world are you showering at this time?"

"Can I talk to you when I am done?"

I finished my shower, realizing it didn't wash any of the disgust away, nor the disappointment in myself.

Wrapping a towel around my hair like a turban, I reached for another to wrap around my body. Mom was standing at the door with a look of anger.

I brushed past her and said, "Please, Mom, come in my room."

I still felt a bit drunk but mostly just sickened and with a giant headache.

I removed clothes from my dresser, my mother looking at me like I'd lost my mind.

Probing, she asked, "What in the world has gotten into you?"

"Sit down, Mom," I replied somberly.

I put on comfortable sweats and a T-shirt, sat on the bed next to her, clutched her hand, and told her, "Mom, I was just raped…"

Throughout my adolescence, I came to realize tragic upsets like this are just part of our stories unfolding. I realized that "shit happens" and you have to learn to deal with it. You can internalize your shame, guilt, and pain—which I did for many, many years—or the alternative is to process and move through tragedies as they arise. Diving deep into your journey and looking at the occurrences that have shaped us is extremely difficult but essential for growth. As hard as it is to reflect on these tragic events, learning and taking something away from it is what is most important, even if the journey seemed unbearable along the way. During our time on this planet, embracing life and every part of it can be beautiful, even the hard stuff.

When I am faced with what seems like insurmountable challenges in life, I remember the time I was seven and ate shit on the hard asphalt. Cruising down the street on my dark green plastic skateboard, I didn't see the bulge in the pavement. The front of my board jammed in the crevice, and I heard a loud cracking sound. I flew onto the asphalt, planting face-first on the ground, then skidding on my nose for what felt like ten feet or so. With my head hung low, blood and tears dripping from my face, I stared at the ground with fury. I felt defeat in my heart, but knowing I had to persevere, I quickly changed my attitude. Kissing the ground, I stood on my feet, grabbing my broken board. I walked the rest of the way home, where I bandaged myself up.

Sometimes I wonder how I survived my childhood. Looking back, all I can say is that I was somehow able to find that sliver of light and know I could reach it if I fought hard enough.

In Delicia's next book, *Not My Circus,* find out what happens after the rape and learn about TRUSTWORTHY MONSTER #2, Nile's continued success in life, and more as you join her on an adventure to liberation, freedom, and happiness.

Made in the USA
Monee, IL
22 November 2023